Black Chant traces the embrace and transformation of black modernisms and postmodernisms by African-American poets in the decades after World War II. Centering on groups of avant-garde poets, including the Howard/Dasein poets, the Free Lance group, the Umbra group, and others, the study particularly attends to those poets whose radical forms of new writing formed the basis for much of what followed in the Black Arts period. The author also undertakes a critical rediscovery of recordings by black avant-garde poets such as Amiri Baraka, Jayne Cortez, and Elouise Loftin, who worked with jazz composers and performers on compositions that combined post-Bop jazz with postmodern verse forms. Exploring the farthest reaches of black creative experimentation in words and music, *Black Chant* yields an invaluable reassessment of African-American cultural history as it has been shaped throughout the era we now call postmodern.

BLACK CHANT

BLACK CHANT

Languages of African-American Postmodernism

Aldon Lynn Nielsen

San Jose State University

CAMBRIDGE
UNIVERSITY PRESS

PUBLISHED BY THE PRESS SYNDICATE OF THE UNIVERSITY OF CAMBRIDGE
The Pitt Building, Trumpington Street, Cambridge CB2 1RP, United Kingdom

CAMBRIDGE UNIVERSITY PRESS
The Edinburgh Building, Cambridge CB2 2RU, United Kingdom
40 West 20th Street, New York, NY 10011-4211, USA
10 Stamford Road, Oakleigh, Melbourne 3166, Australia

First published 1997

Printed in the United States of America.

Typeset in New Baskerville

Library of Congress Cataloging-in-Publication Data
Nielsen, Aldon Lynn.
Black chant : languages of African-American postmodernism / Aldon
Lynn Nielsen.
p.   cm. – (Cambridge studies in American literature and
culture ; 105)
Includes bibliographical references (p.).
ISBN 0-521-55510-8. – ISBN 0-521-55526-4 (pbk.)
1. American poetry – Afro-American authors – History and criticism.
2. American poetry – 20th century – History and criticism.   3. Music
and literature – United States – History – 20th century.
4. Postmodernism (Literature) – United States.   5. Modernism
(Literature) – United States.   6. Avant-garde (Aesthetics) – United
States.   7. Afro-Americans in literature.   8. Race in literature.
9. Afro-American arts.   10. Afro-Americans – Intellectual life.
I. Title.   II. Series.
PS183.N5N535   1996
811.009'896073 – dc20
96-12762
CIP

A catalog record for this book is available from
the British Library.

ISBN 0-521-55510-8 hardback
ISBN 0-521-55526-4 paperback

To the memory of
C. L. R. James

. . . they held up a banner, groping pioneers
for a native American radicalism.

. . . there is a corner just ahead whose turning
is so badly understood that being
upset is included in the tickets.
Ed Roberson, When

CONTENTS

ix

ACKNOWLEDGMENTS

At a time when material support for research in the humanities is rapidly dwindling from its already negligible levels, I more than ever wish to thank those who have assisted me as I have worked on this book.

Anna Everett has continued her unstinting encouragement of my efforts, and her many criticisms and suggestions have been invaluable. Our discussions have constituted a perpetual collaboration that I would not have been without.

The majority of the research and writing of this study was completed during the period of a fellowship at the Center for Afro-American Studies at the University of California in Los Angeles. The staff and faculty associated with the center provided the kind of enthusiastic support that is only available in a true community of inquiry. I am particularly grateful to Chérie Francis and all the other staff members who made my time at the center so productive. The fellowship at the center was provided by UCLA's Institute of American Cultures. I also wish to thank San Jose State University for my first sabbatical, which made it possible for me to accept the UCLA fellowship.

Professor Eric Sundquist expressed interest in this book before it had become a book, and I want to thank him for his continued confidence. Susan Chang, Anne Sanow, Brett Kaplan, Christie Lerch, Holly Johnson, and the able staff of the Cambridge University Press made the final production of this book a more than usually pleasurable experience. My colleagues and students at San Jose State University have been patient with my endless thinking out loud, and their innumerable acts of kindness during our shared institutional crises have been an inspiration. The faculty and staff of the California State University system have become masters at the art of making do with less and less, and I have had much to learn about working with adversity.

I am more than usually indebted to the helpful staffs of several research collections. Mike Basinski and the staff of the Poetry and Rare Book Collection at the State University of New York at Buffalo helped me complete two of the most productive weeks of my career. Mike, a poet himself, used his extensive knowledge of the collection at Buffalo to lead me to sources that I had not known of previously. Charles Bernstein not only introduced me to the Poetics Program at Buffalo, he also arranged a number of useful meetings and activities during my visit. Charles's own poetry has long been a stimulus to my thinking and writing. The staff in the Special Collections department at the University of California Los Angeles Research Library gave me a second home during my fellowship year, and I am grateful for their extended hospitality and assistance. As always, the staff of the Manuscript Division of the Library of Congress gave me a warm welcome, and the librarians at Howard University's Moorland–Spingarn collection, particularly the Manuscript Division, were enormously helpful. I will continue to rely upon the Moorland–Spingarn materials, many of which were still being processed as I examined them, in the next stage of these investigations. Ethelbert Miller, a longtime friend and another increasingly well-known poet (yes, there is a pattern emerging here), made available to me several crucial items he has collected at the Afro-American Studies Resource Center at Howard.

Readers who go so far as to read acknowledgments should know that this manuscript is two chapters shorter than originally planned, again due to economic considerations. Those two phantom chapters, studies of the poetry of Russell Atkins and Stephen Jonas, will appear in a subsequent book continuing this project.

Russell Atkins has generously granted permission for me to reprint his poetry in this study, and I am particularly pleased to have had the chance to speak with him as this book went to press.

To my great sorrow, I learned that Percy Johnston died on March 20, 1993. On the night that he died of a heart attack, Johnston was returning home after rehearsing a play in Greenwich Village with a theater group he had formed. Johnston was, until his last moment, engaged in the kind of collaborative presentation of the arts to which he had devoted his entire life. I wish to thank Walter De Legall, director of Percy Johnston's foundation and one of the original Dasein poets, for permission to reproduce Johnston's poetry.

New York University Press has granted permission to quote from Norman H. Pritchard's *EECCHHOOEESS*, published in 1971.

DeLeon Harrison's "Yellow" is reprinted from *Dices or Black Bones: Black Voices of the Seventies*, published in 1970 by Houghton Mifflin, with permission from the editor, Adam David Miller. Miller, himself a fine poet, has become a valued friend in the course of my research for this project.

PART ONE

THE LINING OF THE HYMN

are we being called
   (between the lines . . .)

        Bob Fletcher "A Lovedirge to the Whitehouse"

1

"THE CALLIGRAPHY OF
BLACK CHANT"

Witches one Way tspike Mr. Chigyle's languish, n currying him back tRealty, recoremince wi hUnmisreaducation. Maya we now go on wi yReconstruction, Mr. Chuggle? Awick now? Goodd, a'godMoanng agen everybubbahs n babys among you, d'yonladys in front who always come vear too, days ago, dhisMorning we wddeal, in dhis Sagmint of Lecturian Angleash 161, w'all the daisiastrous effects, the foxnoxious bland of stimili, the infortunelessnesses of circusdances which weak to worsen the phistorystematical intrafricanical firmly structure of our distinct coresins: the Blafringro-Arumericans.

William Melvin Kelly, *Dunfords Travels Everywheres*

During the decade since I departed from Howard University to take up a tenure track position teaching English in California, I have often found myself, in widely different parts of the United States, listening to academics at predominantly white institutions discuss a topic they term "Black English." Two points have always been clear to me about these casual observations: (1) the "Black English" these discussants appear to have in mind bears little relation to the spoken language of black students in American classrooms, and in any event was not constructed out of the careful linguistic study of the speech habits of actual black speaking subjects (rather, it seems to reflect some preexisting encoded structure of agreements about what "black" sounds like); (2) whatever else might be said about the validity of white academic paradigms of "Black English," they certainly do not encompass

3

such black expressions as the epigraph to this chapter, an excerpt from William Melvin Kelly's remarkable novel *Dunfords Travels Everywheres*, nor do they offer much to hope for in the way of substantive analysis of such artistic modes. As my white interlocutors earnestly assure me that "Black English" is a distinct language in its own right, only occasionally exercising even so much caution as to term it a "dialect" rather than a language, and never offering any explanation for their professed ability to comprehend immediately, with no formal study, the meanings encoded by black speakers of this distinct language or dialect, I have often wondered what they would make of this novel, composed largely, as one of Kelly's lines has it, of "scribbled eggs and puncakes" (57). In fact, white academics have for the most part chosen to make nothing of it. The novel is long out of print and rarely turns up in the literature curriculum. Academics, black and white alike, have chosen largely to ignore what, to turn to Kelly's usage again, "if we be langleashtically corerect we must call the Second Intergenerational Untralinguistic Antirepublican Cunfrontation" (55), a "cunfrontation" which, almost in passing, also deftly parodies three centuries of American literary representations of supposed black dialects.

Although some might argue, even in a post-Derridean realm of academic discourse, that if we wish to understand the performative mechanics of English as spoken by African Americans we had better not begin our inquiry with such audacious literary experiments as Kelly's (a position that, I believe, comes undone as we read out loud and quote from *Dunfords Travels*), it seems evident that a course of literary criticism that expels such works as Kelly's from among its collection of sample texts to be considered, let alone from its canon, ends by offering readers an anemic and inadequate account of both the history and nature of American literature in general and of African-American literature in particular. At the time of its publication, *Dunfords Travels Everywheres* was recognized as a black, English accomplishment of literary art. A prepublication excerpt from the novel appeared in the October 1969 issue of *Negro Digest,* where the editors, who had by that date adopted a black nationalist aesthetics, hailed the text as "A sly and wry fictional romp through the literal and linguistical regions of a fabled island by a storyteller bent on bending a convention to blackness" (61). This editorial introduction emphasizes the close link between traditions of black storytelling and Kelly's experimental violations of convention; in any event, there seemed to be no doubt in the editors' minds regarding the "blackness" of this avant-garde text. Similarly, the blackness of Kelly's English was not in doubt when his novel received an award from the Black Academy of Arts and Letters, though even their willing suspensions may have been tested when Kelly sent his acceptance letter from Jamaica written in his version of an island patois. He said he received no reply from the awards committee ("Interview" 2).

Dunfords Travels Everywheres meets most thematic tests of literary blackness that have surfaced in published criticism. Its embedding of the thematics and symbolism of the Middle Passage, for example, fits easily into the structural paradigms offered by Stephen Henderson in his 1972 study, *Understanding the New Black Poetry,* and if we accept Henderson's term "saturation" as a descriptor of the "communication of 'Blackness' and fidelity to the observed or intuited truth of the Black Experience in the United States" (10), then we might be tempted to say that *Dunfords Travels Everywheres* is a supersaturated black text. It may be that the novel's language has been held against it by later readers, but its language is its most stunning effect and the formal mode of its communication of observed and intuited truths. The language of Kelly's masterful parody of a central tenet of the doctrine of the Nation of Islam, in one instance, is what differentiates the passage from mere mockery:

> E. M. Fardpull, in his landark steady of the study hobits of the eurly tribs of the eorly Yacuvic Pyreod, THE MESS AGE OF THE LACKMAN, states clearly his bilefe in the theory of mismagination and expelcion, the eeveel reck of the hubristic Jack L. Yacoo, M. D.
>
> But yours trolley huffling professanityr, wool not covering his eyes to the identiquality of the doubtcome, can see a clare noncoilition between the lacke of the sun and the luck of the pepills on that spand of Terrifyrma, both in the Furtherland and the Motorcoloniel, glaceried as the Outterre Wreckwitorial Bolt. (53)

Such parody might well serve as a bracing and effective antidote for those of us who, in recent years, have had to contend with the wide publicity given by the mass media to theories not very different from Fardpull's, advanced by Ph.D.-bearing academics both white and black. But it may be that Kelly's audacious signifying within and upon the English language itself is finally more of an obstacle to the minds of critics than the overt content of the myth of "Yacub's devils" that it travesties. It is in its language, however, that *Dunfords Travels* enacts its thematics. Valerie Babb has argued that "Kelly plays an ironic linguistic trick" on his characters in this novel, "for the truth they seek is contained in the incomprehensible language of their dreams and eludes them in their waking hours. By contrast, the lies they must see through are depicted in standard English" (142). It is a trick that may arouse the resistance of some white readers, for, according to Babb, "The paradox is that only in an elusive language created from the history and struggle of black people can truths about self and identity be found" (142–3). Readers who hope to find in black writing the confirmation of "truths" already "known" about black identity, black self, and black expression may find Kelly's form of linguistic paradox unsettling. Since, for such readers, the construction of "Black English" they maintain in mind is part of the repressive structuring by which they construct themselves racially, and since Kelly's writing does not satisfy those expectations of what black speech can and should be, the languages of *Dunfords Travels Everywheres* are in the end doubly othered, for they are read as the other to the paradigmatic habits of enunciation assigned to the absolute black other by white society's hegemonic discourse agreements (those agreements that must be in place before white people at social gatherings can expect to be understood, when, as they so often do, they assume a "black" voice for the telling of an anecdote or the singing of a song). Kelly's experiments and *Dunfords Travels* often overturn assumptions about what white and black language are, and so it will remain easier for those committed to essentialist views of linguistic racial difference not to read Kelly.

For his part, Kelly was neither simply mimicking a Joycean language of modernist European invention nor merely out to confound readers of his earlier, more widely read novels and short stories. What he attempted in *Dunfords Travels Everywheres* was a resituating of modernist forms within the continuum of African art forms that had given so much inspiration to the modernist moment. "The whole improvisational idea is African art," Kelly remarked to Quincy Troupe and Ishmael Reed in a

1983 interview (2). The novel's epigraphs perform this resiting of modernity by sandwiching a passage of Joyce between two quotations. The first is from Melvin B. Tolson's *Libretto for the Republic of Liberia,* an African-American modernist praise song for an American-African republic. The second is a passage from the Nigerian novelist Amos Tutuola, whose texts were read avidly by a generation of European artists and then reread by a subsequent generation of progressive rock musicians, forming a Euro-American chain of Tutuola-influenced cultural production that meets up again with the African chain of readership and authorship in the scene of late twentieth-century world writing and "World Beat" musics. Although Kelly was not out to create a literary form of World Beat hybridity before the fact, he was setting forth a bold improvisation that took as its impetus a necessarily revised model of what international modernism was. By revealing and reveling in the suppressed Africanity of international modernism, by configuring in his writing a site for the international conditions for modernism's coming back into being with a pronounced difference (both economic and sociopolitical), Kelly accomplished a postmodernity that has yet to be adequately tabulated by existing critiques of the postmodern.

Four years prior to the publication of *Dunfords Travels Everywheres,* Kelly had written to Tolson, sending along a copy of his newest novel, *A Drop of Patience.* He told Tolson, "I especially want you to have it. I have only known you a short time, but already I feel as if we have known each other for 300 years now, all our years in bondage. You are a part of my proud past – the past that my white man's education kept from me" (Tolson Papers). Kelly knew that then dominant modes of black education also tended to marginalize Tolson's works. He told Tolson, "I have never been able to find that MAN, and I didn't expect to find one at Fisk either, and I am moved that I did. Keep going." One might wish that Kelly's praise were less gender-specific, but what he refers to is Tolson's insistence upon his subjectivity, albeit fluid, as a black poet in America, in contrast to the somewhat more assimilationist position that had been asserted at the Fisk Writers' Conference by Robert Hayden just a few months earlier. Tolson was not an essentialist, and he attributed much of the problem of international racism to international capitalism (Farnsworth 298), but he also understood that there was no separating his identity as a poet from his social being as a black man in America; no matter how socially constructed race might be in the United States, it was not, in his view, a casual overlay that could easily be stripped away from the reading of his verse. Tolson knew that he would never be simply a poet who happened to be black. His later poetry had reclaimed a blackness within modernism and posited a populist black modernity in writing. Kelly's subsequent situating of James Joyce in the midst of African and African-American registers of modernist language innovation was a means of revealing the canon of international modernism to itself in a postmodern, postcolonial rupture. This may not be exactly what contemporary critics of postmodernity, some of whom wish to oppose an "authentic" third worldism to an "inauthentic" postmodernity that is wholly Western in conception and complexion, expect from black authors.

Gayatri Spivak has raised the gravest of doubts about that mode of critique. "Neocolonialism," she asserts, "is fabricating its allies by proposing a share of the center in a seemingly new way (not a rupture but a displacement): disciplinary support for the conviction of authentic marginality by the (aspiring) elite" (57), and she wants to know, "What are the implications of pedagogic gestures that monumentalize *this* style [magical realism] as the right Third World style?" (58) One implication in North American literary studies, to judge from the contents of most recent multicultural anthologies, has been that a requisite "realism" of language practice must be adhered to by black authors if they are to be canonized as proper literary representations of the experiences of social marginality. This is not a particularly new development. Kenneth Warren, in his book *Black and White Strangers: Race and American Literary Realism* (1993), has noted that, "Like many of their American Studies counterparts, students of African-American literature have often assumed the necessary connection between an acceptance of realistic methods and social progress in the realm of race" (4). There have always been multiple directions of thought within African-American literary studies, and that dominant direction as identified by Warren has been countered by practicing writers such as Clarence Major, who, in his 1974 collection of essays, *The Dark and the Feeling,* expressed his intention as a literary artist "to invest the work with a *secret nature* so powerful that, while it should fascinate, it should always elude the reader – just as the nature of life does" (16). In Major's counterview, "The social realist can never suggest that 'hidden' system of organization because he has never touched it. But it is present in all life and therefore should be in art" (19). Major's specification of the "social realist" indicates, as well, that realism of representation is not the only sort of realism that might be available. As Marjorie Perloff observes, in her discussion of the poetics of Gertrude Stein and Lyn Hejinian, " 'realism' can be an attitude toward language itself rather than only toward the objects to which language refers" (155).

It is crucial that we recall that realism of linguistic representation, like social and magical realism in the novel, is a carefully constructed literary style, not a scientific recording of actual speech. It is a fictive orthography adopted for the purpose of conveying an entire literary ideology via style. Even the most lifelike literary representations of colloquial speech only infrequently correspond with exactitude to the recorded utterances of actual speaking subjects. Indeed, as Stephen Henderson's critical work and anthology *Understanding the New Black Poetry: Black Speech and Black Music as Poetic References* (1972) gave ample evidence, even at the height of the Black Arts movement's calls for a poetic diction rooted in black speech and black music, the typographic representations of that speech were formulated in accordance with poetic practices already worked out by poets such as Amiri Baraka, Larry Neal, Jayne Cortez, Sonia Sanchez, and David Henderson, black poets whose confrontations with modernist poetics on the ground of language established the formal practices followed by subsequent African-American writers intent upon locating a black aesthetic in traditions of black orality and musical improvisation.

What too many critics and lay readers have failed to notice is the broad definition of "black speech" in this poetics. Henderson wrote in 1972, "By Black speech I mean the speech of the majority of Black people in this country, and I do not exclude the speech of so-called educated people" (31). Recent years have seen a proliferation of critical discussions of "orality" in African-American writing that *begin* by presupposing what the critical limits of that orality are. Current commitments to a critical preference for linguistic "realism" in the study of black writing founder upon precisely this rock; they have, at the very outset, assumed facts not in evidence, assumed that the contours of black orality are already fully known and understood. Too much current theorizing about black poetics secures its success with a critical readership by eliminating from consideration those poetic practices that might disrupt totalizing theories of what constitutes black vernacular.

Statisticians know that although charted outliers may not be said to be representative of a majority population, in fact it is their marked difference from the homogeneity of the rest of the sample that marks them as outliers. Still, they are the very defining boundary terms of that majority; they mark the defining margins of the main. In literary studies, such outliers are works and authors that are suppressed in the process of assigning stable identity and politics to the canonical margins. As Spivak warns, "When a cultural identity is thrust upon one because the center wants an identifiable margin, claims for marginality assure validation from the center" (55). There is always the risk that a call for broadening our consideration of African-American poetics by returning to the study of such neglected works as Kelly's might be seen as another "colonizing" move, another call for revalorizing works at the poetic "margins" of African-American studies. It may, in fact, be impossible entirely to elude such a charge. But the call for a rereading of marginalized texts does not value such texts *because* they are marginalized; rather, the argument is that we cannot claim adequate understanding of and theorizing about the course of black literary history so long as we begin such historicizing and theorizing at a point where we have eliminated from view, in advance, works that might, should they remain in view, challenge our histories and theories.

In the decades following the literary epoch of the Black Arts movement we have vastly expanded the course and print space dedicated to examinations of black literature, but this has oddly, or perhaps not so oddly, proceeded accompanied by a strict narrowing of attention to a few select works by black poets. If American literary scholarship and popular reading practices have finally moved beyond the "one-at-a-time" phenomenon, they have not moved far. The same texts of black poetry appear on syllabus after syllabus (when black poetry appears at all), ensuring the continued presence of a few texts in our newly reformed canons while also ensuring the invisibility of others. Ronald M. Radano, in his study *New Musical Figurations: Anthony Braxton's Cultural Critique* (1992), has noted a similar constriction in the study of modern African-American music, whereby "Important countermovements fall by the wayside; notable chal-

lenges recede into a clutter of ancillary diversions" (270). However, although few chronicles of recent jazz history would be so
bold as to omit from their narratives such innovative artists as
the Art Ensemble of Chicago, the Sun Ra Arkestra, the various
iterations of the Cecil Taylor Unit, Ornette Coleman, Archie
Shepp, or the subject of Radano's book, Anthony Braxton, recently published examinations of the literary past of African
America routinely omit such important poets (many of whom
worked with the musicians just listed) as Russell Atkins, N. J.
Loftis, Julia Fields, Norman Pritchard, Bob Kaufman, Stephen
Jonas, Elouise Loftin, and the members of the Dasein group, all
of whom figure in Eugene Redmond's monumental history of
African-American poetry, published in 1976, *Drumvoices: The Mission of Afro-American Poetry*. Critical historians since Redmond,
both black and white, have too frequently set forth on a less
critical mission. The result has often been that, according to
Warren, "despite its contributions to literary study, canon-based
criticism of African-American literature has entailed a variety of
liabilities, from recapitulating in black vernacular the assumptions of American ahistoricism to taking for granted apolitical
notions of black unity that impoverish our understanding of
our intellectual and political history" (16). It is just such an
impoverished canon that the elimination of Kelly's *Dunfords Travels* from critical consideration accomplishes.

Giles Gunn, in *Thinking across the American Grain: Ideology,
Intellect, and the New Pragmatism* (1992), has noted this as a
general impoverishment resulting from the struggle over the
American literary canon in the past two decades:

> Until new texts and new authors are brought into func-
> tional relations with established ones – relations, in other
> words, that demonstrate how those new authors and texts
> increase, or at least extend, the power of the symbolic capi-
> tal already accumulated by predecessors who have deline-
> ated what else can be constructed, remedied, or revised
> with their assistance – culture doesn't really change; it
> merely grows fat about the middle, or, what amounts to the
> same thing, ingests what it doesn't know how to digest. (6)

Earlier in the century, mainstream anthologies often simply
elided black poetry entirely. F. O. Matthiessen's *Oxford Book of
American Verse*, for example, could find no room in 1950 for

even one African-American poem. As Alan Golding has recently pointed out, this followed a century-long period in America during which anthologies of black poets were published. In Golding's view, "one would expect some cumulative effect on mainstream anthologies to derive from such publications," and since "black poets' work *was* widely available, . . . mainstream editors could hardly use ignorance of its existence as an excuse" (28). It seems unlikely that a mainstream anthology would appear today that did not include at least a token representation of African-American verse, but in the canon-forming motion of the past two decades much of the cumulative effect of the anthologies of the late 1960s and early 1970s has been lost. When one observes how many innovative black poets were included in collections made just a generation ago, it is hard to believe that their absence from contemporary anthologies is truly the result of editors' ignorance of their existence.

Each year the Norton and Harper and Heath anthologies so widely used for college courses in modern literature multiply and grow thicker, yet they seemingly can find no room, even while celebrating the margins and revaluing aesthetic transgression, for the likes of *Dunfords Travels Everywheres* or a poem like Norman H. Pritchard's "junt":

junt

mool oio clish brodge
cence anis oio
mek mek isto plawe

(*EECCHHOOEESS* 28)

William Melvin Kelly has been a much-honored, widely reviewed novelist and has published with a large New York commercial house. If the language experiments of his fine novel have been allowed to fall off the map of the recent past of American literary history, Pritchard, we might suggest, has been pushed off. His poems seem to ask, as did Gertrude Stein's and William Carlos Williams's before him, fundamental questions about the very nature of the poetic. "Words," he inscribed as the epigraph to his collection *The Matrix*, published in 1970, "are ancillary to content." This statement may not get us very far in considering the form-versus-content controversy, but it no doubt explains a great deal about why so few critics of African-American poetry have devoted any time to his works. A more ready explanation presents itself for the fact that Pritchard is not written about as a predecessor to such important American literary movements as the so-called L=A=N=G=U=A=G=E school: critics of white poetry simply seldom look at black writers while compiling their genealogies of aesthetic evolution.

But Pritchard, who to date has never been mentioned by cultural studies critiques of aesthetic transgression, was not always so extremely marginalized. The book in which "junt" appears was published by New York University Press, and his still more unconventional collection *The Matrix* was published by Doubleday. In June of 1967 Pritchard's photograph filled the cover of the magazine *Liberator,* published in New York by the Afro-American Research Institute, an organization with both Old and New Left affiliations. Inside this issue was a collection of Pritchard's poetry, accompanied by a brief commentary written by W. Francis Lucas. The terminology of Lucas's notes is striking in retrospect. He said of Pritchard's work, "These poems decompose the reader by sight and sound" (12). This was in 1967, before English translations of Derrida, Lacan, and Kristeva had become standard fare for graduate literary study, before deconstruction and other forms of poststructuralist critique had had much opportunity to alter the critical vocabulary of book reviewers. More importantly, we see in this instance that Lucas was free of the all too common assumption that experimental approaches to expression and theorized reading are somehow white things. By situating Pritchard "in the balances of language" that include Paul Laurence Dunbar, Geoffrey Chaucer, and Ezra Pound, Lucas manifested, as did Kelly in his epigraphs to *Dunfords Travels,* as did Tolson in his later poems, an understanding of English-language poetic tradition as having been already implicated in blackness. A poem such as "junt" clearly foregrounds the materiality of the means of signification, but critics have been slow to see black participation in the critical vocabularies of that trend in modern and postmodernist verse.

Interestingly, even with the emphasis upon the orality of black verse in the work of so many critics, little critical study has been offered of the relationship between the Pritchard poems as scored on the page and, for an excellent example, the chanted versions of the poems that he recorded for the 1967 Broadside album *New Jazz Poets.* Pritchard's published poems hug to the shifting line between the composed and the improvised. A poem that appeared in the second issue of the magazine *Umbra* shows

Pritchard as early as 1963 worrying that line between text and tongue, between writing and intention, singing and speaking, all saturated in the signifiers of black song traditions:

> "The Lady" utters a cantata in "praise"
> of morning heartaches . . . one more chance
> to realize that it's   the unsung
> that makes the song.   From where the blues?
> Strange, this combat that selects its soldiers.
>
> (51)

The first three words of the second line of this poem exactly follow the rhythm of the Billie Holliday song that is their "real-world" referent. Pritchard's poems meet all the structural criteria outlined by Stephen Henderson in his interpretation of black poetics. They are virtual catalogues of jazzy rhythmic effects, virtuoso free rhyming, hyperbolic and metaphysical imagery, understatement, compressed and cryptic imagery, "worrying the line," and, in both "junt" and "From Where the Blues?", I would argue, black music as poetic reference.

Commentary on jazz history makes copious room for the advent and evolution of scat singing on record, but literary criticism, at least mainstream criticism of black writers, seems either to be left speechless by scat's poetic analogue or simply not to have noticed it. The techniques of "junt" have been adopted by other black writers and sometimes adapted to a yet more overt effort to suggest "Africanesque" language thematics, as in the poem entitled "HER," by Stephen Chambers, which appeared in the *Journal of Black Poetry* in 1969:

> A – JA – BU;
>   A – JA – BU
>   (bu – su)
>   sue/san
>   I – Kemo – San
> Ja – A – Bu
>   Ja – A – Bu
>   i/kemo/no/san
>   San/ (frisco???)
> Bu – A – Ja
>   (jabua)
>
> (21)

Chambers's poem may also suggest similar passages in works by Amiri Baraka, passages that script the vocal elements of jazz instrumental music and voice American accents in imitation of heard African languages, a speaking in tongues often accompanied by humor. Neither Pritchard nor Chambers was among the exhibits in the anthology section of Henderson's book, even though Pritchard was regularly represented in contemporary anthologies of black poetry, including *The New Black Poetry; You Better Believe It; The Poetry of Black America;* and *Dices or Black Bones.* Later anthologies advertising themselves as records of the period, though, steadfastly ignored Pritchard and most other poets who wrote in a similar vein. Even as eclectic an anthology as Michael Harper and Anthony Walton's *Every Shut Eye Ain't Asleep* (1994), which attempts to represent "poetry by African-Americans since 1945," has no room for Pritchard's record of experiment.

Pritchard's penchant for concocting sound texts and his interest in concrete poetry should, by now, have attracted much more attention from critics interested in the infinite permutations of orality in black verse and of those tracing the history of American participation in such international aesthetic movements as concretism. The attention has not come. If Lucas was guilty of anything, in his too short note on Pritchard, it was overoptimism. He argued that "Language and its use in our time" were the conveyors "of larger and more detailed perceptions about life and art" and predicted, "Time inevitably holds a great deal in store" for Pritchard (13). Pritchard has been, to the contrary, nearly wholly forgotten. One of the only critical assessments of him to appear in the last decade was written by Kevin Young, then a student at Harvard University and a member of the Dark Room Collective of poets, in connection with an exhibit at Harvard's Widener Library entitled "Material Poetry of the Renaissance/The Renaissance of Material Poetry." Young advanced several explanations for the nearly complete repression of this once well-published poet, perhaps the most convincing being that "Pritchard seems positioned outside whichever definition of 'concrete' is chosen, whether Black reality or reader-oriented physicality" (27).

There lingers an oddness about this explanation: Why does the concrete existence of poetry so determinedly given to foregrounding the material of its own workings elude definitions of

the concrete? Surely there is something deeply wrong with critical definitions that might have the end effect of repressing the
reality of a black poet by viewing him and his work as being sited
outside of black reality. Writing in *Black World*, in July 1971,
Kalamu Ya Salaam declared, "Something is wrong when we mistake everyday Black rapping about our Black condition and experience for strong Black poetry that expresses our realest selves.
Something is going wrong with this and we'd better find out
now" (28). Although the date and the occasion of this declara-
tion will remind us that the "rapping" he addressed was not quite
what the word calls to mind in the 1990s, the essay was a 1971
review of recent recordings by Amiri Baraka, the Last Poets, and
the Black Voices, the observable fact that essays in cultural studies
today are far more likely to look for their valued transgressive
readings in the realm of Rap than among publishing black poets
should give us pause.

In 1968, Stanley Crouch, who was then giving himself to the
movement "Toward a Purer Black Poetry Aesthetic," offered a
stern binary opposition of his own: "Street speech and street
song are two very different things. Many of the younger Black
Writers do not really understand this, do not develop their ears
so as to tell the difference, a vital difference which, if not understood, most often leads to the flat, ugly sort of thing that Robert
Creeley, Ginsburg [Allen Ginsberg], Frank O'Hara and many of
the so-called 'avant garde' white writers come up with" ("Toward"
28). (Perhaps Crouch has not changed much in the intervening
years.) In the same issue of the *Journal of Black Poetry*, Crouch,
denouncing new poetry collections by LeRoi Jones, A. B. Spellman, and David Henderson, stated with his accustomed air of
certainty, "I am very concerned about Black Literature and do
not believe, as do many others, that we are experiencing a renaissance, but, rather, think that we are falling into the same kind of
slump Black Music fell into during the soul-funk fad of eight
years ago: A whole lot of people are bullshitting under the banner of 'getting down' " ("Books" 90). What comes into view in
the critical comments of both Kalamu Ya Salaam and Stanley
Crouch (though I hesitate to yoke them in this fashion, given the
quite different routes they have since taken from this shared
point) is a growing impatience with some claimed links between
black poetics and daily black performance in speech and song,
as well as a desire to forge other, perhaps more effective links
between those same subjects. Although these debates have for

the most part not been reexamined by the critical establishment
(when I went to check the *Journal of Black Poetry* out of the library
at UCLA I found it had not been requested in twenty years), the
residual effect of the debates continues to shape readings and
discussions of African-American poetry. Mainstream critics today
are far more likely to assume they already know what was said
during the Black Aesthetic period and reargue the issues from
there than to revisit the documents themselves.

For another take on these issues, we might look at Jerry Ward's
1976 article on N. J. Loftis's pioneering volume *Black Anima*.
Ward shared Ya Salaam's frustration: "in searching through all
the writing devoted to this protean phenomenon, one's attempt
to find discussion of the *aesthetics* which inform the Black Aesthetic is a hopeless undertaking . . . Until such time as we do
formulate an aesthetics that will elucidate the concepts involved
in critical judgments about black works of art, we will confuse
moral and ideological attitudes with aesthetic attitudes" (145).
We can say with Jessie Fauset that there is confusion. Ward's
article appeared four years after Henderson's attempt, in *Understanding the New Black Poetry,* to clear a path toward discussion of
the *aesthetics* that might inform the Black Aesthetic. Many of our
finest critics, including Hazel Carby, Houston Baker, Hortense
Spillers, Henry Louis Gates, Vévé Clark, Deborah McDowell, and,
as always, Jerry Ward, have done essential work in the critical
anatomizing of the aesthetics of literary art by black writers. If we
look beyond that important work to the exclusions practiced so
regularly against so many black poets in the decades since Ward's
article, it appears, at least to this reader, that many of them have
been accomplished precisely by masking ideological desire as an
aesthetic judgment rooted in concrete particulars. Ward predicted in 1976 that "*Black Anima* will never become a popular
book" (208); in *The Dark and the Feeling* (1974), Clarence Major
offered a stark definition: "to be a black artist is to be unpopular"
(24). We need, still, to look carefully at the question of why some
are more unpopular, critically unpopular, than others; why, for
example, Ward was so right that *Black Anima,* a book he termed
"an important and necessary document in the tradition of black
writing" (208), has proven to be so consistently unimportant and
unnecessary to those critics documenting and theorizing black
poetics. We need to ask why it is that, given so much talk of the
importance to black poetry of black speech and the avid academic interest in the most popular Rap recordings, so few schol-

ars have been, as Ward was, "caught by the rhythms of black speech rerapped" (207) in *Black Anima*.

One key component of the critical operations that have "deac-cessioned" (to use a term depressingly current in the language of the library and the gallery) broad swaths of the recent past of black experiment in poetics is a series of nearly hegemonic assumptions about the nature of the relationship between African-American oral traditions and writing, with a clear privi-lege given to the prevailing ideal of the oral. This is absolutely not a phenomenon limited to critical discussions of black writ-ing. As Spivak has summarized Jacques Derrida's deconstruction of the speech–writing opposition operative in European thought, "Western metaphysics opposed the *general* principle of speech, on the one hand, to writing in the narrowest sense on the other" (98). That categorical error itself remains observably operative in some of the texts on orality and culture that have assumed the greatest influence among educators and critics in our lifetime. In Walter J. Ong's frequently cited book, *Orality and Literacy* (1982), just to take one of the most prominent examples, there is a strange instantiation of this logic. Ong writes that "Human beings in primary oral cultures, those untouched by writing in any form, learn a great deal and possess and practice great wisdom, but they do not 'study' . . . Study in the strict sense of extended sequential analysis becomes possible with the interiorization of writing" (9). Ong takes care to define "study" in such a way that it only becomes possible with the advent of writing, but at the same time he appears less strictly concerned with the largest of epistemological questions. At the most basic level one has to ask how it is that this highly literate writer has come to possess this truth about primary oral cultures, those untouched by writing in *any* form. Has he received this truth in the form of a series of oral reports from previously illiterate informants who have brought the knowledge to him directly upon leaving their primary oral cultures behind, or is this knowl-edge the result of his reading? Later in this book Ong acknowl-edges quite openly the fact that "Without textualism, orality can-not even be identified" (169), and he does make it clear that his theories of what must have been true for primary oral cultures are derived from his reading of texts. But for all his willingness to engage the debates over textuality, logocentrism, and phono-centrism, Ong never truly comes to grips with the full implica-tions of the transcendent nature of his theories of orality. Simi-

larly questionable assumptions have often been made about the
verbal and educational practices of primarily oral cultures, assumptions sometimes mirrored by late twentieth-century theories
of education.

The relationship between memory and orality is one about
which numerous inadequately tested assumptions circulate. Ronald A. T. Judy, in (Dis)forming the American Canon (1993), finds
a remarkable passage in Theodore Dwight's nineteenth-century
ethnological texts. Dwight reported an interview with Lamen
Kebe, an African-American slave who had been a scholar and
teacher in West Africa. Kebe provided Dwight with a description
of a West African mode of teaching Qur'anic Arabic that may at
first seem to fit with what Westerners generally take to be the
norm in such African scenes of instruction. But, as Judy observes,
"While mnemotechny was emphasized in learning the Qur'an,
what was practiced in Kebe's school was memorization by graphic
reproduction, rather than oral presentation . . . What is most
noteworthy about Kebe's discussion of the . . . pedagogical
method is that the written and not the heard word is memorized
through recitation. The students are taught to be readers before
anything else, and above all readers who can decipher" (173). If
we recall the enormous import of such scenes of instruction in
African-American literature, the regularity with which an atmosphere of nearly religious liberation accompanies the introduction to literacy, we can see that traditions of graphic reproduction
and improvisation are part of an iterative continuum with orality,
not a secondary or elitist and pale reflection of the spoken, and
we can likewise estimate the dangers to our understanding of
African-American literary history implicit in the construction of
an idealized orality in opposition to a devalued writing.

While introducing the poems of Arthur Pfister in a Broadside
Press chapbook, Amiri Baraka took a moment to address the
devaluing of the written, and we can locate in his remarks a
deterritorializing motion against European claims to primacy
over supposedly nonliterate societies. Baraka says, "We talk about
the oral tradition of African People, sometimes positively, many
times defensively (if we are not wised up), and it's always as a
substitute for the written. What this is is foolfood, because we
were the first writers as well . . . Thot is the God of writing, its
inventor, and African" ("Introduction" 4). It is important to
understand that Baraka's statements were made in the historical
context of previous attempts to assert the primacy of African

inscription. Langston Hughes and Arna Bontemps argued, in their introduction to their anthology *The Poetry of the Negro* (1970), that "articulate slaves belonged to a tradition of writers in bondage that goes back to Aesop and Terence" (xxii), and we should remember that it was Terence who was memorialized as a predecessor in the poetry of Phillis Wheatley, the first African American to publish a book of poems. In the nineteenth century Martin Delany, writing in his book *The Origin of Races and Color* (47, 53), copied into his text examples of both Egyptian hieroglyphs and the ancient alphabetic script of Ethiopia (and who can forget the importance of ancient Ethiopic script in the mysterious transcriptions of Edgar Allan Poe?). Delany's figures are an early instance of black efforts to reassert African inscription as a basis for metaphysical philosophy in language:

We here introduce the hieroglyphics, the reading of which will be observed, accord to our version, or that which we obtained from study among the Africans themselves, by learning the significance or meaning of certain objects or things.

The hieroglyphics are letters forming a literature founded upon the philosophy of nature without an alphabet; but that which we shall now present is of a much higher order, being artificial characters based on metaphysical philosophy of language.

THE OLD ORIGINAL ETHIOPIAN ALPHABET.

Alf.	*Zai.*	*Mai.*	*Kof.*
Bet.	*Hbarm.*	*Nabas.*	*Rees.*
Geml.	*Tait.*	*Saat.*	*Saut.*
Dent.	*Jaman.*	*Ain.*	*Tawi.*
Haut.	*Caf.*	*Af.*	
Waw:	*Lewi.*	*Tzadai.*	

In the next century, postmodern poets would again turn to ancient African script for precedents. In a 1967 letter, the poet Stephen Jonas expressed his frustration at not being able to locate a copy of Wallis Budge's guide to Egyptian hieroglyphics at the Boston Public Library and reported that he was ordering a copy of his own from Dover Books (*Four Letters* 14). Little acknowledgment has thus far been given by white critics to this history of black historical recovery, perhaps in part because, as Frances Smith Foster remarks, "Though they have little difficulty acknowledging the complexity of early black music and oral literature, they are reluctant to assume a similar level of sophistication with written language" (28). In positing an African genesis for writing against European attempts to strip the African continent of its history of inscription and its history in writing, Baraka did not offer a simple reversal of the speech–writing opposition. His introduction to Pfister's poetry was, in fact, entitled "Pfister Needs to Be Heard!", a title that links together, in its inscribed ambiguity, the need to hear spoken realizations of Pfister's script and the political need to hear what Pfister has to write.

One problem with continued privileging of orality over the written in the study of African-American writing is that such privileging too often leads to a critique that inadequately listens to the relationships between script and performance. Poet C. S. Giscombe writes, "I'm African-American, a phrase I like because the last 2 syllables of each word are the same & in that I see two near-identical dark faces" ("Fugitive" 51). Giscombe, the writer, sees in what he has written that which can be heard in its enunciation, locating a racial ideology in the syllables of a phrase. He enacts that syllabic ideology in his poem "Giscome Road," where he writes, "I was / Africa & America on the same bicycle" (96). Giscombe's eye has seen the marker of the sound he links both graphically and aurally to the ideology inscribed within his poem. He does not elide the importance of a performative poetics in so doing. To the contrary, he is positively concerned about the relationship between ethos and inscription, the tension that can exist between the encoded values of a lyric and the sea-change they can undergo as they move from page to performance to recorded reiteration. In his essay on "The Fugitive" he turns to Martha and the Vandellas' Motown hit "Nowhere to Run, Nowhere to Hide" for an accessible citation: "because of

the sheer – meaning precipitous – strength & sound of Martha
Reeves' voice the song achieves a virtual truth, one that surpasses
the arguable lie of the lyrics. Willful performance'll *do* that to
absolute value" (49). Unless we are willing to read fully the
nuances of these movements between scripting and voicing, we
cannot hope to historicize the continual unfolding of these problematics in the poems of black writers. We would not know the
precipitous strength of Martha Reeves's voice had it not been
remarked by the recording head and reiterated by the scratching
stylus of post–World War II technology. My younger students,
who have not shared my good fortune in having heard Martha
and the Vandellas live, would simply have had to take my word
for it.

Similarly, when Jonas wrote, in his "subway haiku," published
in a 1967 issue of the magazine *Floating Bear,* "i tell you the
sentence is doomd" (433), we have to read what we cannot
hear. We have to see the cummings-like lower-case first-person
pronoun and the elision of the letter *e* in "doomd." Most of all
we have to read the absence that cannot be heard, the absence
of a closing period, the missing punctuation that poetically carries out the prophecy written in the poem. None of these are
specifically "oral" features of Jonas's poetics, but neither are they
antithetical to the improvisatory impulses of African-American
orality. Such graphic techniques are, instead, part of the general
economy of language that encompasses oral and written in an
ever expanding grammatology. As Nathaniel Mackey argues, in
Discrepant Engagement (1993), "The rush to canonize orality as a
radical departure from the values of an 'eye-oriented' civilization
runs the risk of obscuring the attention paid by recent poets to
the way the poem appears on the page. This 'graphicity,' moreover, [is] hardly at odds with the 'oral' impulse" (122).

One risk run by those who would canonize orality, the same
risk run by all canon formation, is that even many oral phenomena may be left out. It is commonly the case that a privileging of
the oral in examinations of black writing is accompanied by a
severe restricting of the registers of English considered availably
"black." It was the concern about such a constricting of registers
that brought Bobb Hamilton, in 1969, to feel the need to explain
his use of the word "whilst" in his poem "For Malik:"

> In Cleveland, Ohio, in the ghetto, where I grew up everyone
> said whilst in spite of all that the teachers could do to

"civilize" us ... There are lots of other archaisms that I used until I went to college and then became self-conscious behind my degree! My neighborhood was really a southern black community moved north, and the language there was often "quaint" so to speak. What I tried to capture in the poem was the flavor of the black storefront preacher and his female congregation ... My use of the term ["whilst"] was not pretentious but an attempt to go back, so to speak, to the way our people responded to an emotional shock as I remember it. Malcolm did have that kind of appeal to the older people – I've seen them shout at some of his indoor speeches. (100)

Hamilton wrote this note because he knew that some readers would condemn his use of the word "whilst" in a poem about Malcolm X as a pretentious archaism, an overly literary, perhaps even white, elitist affectation. He wanted readers to know that the word *is* archaic, but that it is an archaic usage that lives in the oral tradition of his black community, one that carries an emotive value which is contemporaneously available to black reading subjects.

Just such a constricting of registers considered to be available to black orality continues to motivate much current critical discussion of literary history. In an essay in a recent issue of the *American Poetry Review,* John Yau condemns Eliot Weinberger on just these grounds. Yau is responding to an historical essay in Weinberger's anthology *American Poetry since 1950: Innovators and Outsiders* (1993). The anthologist's criteria in selecting poets for the anthology might have been expected to exclude some innovators at the outset. He limited his selections, he explains, to poems published in books since 1950, written by poets born before World War II. Even with that limitation granted, it would appear there must be other exclusionary criteria at work, since the only two black poets whose works Weinberger included were Hughes and Baraka. Yau indicates the enormity of Weinberger's exclusions with a list: "Both in his selection and in his accompanying essay, Weinberger fails to acknowledge the importance of Sterling A. Brown, Henry Dumas, Robert Hayden, Stephen Jonas, Bob Kaufman, Etheridge Knight, Larry Neal, Lorenzo Thomas, Melvin Tolson, and Jay Wright" (50). Though Thomas is close to the cutting edge of Weinberger's criteria, having been born in 1944, every poet on Yau's list has published books since 1950, has been recognized as a poetic innovator, and has spent much of his career as an "outsider" by any critic's definition.

Part of Weinberger's exclusionary tactic is patently motivated by his privileging of orality, accompanied by his extremely narrow notion of what constitutes black speech. According to Yau's analysis, "by valorizing orality and performance in African-American poetry at the expense of all else, Weinberger upholds a degrading view of African-Americans and African-American literature; they can talk jive, but they can't write. They can swear, but they can't spell. This is the liberal, postwar update of Rousseau's notion of the relationship between the pure self and corrupt society, as well as the valorization of the Noble Savage" (51). Weinberger, of course, rejects this imputation of racist motives to his work as a literary historian. In his letter to the editors of the *American Poetry Review* responding to Yau, he terms Yau's article "a nervous breakdown in print," "demagoguery," "crazed invective," and he calls Yau a liar (43). Curiously, though, his only real response to Yau's central charge is to deny it and to assert that Yau offers "*no other corroborating evidence whatsoever* [of Yau's accusation of bias] (because there isn't any)" (emphasis in original). But we have only to look at his own explanations of his inclusion of Baraka to see that there is much truth to Yau's charges. In the "Very Brief History" Weinberger has written to conclude his anthology, he speaks of black nationalist poetry, whose only representative in the anthology is Baraka, as "The movement [that] effectively admitted African-American speech into poetry (something the Harlem Renaissance, with the notable exception of Hughes, had refused to do)" (401). Yau quite accurately takes Weinberger to task for this remark, not only for excluding other poets during the period of the Renaissance who clearly and consciously attempted to effectively "admit" African-American speech into poetry (Jean Toomer? Helene Johnson? James Weldon Johnson?) but also because Weinberger's history ignores poets such as Sterling Brown and Melvin B. Tolson, who published books in the period between the Harlem Renaissance and the Black Arts movement. If Weinberger were correct that, with the exception of Hughes, the Harlem Renaissance had refused admission to African-American speech, then we would be hardpressed to understand why later black writers such as Sarah Webster Fabio would feel that "The Harlem Renaissance period closed the credibility gap between the Black man, his articulation of his experience, and his selfhood" (177). Perhaps the other

poets of the Harlem Renaissance just are not black enough for
Weinberger. It may be that he prefers poems in which, to quote
a satire by Helene Johnson, "Some bozo's been to Africa to get
some sand" (97). But there remains a larger, racially marked
fallacy in Weinberger's "Very Brief History." If, during the Harlem
Renaissance, all but Hughes refused to admit African-American
speech into poetry, then all speech admitted into poetry by black
writers other than Hughes in that era must be viewed as something
other than black speech. Not only would Weinberger need to have
read much more poetry than he gives evidence of having read in
order to make such a claim; he would have to believe that he
knows what black speech was during the Harlem Renaissance,
what it was during what he calls "the decade of black nationalist
poetry" (401), and what it was during the intervening years. Fabio,
in contrast, viewed black writers as recording angels of black orality. "Black writers," she insisted, " – most of them poets plus – have
always been barometers, even when America kept bell jars on
them. Have always been/still are/will be. Always traveling with
ears to the ground; attuned to the drumbeats of the age" (181).
Even Fabio, we must concede though, had a hard time with the
registrations of Tolson's barometer.

But this emphasis upon the ear will still miss a great deal that
black poets are doing and have always done. It will miss, as most
criticism to date has missed, this passage from Julia Fields's long
poem "When That Which Is Perfect Is Come" (*Slow Coins* 132):

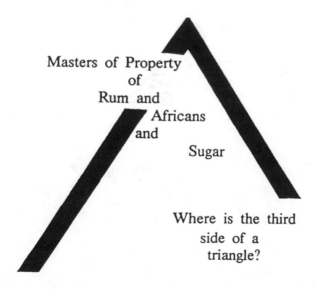

Here Fields writes across the Triangle Trade. It is a writing that disrupts the mastery of the trade it represents, and it is an opening out of the Middle Passage onto contemporary readings. This is a poem that graphically remasters history, using oral *and* graphic tradition, orature and historical document, but using them in a fashion that must be seen to be heard. It is a poem that follows some of the same formal imperatives Nathaniel Mackey has discerned in the poetics of Charles Olson. It is a work that "tends to be tempered by a visual intelligibility ('impenetrable to anything but the eye'), a sense of coherence that resides in shape rather than message or paraphrasable statement, a sense impressed upon the reader by the placement of the words on the page" (*Discrepant* 134). Likewise, the rest of Fields's poem works with an almost unspeakable, though rebuslike, play between eye, ear, and tongue (139):

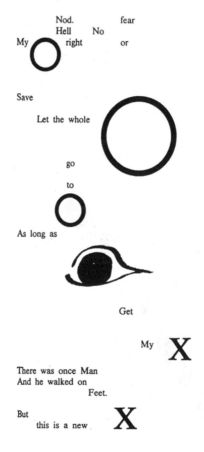

In this passage we *can* read "As long as / 🐍 / Get / My X" aloud to one another, but the graphic texture of the poem is essential to its effects; the texture can be read from the page but cannot be read to another. We must look at this poem to see the "wholes" become eyes (Olson's polis was composed of eyes in heads to be looked out of), to see the *X* mark itself as absence, burial, and rechristening. The advent of the *X* in Fields's post-Malcolm poem signifies for us in ways that were unavailable before Malcolm X. As the *X* emblazoned as both commodity and historic claim on the caps of so many young people in the early 1990s signified so loudly within the silence it marked, the *X* in Fields's poem is an *X*-ing out and a crossing over. The new *X* of Fields's "When That Which Is Perfect Is Come," though, continues to be *X*-ed out of critical history, and I doubt that it can be reclaimed by an ethnopoetics that awards primacy to orality. Fields herself commented upon similar impoverishments of American reception of African-American literary arts. Writing to Rosey Pool to express her dismay at the lack of response to Paul Bremen's Heritage series of chapbooks, Fields remarked, "I think that in the future one of the great regrets of the U.S.A. will be the great snobbery and stupidity of manner in which it has behaved toward Negro creative expression" (Pool Papers 52).

"It is instructive to listen," writes Mackey, "to others who . . . come from communities we tend to think of as oral. Their remarks on the orality versus literacy question provide an antidote to the either/or, too easy infatuation with the oral that ethnopoetics might lapse into" (261). Whereas the ethnopoetics movement may be seen as a temporally locatable trend primarily associated with first-generation postmodernist American writers (Gary Snyder, Jerome Rothenberg, etc.), the either–or opposition that worries Mackey extends well beyond that field into the very different regions of ethnic studies and racialized cultural criticism.

One of the more prominent recent examples of this is Lindon Barrett's essay "(Further) Figures of Violence: *The Street* in the American Landscape" (1993). It is important to note, at the outset, that Barrett has much of value to say about Ann Petry's too long neglected novel *The Street* and its itinerary through critical discourse. In the midst of his historical tracking, nonetheless, Barrett produces an argument opposing "singing" to "signing" and not just privileging the first of these terms but adducing it as a "peculiarly African-American possession" (220). This peculiar institution of essentializing binary oppositions is all the more surprising in an essay that attempts to engage Derrida's deconstruction of such oppositions. In order to advance this type of argument, Barrett has to establish a series of rather startling assumptions:

> By highlighting the enunciative or vocative aspect and moment of the voice, the singing voice marks the absence of iteration and repetition. The singing voice iterates or repeats nothing per se, because speech is declined insofar as the singing voice does not intend to effect, or direct, the meaningful word but instead to affect, display or deploy – even to displace – the meaningful word . . .
>
> The revisionary allowance of the singing voice depends chiefly upon suspending meaningfulness understood as the *sign*, a suspension readily apparent in virtually all African-American vocal performances – and most especially, and most vividly, in a blues and jazz tradition in which scatting abandons meaningful speech altogether and turns freely and ludically to the charged instrumentality of the voice – an Other and novel realm of meaning. (219–20)

The claim that the singing voice "iterates or repeats nothing per se" is sufficiently peculiar in itself, seemingly rendering repeat performances either impossible or nonsinging. No matter how varied her improvisations upon "Perdido," Sarah Vaughan's versions of that song continue to exist in some relationship of reiteration to one another, recognizably so to most experienced ears. But more remarkable yet is the assertion that the singing voice repeats nothing per se *because* it declines speech. It is difficult to ascertain just where this argument draws the line between speech and song. By this logic, Norman Pritchard's "junt" might be judged singing, and "Lift Every Voice and Sing" might not measure up. It is true, as C. S. Giscombe's citation of Martha and the Vandellas confirms, that the singing voice affects, deploys, and even displaces the meanings of the meaningful word, but it does not in so doing leave the meaningful entirely behind. Scat singing does turn ludically and freely "to the charged instrumentality of the voice," but this does not mean that meaningful speech has been wholly declined. The vocables of scat singing retain a differential relationship to both sung lyric and speech, and there clearly exists a conventional vocabulary of scatting. If this were not so, then there would be nothing to remark when a singer expands the vocabulary of scatting by introducing previously uncommon vocables. Further, although musical vocabularies may be considerably less denotative than the lexicons of spoken languages, it remains the case that conventions evolve linking musical figurations to connotative values (which is why the "Devil's interval" sounds so much less devilish to us today). The singing voice does arrive at another realm of meaning, but this is not accomplished by leaving meaningful speech altogether. For Barrett, "the singing voice is the peculiar moment that is original and negative to speech" (219), but this would require that this peculiar and originary moment have the existence of speech as its originary other upon which to depend for its identity. In order for the singing voice to be the original moment negative to speech, it must be founded upon the possibility of speech, and thus could never wholly leave speech behind; rather it would always and forever carry the meaningful word within it.

Further yet, when Barrett argues that the *singing voice* comprises the primary legacy of the New World African, his logic pushes beyond a simple claim that the New World African contribution to music somehow exceeds contributions in other realms to the essentialist proposition that singing is a peculiarly African-American possession. The American Indians, when they sing, must be doing something even more other than any of their auditors from other ethnic groups ever supposed. In the same way that Ong secures part of his argument upon a definition of "study" that limits it, strictly speaking, to literate societies, Barrett must redeploy "singing" as a term so that it will function only as he wishes it to. Thus he can explain in a note that "The newest correlate of 'signifyin(g)' [which, he cautions, we are not to mistake for 'singing'], rap music, is similarly an extension of the 'singing' performance" (235n). Just how peculiar Barrett's defining logic is becomes evident when he offers a summary of his idea of "singing": "My formulations on the singing voice might be summarized as follows: the sign is iteration; iteration is closure; closure is power; and the singing voice, for the diasporic African, undoes all three in a landscape in which iteration, closure, and power belie her or his presence" (220). Here, again,

Barrett has secured these formulations upon the most radical of misprisions. Most authorities on English usage, as part of their definition of "iteration," indicate that it refers to repetition and recurrence, saying or doing something again. To "say or to do again" is to say or do with a difference, temporally and topologically at the very least, so that there is always repetition and difference. Iteration is Baraka's "changing same." It is *not* closure. The oddness of this misprision is underscored by Barrett's locating of his binarism in the graphic difference between "singing" and "signing," which is to say that the difference between the singing and signing voices that Barrett wants us to hold to is *not* an audible phonetic binarism, though it is an audible difference. The phonetic difference between his terms is multiple and scriptable.

This brings us to a fundamental argument that song, chant, and poetry have with those who would divide them against themselves in an attempt to divide the oral from the written. Chant, and this is true equally of such terms as "song" and "tradition," in order to be *heard as* chant, must present itself to us as the at least vaguely familiar, the already heard, for it must have presupposed the possibility of reiteration, response, recall, re-rapping. It is not chant if not repeated, nor is it orature unless it is transmitted, remarked, redeployed. Each member of the inheriting chain of tradition repeats the chant in a different voice, replays it in a different register, alters its rhythmic patterns. In this respect, chant, and indeed all orature, bodies itself forth in the garb of the mark, inscription, calligraphy. Orature is not opposed to writing; lecture is not opposed to listening.

"There should be, of course, a way of speaking about all kinds of Black poetry" (10), according to Stephen Henderson. Such a way must be intertextual and polyglot if it is to address itself to what the narrator of Clarence Major's novel *No* describes as "Creolized language, trade language, contact vernacular, *our* thing" (83). Such a future way of reading and historicizing must retrace what Ed Roberson, in *When Thy King Is a Boy* (1970) has called "The Calligraphy of Black Chant" (74). It may not be a criticism that, as in Roberson's "Four Lines of a Black Love Letter between Teachers," comes to a halt at the question "but but / is it   black" (*When* 67). It will have to be a criticism capable of encompassing works such as Russell Atkins's "Nocturne and Prelude" (qtd. in High 26):

By N x   x   x   x   x
    x   x   x   O   x
      x
  x

           x
    (ight   rE
               o
from the (((((((((((((Slɪ///
you may very reverently
begin /// wa lk // Ing
com mmm mmmmmmm mmmmmm mmm

Undoubtedly, early readers of this poem, when it appeared in the *Beloit Poetry Journal* in 1951, were put in mind of e. e. cummings, and the poem clearly bears the imprint of that influence, among others. In retrospect, there seems something proleptic about those nocturnal *X*'s filling the sky of the page like so many stars, almost as if the poem had intuited the significance that the letter *X* would soon acquire for African-American writers and readers, almost as if it were calling into being the chiasmatic poetics of Julia Fields. A criticism more effectively engaged with the entire breadth of black literary expression must not sit idly awaiting the wider circulation of "interactive" texts so long as we have not begun our analyses of poems such as this one, from Atkins's 1960 chapbook *A Podium Presentation* (n. pag.):

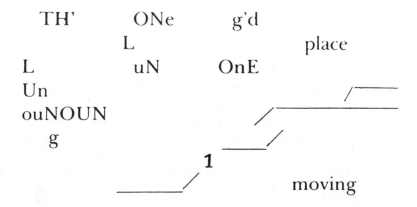

This poem's iterations and delineations do not assume, nor will they be subsumed by, the powers of closure. Neither can the poem, taken as score, be limited to one mode of performative realization. The inscribed lines of the poem can be read, but they cannot be read aloud in any usual sense of the term. The calligramic shapes of this section of a larger poem, entitled, appropriately enough, "Lines in Recollection," recall the formal innovations of Apollinaire, while at the same time they appear to graph the anagrammatic planes of the alphabetic text around them. Atkins's lines also seem to chart, in a fashion orally unreproducable, "the coy farm settled heavy shapes" of the hills described in the more nearly normative lineation of the stanza facing them on the opposing page. The terraced stanzas moving upon the word "moving" at the end of the poem are no problem to look at, to remember, to recollect, or to reiterate. As is true of the poet "just arrived on the advanced slope" in the first part of the poem, a reader arrived at this prospect finds that it is "no trouble at all/to see the around'd spanned circular far/moving hills" (n. pag.). As Ronald Henry High reads "Lines in Recollection," "At the word 'moving,' there is a diagram which gives visual meaning to the reader," and what Atkins has done with his structuring of his verbal materials is to place "the words so that one has to visualize the 'long place' that is referred to in the passage" (28). Such techniques typify the poetics of Atkins, who had, by 1951, publicly elaborated a theoretical stance of his own that he termed "psychovisualism," a theory he applied to his work in poetry as well as music. Although Atkins's psychovisualism has enjoyed considerably less critical assessment and practical currency than Charles Olson's much better-known statements on "projective verse," Atkins's practice of his theory has had far-reaching influence. In a 1973 issue of *Black World,* Leatrice W. Emeruwa went so far as to claim, "Unsung though he may be at present, the truth of the matter is that Russell Atkins has been to poetic, dramatic and musical innovation and leadership what John Coltrane has been to jazz avant-gardism" (26).

In point of fact, the type of experimental poetics attempted by Atkins (and he was among the first African-American poets to pursue such techniques as concretism and sound texts) closely paralleled innovations in black music during the same period. It was in 1959 that Ornette Coleman appeared with his pianoless band of musicians at New York's Five Spot Cafe, and it was in

1960, the same year in which Atkins published *A Podium Presentation* as a chapbook, that Coleman recorded *Free Jazz*. Not until 1965 did John Coltrane's *Ascension* recordings appear. These forays into Free Jazz, like early appearances of free verse, often met with initial incomprehension. Yet there were always listeners and critics who recognized the "changing same" in this latest iteration of black music. Radano, in his book on Braxton, saw, in retrospect, that "Free jazz represented not an aberration, but a fracture in the continuum of a tentative, constructed mainstream" (4). Critics of African-American verse have been somewhat slower to recognize the significance of similar fractures in the constructed mainstream of their literary histories. Poems such as "Lines in Recollection" may disrupt the construction in progress of an African-American critical canon, but they form a continuum within a tradition of such fractures.

De Leon Harrison is, like Atkins, an experimentalist working in several media. He has been a filmmaker and a painter, along with writing poetry, and was a founder of Cinema Blackscope. He also follows Atkins in composing poetic texts that might well be termed psychovisual, texts that, though yielding none of their ineluctable textuality, call for a performative reading. They are not lines that can be recollected in tranquillity. Those who have made a study of the diagrammatic titles of the musical compositions of Braxton will recognize a similar mode operating in a poem like Harrison's "Yellow" (see page 34). The "picture titles" (Radano 277) of Braxton's pieces are unpronounceable (and were so long before Prince rechristened himself with a picture title of his own), and Braxton's titles give shape to the compositions as much as they "name" them. We can pronounce, and even spell, the title of Harrison's piece, but that title names a succession of possible improvisatory performances, no two of which will be realized identically, and each of which will exist in a describable formal relationship with the original text (395).

Without having yet read Roland Barthes or Jacques Derrida or the other critics of textuality whose works began to be circulated widely in English translation during the years in which Harrison began to write his poems, Harrison, working out of traditions of African-American vernacular and aesthetic signifying practices in both music and literature, enacted a poetics that opposes itself to the artifactuality of the lyric as defined by the New Criticism while working out the implications of modernist and postmod-

Yellow

birds & sunlight
a piece for *bird calls* , *bells*   apprx. time 3 min.
  & *silence*

bells should be light tinkle or chime like to
medium ring

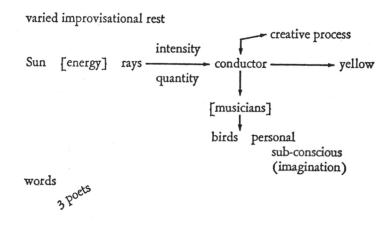

varied improvisational rest

ernist formal innovations. Were it not for the presence in print of an Atkins we might be tempted to say that such a poem as Harrison's "Yellow" would have been inconceivable without the example of Baraka's confrontations with the languages of modernism in the preceding decades. Once we have begun the work of recovering the poetics of Atkins and other African-American avant-garde writers, we will see more clearly what was always clear in Baraka's own commentaries: that African-American traditions of orality and textuality were not opposed to one another and did not exist in any simple or simplistic opposition to modernity and postmodernity. African-American poetics both birthed and fractured modernist and postmodernist practices. Poets like Harrison did not have to wait for poststructuralist critics to pronounce the death of the author or for cultural studies to problematize humanist conceptions of subjectivity and agency before writing poems that might be seen as countering now prevailing notions of the unity of minority subjectivity and its relationship to the lyric. In "The Room" Harrison writes, "I leave through a tear in the Paper/so as Not to disturb the rhythm" (395). Harrison's "Yellow," with its geometric rays and instructional modes of address, invites the reader to enter into the improvisation as an instrumental member of the cast. "The Room" inscribes one of those aporia, the invisible tear in the paper, as an exit for the "I" as disturbing to more conventional views of the lyric subject as the fractured perspectives in "Yellow" are disturbing to the eye trained to take in the regularity of stanzaic patterning. The traditions of such effects remain obscured by current historical practices in literary criticism that continually occlude the once better-known progression in black writing that included Atkins, Fields, Kelly, Pritchard, and Harrison. If we are to continue to claim to theorize African-American literary history, we will one day have to develop vocabularies and paradigms that will permit us to read and make sense of the sound texts, pattern poems, and unpronounceable delineations of these poets.

A powerful beginning in this direction has been offered by Harryette Mullen in her recent work as both a critic and a poet. In "Visionary Literacy: Art, Literature and Indigenous African Writing Systems," a lecture presented in 1993, Mullen moves beyond the standard explanatory models of African-American vernacular orality that have dominated much thinking about African-American literary history. She begins by differentiating her approach from that of critics who assert

> that black literary traditions privilege orality. This critical position has become something of a commonplace, in part because it's based upon what seems to be a reasonable and accurate observation . . . Presumably, for the African-American writer there is no alternative to production of this authentic black voice but silence. This speech-based and racially inflected aesthetic that produces a black poetic diction requires that the writer acknowledge and reproduce in the text a significant difference between the spoken and written language of African Americans and that of other Americans.

Mullen's thesis is that this approach has indeed produced an impoverished and narrowed view of black cultural activities, not the least because of its questionable assumptions about the construction of African cultural histories. "The illiteracy of Africans cannot be accepted as given," she argues, "although to speak of

non-Islamic Africans as literate would require broader definitions of writing than Western scholars such as Walter Ong might
find acceptable." What Mullen proposes in her work is "an attempt to explore connections between African spirit writing and
African-American signs." I would argue in turn that her historicizing project has much to tell us about the falsity of the assumed
opposition between singing and signing in both Africa and
America, about the traditional contexts for such seemingly nonrepresentational poems as Pritchard's "junt," and about the
graphic marks that cross the pages of poems by black poets like
Atkins, Fields, and Harrison.

I quote at length from Mullen, because she has posed important critical and historical questions more forthrightly than
most recent writers attempting to reconfigure our understanding
of African-American cultural productions. She announces her
intention in this ongoing project as follows:

> The larger question I am asking is this: How has the Western
> view of writing as a rational technology historically been
> received and transformed by African Americans whose pri-
> mary means of cultural transmission are oral and visual,
> rather than written, and for whom graphic systems are asso-
> ciated not with instrumental human communication but
> with techniques of spiritual power and spirit possession . . .
> In order to construct a cultural and material history of
> African-America's embrace and transformation of writing
> technologies one might ask how writing and text functioned
> in a folk milieu that valued a script for its cryptographic
> incomprehensibility and uniqueness rather than its legibil-
> ity or reproducibility.

Similarly, it will become increasingly important that we begin
to understand the eventual transmutations of such a vernacular
or folk milieu in a still more self-consciously writerly and literary
milieu in the last half of the twentieth century. Additionally, if an
intertextual history of African-American poetics is to succeed, it
must also take as part of its assignment a study of the multitudi-
nous ways in which black writings relate themselves to those
writings by whites that seem to afford openings for transracial
signifying practices. If American postmodernity is to be compre-
hended in its transracial plenitude, critical readings will have to
follow black poets as they read and transform the texts of whites.

As always, it is in the writing itself that we will find our way to a retracing of the motions between black and white, between script and speech, between page and performance. Stephen Jonas, in his poem "Morphogensis," offers just such a moment as he reads the poetics of Jack Spicer: "I take it that Jack Spicer's 'phonemes' carry / the printed circuitry that upon utterance / reproduces the visual impression" (*Selected* [1994] 158). Jonas's reproduction is not, strictly speaking, mimesis; what is reproduced phonically here is the visual impression hard-wired into the graphic text. Like the folk spirit texts and visual glossolalia explored by Mullen, Jonas's poem theorizes a graphic system of markings that link text, body, spirit, and voice. It is a calligraphy, not wholly phonetic, that compels, but is not limited to, speech and song. It becomes, as Jonas transforms his readings of Spicer into his own spirit texts, the calligraphy of black chant.

Eventually we will need to devise categories of cultural studies that will open for reading the continuum that links the line of Free Jazz to the lines of psychovisualism, that finds in Harrison's "tear in the page" not just an allusion to the bottom of the bag through which William Carlos Williams's poet pulls his disappearing act in *Paterson* but also a reiteration of the openings in the surface of African masks and African song. To make a beginning in the direction of such a criticism, to begin to reread the lining of the hymn in poems like "Lines in Recollection," requires first of all a recollection of the history of fractures. Excavation, restoration, and rereading must proceed simultaneously, provoking and informing one another. To reiterate, first we must reread and rewrite.

2

"OUTLANTISH"

Goodbye, crackers, Tom Russ is leaving your town. His grandson'll
be back to correct your grammar and throw stones in your wells.
Fifty years ain't so long.

> Amiri Baraka, "Suppose Sorrow Was a Time Machine"

    i have come to
chew up yr language

> Stephen Jonas,
> "Exercises for Ear"

So this was a time, I think, of transition ... And I myself was a
transitional figure.

> Amiri Baraka, *Autobiography*

As Langston Hughes and Arna Bontemps worked on the selections for their anthology *The Poetry of the Negro,* it became evident
to them that something new was appearing in the networks that
linked black poets to one another in the United States. Writing
to Bontemps on November 19, 1947, Hughes reported,

> In Cleveland I got some good poetry from Helen Johnson.
> Also Russell Atkins (who publishes in 'Verve' etc. and is
> 'more so' even than O'Higgins) promises some soon. Looks
> like we are in for a set of Negroes who will out-do the most
> *avant-garde* whites! Which delights me! And if we don't have
> them in our Antho. we'll be behind the times by 1950.
> (*Letters* 226).

Looking back to that moment now, we can see that Hughes was well ahead of the times in his worry about being behind the times. Anthologies representing themselves as representative of American verse continued for some years to be all-white projections, ignoring both avant-garde and more traditional African-American poets with stunning even-handedness. Further, with the exception of Hughes's and Bontemps's anthology, most publishing venues open to black writers on any sort of regular basis were really open only to those who remained within more mainstream modes of composition. Typical of an older generation that, for all its accomplishments, had not yet even absorbed Gwendolyn Brooks's variety of modernism, is a poem entitled "Resolution," by Georgia Douglass Johnson, published in *Phylon* in 1960:

> With but one life full certified
> And that of every gleam denied
> My portion,
> Close to the unrelenting sod,
> Just as my fathers dumbly trod
> I've slumbered.
>
> (265)

There is little, other than its sincerity of tone, that would lift this poem to our attention from among the hundreds of similar, staid exercises that dominated the poetry pages of American journals for much of this century. Even when turning to such contemporary subjects as the advent of the nuclear age, many publishing black poets at mid-century seemed hamstrung by their commitment to standard British metrical forms. Somehow the "Atomic Bombs" that are the subject of this 1960 poem by Mary Graham Lund, also published in *Phylon,* appear less ominous as we contemplate them within stanzas that, formally, recall a much earlier era:

> These lovely ones who wander in the park,
> > Their movements measured and their faces dead,
> > These lost ones carried as the current led –
> > What burning nausea penetrates the dark
>
> Recesses of a cumbered brain? What spark
> > Ignites rancidities on which it fed?

> What slow fuse burns the economic bed
> In which they lie like corpses cold and stark?
>
> (143)

Though there are some promising flashes in the poem ("the economic bed"!), those moments seem as encumbered by their formal constraints as the brain described in the poem.

It is, of course, possible to write effectively of new thematic materials in old forms. One might well, for example, use the stanzaic constraints of metrical verse ironically to oppose the violence of the subject matter. Hopkins might be a good model here, or Robert Hayden. Instead, this poem's form, which gives no hint that the modernist revolutions of Williams and Stein and Hughes had even occurred, ends by foregrounding the clichéd diction of the discourse. Even a poet such as May Miller, whose more traditional poems are sometimes still compelling, becomes maudlin when she attempts to set such unruly contemporary detail within a verse pattern that seems to have progressed no farther than the modernism of Masters or Robinson:

> We wake on the wrong side of morning
> From a nightmare of wings
> And mushrooms of huge death.
> Weep for us whose lives are caged
> In concrete, for our straw images
> Seen through glass walls
> Are you and you tomorrow.
>
> (316)

Not only does such writing, whatever its other merits, give no indication of the revolution in prosody and thematics that was raging around it, not only does it yield little sense of the impending Black Arts movement in poetry, but this poem, had the *New Yorker* of its time only been open to black poets more often, might *be* the *New Yorker* poem Amiri Baraka remembers reading that "had no feeling I could really use" (*Autobiography* 118). For Baraka in those days, such verse "spoke of lawns and trees and dew and birds and some subtlety of feeling amidst the jingling rhymes that spoke of a world almost completely alien to me" (118).

Neither would one get any sense from reading most anthologies that appeared before 1965 that there existed entire commu-

nities of African-American poets who both shared in the poetic
revolutions subsequently canonized as the Black Mountain
school, the New York school, the Beats, and the San Francisco
Renaissance and initiated revolutionary programs in poetics of
their own that would have importance for later developments
among white writers; for the soon-to-explode-on-the-scene Black
Arts movement; and for subsequent groupings of Latino, American Indian, and Asian-American poets. Donald Allen's nearly
canonical mapping of post–World War II avant-garde movements, his anthology *The New American Poetry,* published in 1960,
included only one black poet, Baraka, then becoming known to
a reading public as LeRoi Jones. Allen's project seems to have
established a paradigm, for most similar anthologies of the period included either no black poets or only one, Baraka. If one's
readings were limited to anthologies such as *A Controversy of
Poets* or *Naked Poetry,* let alone even more academically oriented
anthologies like the various Norton anthologies of literature, one
would be hard-pressed to understand how, in just a few short
years, there could appear such a profusion of black poetic stylings as to fill the pages of anthologies that seemingly were appearing everywhere at once: *We Speak as Liberators, The New Black
Poetry, Soulscript, Dices or Black Bones, Black Fire, The Poetry of Black
America, The Black Poets, For Malcolm, You Better Believe It,* and
Understanding the New Black Poetry. If some white readers (perhaps
even some black readers) got the feeling that the poetries of the
Black Arts movement had emerged fully formed in the immediate wake of the Civil Rights movement, it was an impression
fostered by the nearly total exclusion of black poets from earlier
anthologies and critical histories of American literature, combined with a continuing lack of interest, both popular and academic, in reading the many small-press journals and booklets in
which black poets, even avant-garde black poets, appeared with
some frequency, publications such as *Dasein, Free Lance,* and *Floating Bear.*

Hughes, however, read such little magazines assiduously. Like
Coleman Hawkins in jazz, Hughes was a bridge between generations of black artists. He had been a prominent influence on
younger writers like Baraka, Russell Atkins, and Julia Fields, and
Hughes joined these younger writers in the newer magazines,
where his prominence gave added force to their stand for a new
poetics. When Hughes began to edit his 1964 collection, *New*

Negro Poets U.S.A., he knew where to find the poets whom Allen and so many others could not be bothered to find. Hughes understood that the presentation of some of these newer poets would meet resistance, and he understood that much of this resistance would be racially defined. His experience had taught him that many white readers had fixed notions of what was an appropriate poetics for a black writer. It was this experience that formed the suspicion Hughes expressed to Bontemps when Indiana University Press seemed to be delaying its decision about publishing the anthology. The press still had not "made up its mind on the *New Negro Poetry*," Hughes wrote to Bontemps in March of 1961. "I guess they [the *New Negro* poets] write too much like white folks, which is Eva Hesse's complaint in Germany, too, in trying to put together a contemporary cullud anthology" (Hughes and Bontemps, *Letters* 411). (Another problem Hughes encountered in putting together his anthology is represented in an amusing exchange of letters in which he and Bontemps contemplated various means they could use to determine whether or not "black" poet Mason Jordan Mason was really, as they suspected, the white poet Judson Crews. He was. [*Letters* 316–17])

It has to be conceded that Bontemps and Hughes themselves felt some resistance to the experiments of their younger colleagues. Bontemps's immediate response to Hughes's suspicions about the Indiana University Press delay was to write, "I suspect you-all are right about the *newest* Negro poets writing too much like white folks – and not always the best white folks. In other words, the beat ones" (413). While editing *American Negro Poetry*, Bontemps wrote to Hughes, "I've read the LeRoi Jones poems you sent. I find a sameness about his poetry. However we must represent him adequately, without using anything that will knock us out of the high schools of the nation" (472). Bontemps, indeed, declared his readiness to "close the door" on what he referred to as "the Allen Ginsberg cabal" (478). Hughes may have proved considerably more open to the innovations of the younger poets than Bontemps, but even he drew back from some forms of experiment. In 1966, as they were revising earlier anthologies, Hughes told Bontemps, "Tonight I've been returning unusable manuscripts, some so beautifully typed I hated to send them back – particularly Norman Pritchard's (who sounds better than he reads in type – on a recording with Calvin

Hernton and others, called DESTINATIONS, they sent me)"
(479).

The more radical experiments of Norman Pritchard and Russell Atkins did not appear in *New Negro Poets U.S.A.*, though
Hughes was a longtime supporter of Atkins. As early as 1949
Hughes had written to Atkins "remarking how much the students
in his survey of American poetry class in Chicago were 'in-
trigued' " by one of Atkins's poems (High 30). Yet even with the
elision of such formally challenging works as Pritchard's and
Atkins's, *New Negro Poets U.S.A.*, which was finally published by
Indiana University Press in 1964 and went through numerous
printings, brought together a number of avant-garde younger
poets with more traditional older poets whose works would still
be "new" to most American readers today. What should have
become instantly apparent to a larger readership with the publication of Hughes's anthology was the fact that there had now
existed for some time a nationwide convergence of innovative
poets whose formal accomplishments were a break from the
conventions of their predecessors, but whose breaks with convention must be read in the dynamic context of the writings that
preceded theirs. Speaking of Anthony Braxton's appearance on
the music scene, just a few years after the publication of *New
Negro Poets,* Ronald Radano argues that "His articulation of a
vital, dynamic art that referred to the modernist legacy but in a
distinctly African-American creative voice signalled the appearance of a dramatically new kind of musician: the *black experimentalist*" (5). Although the newness of the figure of the black experimentalist might be questioned, a similar articulation can be
read in *New Negro Poets U.S.A.* Here the "changing same" inscribes itself as an emergent black postmodernity in colloquy
with the still evolving black modernisms of its antecedents. Few
poets of the Harlem Renaissance demonstrated as severe an
epistemology as that legible in the LeRoi Jones poem "Epistrophe," whose title pays tribute to that severest celebrator of the
modern, Thelonious Monk: "What I know of the mind / seems
to end here; / Just outside my face" (73). Few poets of the
Harlem Renaissance, or the decades that followed, exhibited
David Henderson's ironic self-regard as he charted his location
on the cultural map of American history: "Downtown-boy
uptown / Affecting complicity of a ghetto / And a sub-renascent
culture" (99). Despite the modernist fascination with various

orientalisms, we would probably not expect pre-Beat black poets to place Buddha, as Thurmond Snyder does, in a Beale Street poem. If Beale Street could talk, the earlier generation of modernists might not have heard it announcing, "Gautama has returned / From the mountain" (54). In "Return of the Native," Baraka wrote that "Harlem is vicious / modernism" (*Black Magic* 108), a statement that places black life in a "post-" relationship to modernity even as Baraka was including himself in a fiction anthology he entitled *The Moderns.*

New Negro Poets U.S.A. bears a foreword by Gwendolyn Brooks that might serve as a boundary marker between two thematic epochs in black writing, were such things so readily demarcated. "At the present time, poets who happen also to be Negroes are twice-tried," Brooks notes. "Often they wish that they could solve the Negro question once and for all, and go on from such success to the composition of textured sonnets or buoyant villanelles about the transience of a raindrop, or the gold stuff of the sun" (13). The first part of this formulation probably fairly represents the view of double consciousness held by many middle-class black poets of Brooks's generation. It was the description of himself as a poet who happened to be a Negro that aroused such vocal criticism of Robert Hayden at the Fisk Writers' Conference just a few years after Brooks's foreword was written. By that time, however, Brooks herself, largely influenced by the younger writers at the conference, would vociferously reject the second part of her own observations. The younger poets would soon rebel against both the prescriptive restraints of the buoyant villanelle and the view that somehow the transience of a raindrop was an inherently poetic subject for their art. Brook's foreword graphs a portion of that transition the younger poets were making in its insistence that even those few poets who have renounced the "flags and emblems" of racial responsibility "have in effect spoken racially, have offered race-fed testimony of several sorts" (13). The older of the poets Hughes featured in his 1964 collection, such as Dudley Randall and Conrad Kent Rivers, though they may have adhered at the time to formalist aesthetics closer to those of Donne than of Don L. Lee, were programmatically in the tradition of polemics such as Hughes's "The Negro Artist and the Racial Mountain." The younger poets in the anthology had, if anything, furthered that tradition in the process of seeking out newer forms they felt were more suited to the altering circumstances of their own times. Brooks was to decide later in the 1960s that this was no longer a time in America for the "composition of textured sonnets." Randall, whose own poems continued to honor an academically respectable syntax even when he did not write in metered stanzas, would form Broadside Press in Detroit, the most successful distributor of black poetry in the 1960s and early 1970s. There is a fracture detectable in *New Negro Poets U.S.A.,* but it is a fracture that is, if anything, encouraged by the example of the older poets. The formal differences between poetic generations, between a Dudley Randall and an A. B. Spellman, are as pronounced as those more frequently anatomized differences between the white "redskins" and "pale faces," the "academic" and the "outside" poets of the 1950s and 1960s, but the formal differences among the African-American poets can be read now as almost a call and response. Though there were to be heated, perhaps even vicious, critical debates between a J. Saunders Redding and an Amiri Baraka, there was a general unity of thematic purpose in a book like *New Negro Poets U.S.A.* that established a continuity between metrical formalism and the radical formalisms of projective verse and the Black Arts.

Too many of the names that appear in the table of contents for *New Negro Poets U.S.A.* have been forgotten by later chroniclers of the period. James P. Vaughn, Lucy Smith, Vilma Howard, Isabella Johnson, George Love, Solomon Edwards, Vivian Ayers, Thurmond Snyder, Carl Gardner, and Helen Morgan Brooks are names that will carry little meaning for today's students of literature, even for students of African-American poetry. Other names, better known in other contexts, will evoke surprise by their appearance here: Lerone Bennett is far better known as a journalist and historian, and how many literary critics now remember that Julian Bond, son of educator Horace Mann Bond and himself a prominent political leader, once published lyric poems? Other names will be more recognizable as belonging to key personalities in the recent history of black poetry, including Samuel Allen, Mari Evans, Naomi Long Madgett, Margaret Danner, Ray Durem, and Raymond Patterson. It is important, too, that this anthology allows us to see a poet like Audre Lorde in the context of her early publishing history. Too often her body of poems and prose works is considered in isolation from the community of poets in which she first became known as a poet. It remains imperative that we read Lorde within our historicizing of feminist poetics and lesbian aesthetics, but it is a grave error to assume that we can understand those traditions apart from the many converging lines of development that meet around her poems. Lorde's works must be read alongside those of Gloria Oden and Julia Fields, and they must also be read alongside the work of other poets in this anthology, David Henderson and A. B. Spellman, whose early chapbooks, like Lorde's, were produced by New York's Poet's Press. Similarly, seeing Baraka's poems reprinted along with those by poets like Tom Dent, Oliver Pitcher, and David Henderson makes it more difficult to accept the picture of Baraka's work given by many mainstream anthologies. Baraka is clearly the most significant figure in the early stages of postmodernist black American poetics, but, as is evident here and in his autobiography, he was hardly an isolated phenomenon. There was, to use his own terminology, a united front pushing together for a populist modernism.

Gloria C. Oden's poems in *New Negro Poets U.S.A.* indicate one other path taken by the poetics of modernity among black writers that has been little attended to by historians of twentieth-century verse. Her aesthetics are at times strikingly like those of another poet whose mostly traditional forms operate at a slight skew to the direction of late modernism seen in a Lowell or a Roethke, Elizabeth Bishop. Bishop's works have spawned a minor industry of biographers and explicators since her death. Oden's poems, which in their ideological development pose intriguing crosscurrents to the similarly structured poems of Bishop, on the other hand, have found few readers and even fewer critics. Her inclusion in the recent anthology *Every Shut Eye Ain't Asleep* may help bring her poems again to a wider audience. "The Map," Oden's contribution to the second of Hughes's thematic sections in his anthology, presents an interesting corollary to Bishop's work in books like *Questions of Travel* and *Geography III.* Here Oden interrogates, to use a critical term not then given much currency, the relationship between the world and its representations:

> This map is of the world.
> It says so. In type ½″ high: WORLD;
> and with what I know of maps I do, in-
> deed, believe it – though over it, in type

now smaller by one-half, I read the word
"COSMOPOLITAN," and over that, in
type yet smaller by one-half, these gentle
modifiers "RAND McNALLY"

(47)

Like the poem, the map is simultaneously in and of the world, and it is both owned and sponsored. Oden's formal practice seldom becomes more transgressive than the enjambment here breaking the word "indeed" between two lines, but the poem's reflections upon the workings of words in the world, and their political imbrications, is of a piece with more commonly cited instances of postmodern reflexivity. With what Oden knows of maps, as with what she knows of poems and words, she does indeed believe what the map "says," that it is a map and that it is of the world. Oden does not doubt that representation takes place, that the map is indicative of certain relationships in the material world, but there is always that nagging "though." For Oden, representations can never quite be taken at their word, and thus can never take the place of that which they indicate; maps are mediating ventures, always instrumental, always modified, interested, and modifying. Her map "soldiers" the white wall behind it, and its "clear hues" give her a certain notice of the world she can move about in. Like so many other poets, she reads the shape of Africa. Where Melvin B. Tolson saw the continent on a map as raising a question mark, Oden reads a head, housing a mind, whose fever "will blaze the length of continent as / now it fires breadth" (48).

This poetic reflection within quiet formalism is Dickinsonian in spirit, if not in stanzaic pattern, and it typifies Oden's poems throughout her career, most visibly in her two almost universally unavailable books *Resurrections* and *The Tie That Binds*. Although those who know her primarily as a long-time faculty member at the University of Maryland, Baltimore County, might be surprised to find that Redmond's critical history of black poetry, *Drumvoices*, groups her as a "Village" poet, along with Baraka and Ted Joans (321), the fact is that this quiet and quite unheralded poet, who describes herself on the back cover of *Resurrections* as a "Black Puritan," was early on an active reader on the Greenwich Village coffeehouse circuit. Her mode of experiment never became as formally audacious as those of A. B. Spellman and

Baraka, but in her own way she represents a significant break with the poetics of a May Miller or a Georgia Douglass Johnson every bit as remarkable as Sterling Brown's or Melvin Tolson's. In her Village days Oden did editorial work for the American Institute of Physics and was on the staff of the *Urbanite*. Both Oden and the San Francisco poet Kenneth Rexroth contributed to the special March 1961 issue of the *Urbanite* entitled "Images of the American Negro," for which Oden was a member of the initial editorial staff, and the two of them engaged in an intense love affair during Rexroth's time in New York. According to his biographer Linda Hamalian, Oden and Rexroth "seriously considered marriage, but Oden's strong sense of identity kept her in New York" (308). Here we find a more than usually literal transracial influence among what might be termed a "middle-generation" avant-garde. Undoubtedly Oden influenced both Rexroth's poetics and his views on race in America, just as his encouragement and interest were equally of value to her development as a poet.

Oden's fellow Village poet Ted Joans appears in Hughes's 1964 anthology with two poems, "It Is Time" and "The .38," perhaps the most "Beat" poems in the volume and evidencing the influence of Walt Whitman as well as Hughes. But the clearest signs of the new in *New Negro Poets U.S.A.* came from poets of the "Umbra group," soon to be much more widely known, such as Tom Dent and David Henderson; from Village poets who were at that time signing their works as LeRoi Jones and Alfred B. (later "A. B." Spellman); and from poets who remain largely unknown, such as another Umbra group member, Oliver Pitcher. Pitcher's poem "The Pale Blue Casket," with its startling opening line, "Why don't we rock the casket here in the moonlight," strikes what became a characteristic chord for a generation of avant-garde black poets. Pitcher's mixture of surrealism with African-American vernacular terms and rhythms is recognizable in retrospect as a dominant mode linking the poetics of new black poets in the Dasein and Umbra groups to Village poets like Spellman and Baraka/Jones.

That mode continued to characterize African-American poetry through the Black Arts period and beyond, Baraka's poem "Black Art," with its images of teeth, trees, or lemons piled on a step offering perhaps the paradigmatic example (*Black Magic* 116–17). It may well be the case that surrealism found such an intense welcome among black poets because, with its hyperbolic, compressed, and cryptic imagery – traits Stephen Henderson, in *Understanding the New Black Poetry*, describes as common signifiers of black verbal traditions – it was recognizably kin to black lyric traditions like the blues. Songs such as "Sometimes I Wonder Will a Matchbox Hold My Clothes" and "Smokestack Lightning" demonstrate that this kind of imagery abounded among folk lyricists. Henderson cites Big Bill Broonzy's "Hollerin' the Blues" as an instance: Broonzy's lines "I hear my hamstring a-poppin, my collar cryin' " (110) unquestionably form a part of the tradition of compressed blues imagery that lies behind Pitcher's "Why don't we rock the casket in the moonlight?" (For that matter, Lewis Black's "Spanish Blues," also cited by Henderson (112), whose lyrics consist almost entirely of humming, might be read and heard as offering a blues origin for such linguistic experiments as those of Norman Pritchard, which Hughes elided in his gathering of *New Negro Poets*.) Although white poets of the period were also greatly influenced by surrealism, and by the blues, Rexroth being a ready-to-hand example, and although they also turned these influences to overtly political ends at times, black American poets appear closer in their adaptations of surrealism to the Caribbean poet Aimé Césaire than to more popular white American adapters of the surreal such as Robert Bly and Mark Strand. For Baraka there was a political as well as an aesthetic logic in the turn to surrealism, a logic that easily placed itself in relation to grassroots movements in the larger black community. In an interview with Michel Oren, Baraka said,

> We thought that Naturalism was a musty, non-adventurous kind of pursuit, a kind of academic status-quoism. A lot of us ... like I was always interested in Surrealism and Expressionism, and I think the reason was to really try to get below the surface of things ... The Civil Rights Movement, it's the same thing essentially, trying to get below the surface of things, trying to get below the norm, the everyday, the status quo, which was finally unacceptable, just unacceptable. (189)

In another interview conducted by Oren, Ishmael Reed went a step farther in connecting the radical aesthetics of the new black writings to African-American and African traditions. Reed's maneuver, a characteristic intertextual reterritorializing by which he established an African claim of priority for an aesthetics that might otherwise be regarded, mistakenly in his view, as Euro-American modernism, denied the label of experimentalist altogether and, as Tolson had done before him, found in African tradition the defining principles of Reed's own work:

> I consider myself a classical Afro-American writer. I work out of the Afro-American cultural tradition, out of the folklore, and my work probably has more in common with black folk art, the visual . . . which emphasizes fantasy, humor, and satire . . . The distortion of my characters also originates from African tradition, if you look at the sculpture . . . I wouldn't call myself an avant-garde writer . . . [*Mumbo Jumbo* is] not experimental writing . . . It looks different but that's because people don't know our tradition . . . Even in Scott Joplin you get a mixture of European parlor music and ragtime. (189–90)

There is an ineluctable historicism and political motivation at work in poems such as Spellman's "Zapata and the Landlord:"

> the mexicans, emiliano
> & anthony, touched
> by the thief, run off to the
> mountains by the thief, returned with their 3000
> brothers
> & brought back the mountain.
> well, i
> have only one
> brother, roland, 18,
> & he has never fought
> a thief.
> (Hughes, *New Negro* 60)

In the imagery of surrealism, the poetics of Pound, Williams, Hughes, and Olson, the verbal inventions of black blues traditions, and the rhetorical traditions of black political thinkers, poets like Spellman and Baraka located an alternative space within which they could inscribe what they at the time thought of as a populist modernism. In Baraka's memory, "The various 'schools' of poetry we related to were themselves all linked together by the ingenuous. They were a point of departure from the academic, from the Eliotic model of rhetoric, formalism, and iambics" (*Autobiography* 158). Spellman's poems in *New Negro Poets U.S.A.* show us a poet who weds the epistemological concerns of the Objectivist poets to the compressed imagery of the blues and of surrealism in the context of innovative black musical imperatives. Seldom is this powerful mixture more plainly in evidence than in these lines from "John Coltrane: An Impartial Review:"

> around the back of the mind, in its closet
> is a string, i think, a coil around things.
> listen to *summertime*, think of spring, negroes
> cats in the closet, anything that makes a rock
> of your eye.
>
> (57)

Significantly, Spellman's poem does its thinking about the mind and its grasp on things in the context of a meditation upon one of black music's most fecund jazz composers and innovators, just as Baraka does in his poem "Epistrophe" ("What I know of the mind / seems to end here" [73]) in the same anthology. Though these poets pursued a freer free verse than did Oden, they shared her concern for a poetics that might track and speak the mind's motions in the world. The formal differences are analogous to the differences between hard Bop and its musical successor, Free Jazz.

All of these features figured in the repertoire LeRoi Jones / Amiri Baraka drew upon in his infrequently studied poem "Lines to Garcia Lorca." The other LeRoi Jones poems in *New Negro Poets U.S.A.* reappeared in his widely circulated and discussed books. "Preface to a Twenty Volume Suicide Note," the poem written to an at-the-time nonexistent daughter, had already appeared in Judson Crews's magazine the *Naked Ear* and was the title poem of Baraka's first Totem/Corinth chapbook. "Epistrophe" and the fourth section of "Hymn for Lannie Poo" have also received extensive critical notice. The Lorca poem, the first LeRoi Jones poem in *New Negro Poets U.S.A.*, had already been published in the initial issue of Baraka's own little magazine, *Yugen*, in 1958. The poem is significant, among other things, for its dedication to the most constant and fertile influence of any surrealist poet among black American writers of the late twentieth century, Federico Garcia Lorca.

Lorca's *Poet in New York*, the surreal but engaged lyrical record of the visit to Harlem of a poet who spoke practically no English, has been prized reading for black poets from Hughes to Lorde, Wright, Kaufman, Jonas, Spellman, and countless others. Lorca's "Verde que te quiero verde" (*Selected* 64) has been a thematic and stylistic touchstone for African-American writers, though one insufficiently attended to by historians of black writing possessed of what Hughes described to Bontemps as "the curious psychology that our white folks have that everything written by a Negro has to be definitely colored colored" (*Letters* 185–6). But Baraka had heard Africa in the colorations of Lorca's *cante jondo,* as Tolson had read Africa in the space symbolism of modern art after Picasso; Baraka had discerned an echo of his own black music in the Spanish poet's *duende.* Like Jonas, Baraka had a sense that

> The blues came to Spain with the gypsies
> who joined the jews & the moors in the Hollywood
> hills back 'o El A afta the expulsion
> the which might as well be Grenada!
>
> (Jonas, *Selected* [1994] 161)

Listening to Lorca's lyrics, Baraka could have said, with Jonas, "that's black singing. 'eso es canto moro' / negros, negros, negros, negros" (Jonas, *The Poetry* 77). Baraka begins his own "Lines to Garcia Lorca" with an epigraph drawn, as were the epigraphs to the chapters of DuBois's *Souls of Black Folk,* from a Negro spiritual, driving home the identification between Spanish *cante jondo* and African-American "soul." Baraka's lines linger in the corridors of Lorca's lyrics only to, as so often in early Baraka, use the occasion to mark the passage work of his own evolving consciousness:

> I live near a mountain, green mirror
> Of burning paths and a low sun
> To measure my growing by.
> There is a wind that repeats
> A bird's name and near his
> Cage is a poem, and a small boy herding
> Cattle with diamonds
> In their mouths.
>
> (Hughes, *New Negro* 55)

(Is it going too far to suggest here that Lorca's *verde*, reflected in Baraka's "green mirror," was close cousin to one of Baraka's favorite childhood pop culture myths, that of the Green Lantern? Are the green lights of Wallace Stevens's florid imagination refracted in the crime-fighting lantern-and-mirror light of a Newark child's first poetic fictions?) The song cited by Baraka at the opening of his "Lines" encodes the joyous fatalism historically associated with black lyric. It is the song's premise that we "Didn't come here for to stay," and in Baraka's poem Garcia Lorca is always dying again. Baraka also establishes a formal relationship of call and response between the Negro spiritual and his own poem. The spiritual opens with a four-stress line: "Climin up the mountain, chillun." Baraka's poem responds to the spiritual with another line in which the variations of the feet from those of the spiritual are syncopated improvisations upon the lining of the hymn: "Send soldiers again to kill you, Garcia." Baraka's line hangs in the air between the four-stress line of the spiritual and a variant on English pentameter (depending upon individual variants in the recitation of the word "soldier"). The result is a shifting rhythmic bottom line that the rest of the poem works against, one that underscores a sense of spiritual suspension throughout the poem. Baraka's poem is determinedly literary, but its sonic effects rely upon the lessons of oral tradition. For Baraka at the beginning of his career there was no real opposition between taking Pound's advice about following the musical phrase in poetic lineation and listening to the lessons of the blues; no true exclusivity between following Williams's polemics about the variable feet of the American idiom and following the example of African-American vernacular (and sacred) song.

Hughes's *New Negro Poets U.S.A.* is certainly less programmatic than Allen's *New American Poetry*, and Hughes's collection encompasses a larger share of more mainstream, perhaps even academic, verse forms. Nevertheless, the appearance of the Hughes anthology in 1964 announced to a larger reading public a fact that was already apparent in small-press circles: Following World War II, a vital network of black experimentalists had taken to the stage of American letters. These practitioners of new writing were not only drawing inspiration from many of the same sources (Lorca, black music, Williams and Olson, African-American vernacular stylings); they were also reading and engag-

ing with one another. They were not a newer, postmodern mockingbird school, merely adopting the fashionable trimmings of
newly notorious white writers, such as the Beats. Instead, these
new black writers were often providing leadership and places to
publish to white writers, such as Olson and Ed Dorn and Diane
di Prima. In some places – Cleveland, Washington, D.C., New
York – actual organizational structures were in place for the
furtherance of new black writing, much like the Association for
the Advancement of Creative Musicians that would soon appear
to promote innovative black music in Chicago. Additionally,
there were individual poets, often peripatetic, who, like Hughes
in earlier decades, moved through and with those localized structures without ever really aligning themselves with any particular
school. Much of this trajectory has been temporarily lost sight of
by many critics currently theorizing black poetics, despite the
valuable record of these phenomena made by Redmond in *Drumvoices*. The loss has been partly intentional and partly the result
of a critical inability to see back past the Black Arts movement to
the dynamic interchanges of poetic groupings that prepared the
ground for the Black Arts. Because we have tended often to look
at the careers of individual poets (a pattern to which I will return
in the latter portion of this study), or to look at poets as they may
embody particular issues that concern us now, we have too many
times tended to lose sight of the historical importance of black
avant-garde movements in writing. Thus Lorde is routinely cited
and studied, but less often appreciated in contexts that might
include Jayne Cortez, Elouise Loftin, Jay Wright, and Julia Fields.
Baraka is perhaps the most frequently anthologized black poet
of our time, and justly so, but few critical discussions, even those
written by authors familiar with Baraka's autobiography, examine
his poetics in contexts that include Russell Atkins, Norman
Pritchard, Harold Carrington, Clarence Major, or, for that very
curious matter, Diane di Prima.

   To make a start toward a rejoining of the histories so ably
outlined by Redmond is to make a start out of local particulars.
Russell Atkins was never a "poet of place," but he was, like Williams, a poet who remained close to a very particular place,
Cleveland, and a very important literary phenomenon, *Free Lance*
magazine and the group of Cleveland artists who sponsored it.
In the course of her report on "Black Art and Artists in Cleveland" for the magazine *Black World,* Leatrice Emeruwa noted that

"At times, *Free Lance* was the only Black literary magazine of national importance in existence" (25). Like the later *Umbra* magazine, *Free Lance* was in fact an interracial publication, but at a time when, as Abby and Ronald Johnson put it in *Propaganda and Aesthetics,* "the color washed out of" black literary journals, only "two small magazines – *Free Lance* and *Yugen* – had black editors and contributors in significant numbers" (155). According to Atkins, *Free Lance* grew out of a poetry and prose workshop begun in Cleveland by librarian Helen Collins in 1942. Atkins, who describes himself as a charter member of the group and who, at age twenty-one, had work included in the Hughes–Bontemps anthology *The Poetry of the Negro,* suggested the publication of a magazine to the workshop in 1950. Both the workshop and the magazine filled a void in Cleveland's cultural life that Atkins described unsparingly in a letter for the special Cleveland issue of *Input* magazine:

> No "little" magazines could be found here save those hoary with respect, the conservatively dull plushes, etc. Lecturing celebrities of the literary world seemed to come to Cleveland as one might have gone to Anchorage, Alaska. Bookstores knew nothing of *Beloit, Experiment, Trace* etc. They knew only the dignity of the hardback book where the poet and even the novelist were concerned: very square hardbacks. *Free Lance* worked indefatigably to change this. ("Letter to *Input*" 6)

Early issues of the new magazine circulated only in Cleveland and gave only a hint of the more experimental course it was to embark upon. The description of those early issues offered by Abby Arthur Johnson and Ronald Mayberry Johnson in their history of African-American literary magazines, *Propaganda and Aesthetics* (1991), gives a sense of the frustration that Atkins must have felt at the beginning of his editorial life: "[*Free Lance*] published primarily traditional verse written by local writers, such as Harvey Leroy Allen, Finley Nix, Helen Collins, Mary B. Langrabe, and Vera Steckler" (156). By 1952 the magazine was circulating outside Cleveland, and disagreements between the more aesthetically conservative members of the Free Lance group and the experimentalists were becoming more pronounced and frequent. Atkins and Collins were joined in their avant-garde interests by Casper LeRoy Jordan, a teacher and librarian at Wilberforce University and, in 1953, by Adelaide Simon, a white woman who had relocated to Cleveland when her husband, cellist Martin Simon, was hired by the Cleveland Symphony. Simon and her husband had found a home in the heart of a black community and became active in neighborhood work. In the 1940s Adelaide Simon organized a community action group. Even after the Simons moved to another neighborhood, a house on Milverton Road, Adelaide continued her participation in an inner-city playwrights' club. Simon and Atkins were eventually to become the primary editors of *Free Lance*. In the early 1950s there was a struggle within the Free Lance workshop between the conservatives and the avant-gardists that eventuated in the breakup of the workshop. The magazine, however, continued under the avant-garde leadership. As the editors recalled in the thirteenth issue of *Free Lance* in 1969, "The 'avant garde' board was not compatible with the remaining Kipling zealots and the Paul Laurence Dunbars, the Tennysonians . . . [A] minister, whose poems began and ended with James Weldon Johnson and Elizabeth Barrett Browning, would not associate with 'atheists' " (22). The avant-garde editorial board took considerable pleasure in troubling the waters. Atkins was fond of pointing out that they had printed the word "fuck" as early as 1955 (in a poem by Irving Layton) and that they had presented his own salon play *The Abortionist* at a time when the word was unmentionable in Cleveland. The *Free Lance* editors also took some pride in their furtherance of their theoretical explorations. Atkins's letter to *Input* claims that "few 'little' magazines had launched as complete and original a bid for a 'scientific aesthetic' " (7). Casper LeRoy Jordan, in his afterword to Atkins's 1961 book *Phenomena,* says of the latter's theory of psychovisualism, which Atkins explained in essays that appeared in two issues of *Free Lance* in 1955 and 1956, "It is worth remarking that this 'music' space theory of eye and brain was prior to both Space-age and the Beats" (76). Not content to have unleashed psychovisualism upon the world, Atkins went on to develop a theory of "egocentrical phenomenalism," which he defined in *Phenomena* as "an objective construct of properties to substantiate effect as object" (79). Here Atkins rejected the poetry of insight into experience as subject matter. Atkins's arguments for artifice and conspicuous technique were aimed simultaneously against the New Criticism and against certain notions privileging presumably "ordinary" language. For Atkins, "A technique should not serve meaning but rather meaning must not only *be* but SERVE technique" (79).

Not all the work appearing in *Free Lance* adopted Atkins's theoretical prescriptions, but all of it was in some sense opposed to the sort of poetry club insularity that had prevailed prior to the rebellion in the Free Lance workshop. The editors of the thirteenth issue remarked that "Poetry here had been an insulated sewing-bee phenomenon for years" (27). Simon revived the workshop in 1960, and her home became a headquarters for avant-garde cultural production. Poet d. a. levy operated his Renegade Press out of her basement, and several issues of *Free Lance* carried descriptions of the salons held in her home. She died in 1967, but *Free Lance* continued well into the next decade, making it unusually long-lived for a small-press journal. Among the writers to appear in its pages were Hughes, John Oliver Killens, Conrad Kent Rivers, Robert Creeley, Dudley Randall, Charles Bukowski, Mari Evans, Judson Crews, Rosey Pool, Julian Bond, Don L. Lee (Haki Madhabuti), Clarence Major, and Irving Layton.

Hughes was a valued friend of *Free Lance* from the outset. He and Bontemps gave assistance to the group when they were beginning the magazine, and Hughes wrote an introductory statement to the first nationally circulated issue. "Here are people," he wrote in a characteristic tone. "Here are poems. Here is revelation" (1). Following his death a special issue of *Free Lance* was published as a memorial to him. Even on an occasion such as this the magazine was boisterously out of the mainstream of memorial responses. On facing pages, for example, this issue offered Lee's platitudinous "Only a Few Left," a poem irretrievably marred by clichés, contrasted with a Clarence Major piece that has been almost entirely forgotten, his "Petition for Langston Hughes." Major's irreverence marks a certain form of sincerity in his tribute:

> Hughes was not my hero
> tho I sensed he was a representation. Could
> have majored, demands of circumvented black arts
> for self-determination of the future of black art
> as black art/black art. The process of big sea
> & Harlem of no human neighbors

> (I wonder if anybody in that block of brownstones
> structured with eyes his grandness, downtown?)
>
> (49)

Major's contribution also gave the *Free Lance* editors yet another
chance to print the word "fuck."

Hughes figured prominently in *Free Lance*'s aesthetic program
as well. "Langston Hughes and the Avant-Garde," an essay Atkins
contributed to *Podium* in 1965, places Hughes at the head of a
tradition of innovation:

> There have been three general lineages for American po-
> etry: (1) the Emerson–Thoreau, Whitman, Sandburg–Frost
> one; (2) the Americo-European one (viz., Eliot–Laforgue,
> Pound–Italy and even China); and finally (3) the Langston
> Hughes thirdstream – neglected until recently, but as origi-
> nal and as experimental as either of the former lineages.
> (14)

Crucial to our understanding of Atkins's use of Hughes is the
fact that Atkins singles out Hughes's typography and his sudden
juxtapositions of tonal materials for attention, along with the
more frequently appreciated aspects of Hughes's works. What is
under way here is the construction of a particular black modernism in Hughes's work to which Atkins sees himself as being in a
"post-" relationship. Atkins finds in Hughes both precedent and
point of departure. One thesis of Houston Baker's *Modernism and
the Harlem Renaissance* is that "The blending . . . of class and
mass – *poetic* mastery discovered as a function of deformative *folk*
sound – constitutes the essence of black discursive modernism"
(93). What I believe can be discerned in Atkins's positioning of
himself as coming after Hughes in a distinctly African-American
"thirdstream" of experiment is the coming into being of one
form of black postmodernism. By means of this thirdstream
positioning, Atkins can reassert the traditional as a source for his
poetics while continuing to reject the sort of "natural" language
poetics we might ordinarily expect from a follower of Hughes.
Within the avant-garde Free Lance faction, the modernist typography of Hughes and his shifting tonal registers were the model
for a deformative folk sound and an experimentalist folk chirography, not a reconstructed simple register of everyday speech. As
Atkins explained in his letter to *Input,* the Free Lance group

"never had any particular sympathy for that concern with 'ordinary language': a dead-end seemingly" (7).

Free Lance, while it lasted, was "Cleveland's hard core for poetry" (7), but its effect was felt far more widely than would be evident from current literary histories of the period. A regular feature of the magazine was a column simply entitled "Of," which chronicled the myriad activities of the group and also served as a forum for their theoretical speculations. There we can read of the almost missionary travels in the interest of new writing of the Free Lance group. In a 1964 issue, for example, it is noted that Free Lance members had visited New York, gone to readings at Le Metro, and made contact with members of the Umbra group. As it happened, another outpost of the black avant-garde was moving northward at the same time. *Dasein* magazine had followed its editor from Howard University in Washington, D.C., to a new home in New York.

Though Abby and Ronald Johnson, in their *Propaganda and Aesthetics: The Literary Politics of African-American Magazines in the Twentieth Century* (1991) have classified *Dasein* as a "college review" – indeed they make a point of remarking in a footnote that *Dasein* "fits the label of 'college review' much better" than does *Phylon* (226–7n) – the fact is that this magazine had a lengthy, albeit sporadic, existence beyond its early years at Howard University, where it began with the advice and encouragement of Professors Sterling Brown, Arthur P. Davis, Owen Dodson, and a new instructor in the Department of English, Antonia Wofford, who would later be awarded the Nobel Prize under her better-known pen name, Toni Morrison. Winston Napier, who has written the most thorough account of the *Dasein*/Howard poets group to date, conducted an interview with Oswald Govan in which the Howard poet remembered that Morrison "had just come down from Cornell, had not published anything, and no one took her seriously as a writer. But she took us seriously. She spent a great deal of time with us. She was one of the few faculty members. . . . who would attend parties that we had, and she heard a great deal of our poetry" (58). The campus of Howard University was, and is, a remarkably overdetermined locus for the development of black intellectual life. In the late 1950s, when the poets who began *Dasein* arrived there, the faculty included such renowned figures as Owen Dodson, Ralph Bunche, John Hope Franklin, Mercer Cook, E. Franklin Frazier, Rayford Logan, and, of course, poet, critic, and incomparable raconteur Sterling A. Brown, who came about as close to being born into a Howard position as could be imagined. Acknowledging the profound importance of the Howard setting to the genesis of *Dasein*, however, it is important to keep in mind that it was not the "official" campus arts review and that its editors took it with them when they left Howard. As late as 1988, *Dasein* enjoyed another in its series of incarnations when a quadruple issue appeared as *Dasein/Muntu*, an issue that, in keeping with the eclectic reach of earlier iterations, combined the visual and literary arts with political and philosophical commentary. The "midsummer" portion of the issue, counted as *Dasein/Muntu*, volume 12, contains an excerpt from Percy Johnston's long essay on Jupiter Hammon as philosopher and theologian.

One particularly notable feature of *Dasein* throughout its history was a commitment to examining the philosophical texts of African-American thinkers. Redmond, in his discussion of *Dasein* in *Drumvoices*, said that "As a group, the Howard poets . . . represent one of the toughest intellectual strains in contemporary black poetry" (314). That intellectual "toughness," which will be instantly recognizable to those familiar with teaching practices during that era of Howard University's history, found its expression in both the poetry and the prose published by this group. That avidly intellectual outlook, which they shared with Atkins, may also account for the fact, recorded by Redmond, that "little critical attention has been given the Howard group" (318), a fact that had only become yet more glaring by the time, a decade later, that Winston Napier opened his essay on these writers by lamenting the "prevailing omission of the Howard Poets from general surveys of American poetry" (57). Again, current editions of the Heath, Harper, Norton and McGraw-Hill anthologies used to teach American literature contain no writing from this group and omit *Dasein* from their historical essays. The Howard poets also were left out of most commercial anthologies of black poetry (a very recent exception being E. Ethelbert Miller's collection *In Search of Color Everywhere* [1994]), despite the fact that representatives of the group had appeared with regularity in earlier anthologies such as *Black Fire, Understanding the New Black Poetry, The Poetry of Black America, You Better Believe It,* and *The New Black Poetry.* Once more we see repeated a pattern whereby entire groupings of African-American poets once widely anthologized and seen as contemporary contributors to the innovation of new black poetries are deaccessioned from the steadily constricting canon of black poets available for critical attention and university instruction.

In the case of both the *Free Lance* of Atkins and the *Dasein* of the Howard poets, the reasons for this may be both formal and thematic. The avant-gardism of the *Dasein* poets, though not nearly as experimental as that of Atkins, may have rendered them invisible to mainstream criticism. Perhaps more fundamentally worrisome is the possibility that the philosophical commitments of the group may have subjected them to other racist exclusions, for, after all, they have also been generally absent from critical discussions specifically directed at historicizing American avant-gardes. Scholars truly conversant with folk traditions will know that there is no contradiction between an interest in folkways and an interest in intellectually rigorous literary works. But those who expect black poets to present them with an already constructed and "known" vision of folk authenticity may simply not see poets who reenact black traditions of public thinking. It was against such paradigms that Percy Johnston addressed much of his prose work. His 1988 essay on Jupiter Hammon, for example, reemphasized Hammon's position as a thinker and theologian for readers who might have wished to view him only as an assimilationist mockingbird. Johnston's estimation of Hammon attempted to complicate and question the views of earlier critics, such as J. Saunders Redding, whose highest praise of Hammon was that "When he is most lucid there is force in the quaintness of his thought evocative of the highly personal flavor of early American letters" (8). Johnston knew that the even more likely response of mainstream criticism would be simply to record Hammon's existence among the very first American-born black poets and then not read him at all. Johnston also wanted to bring greater attention to those generations of African-American scholars and thinkers who came between the time of W. E. B. DuBois and our contemporary scholars, thinkers who remain invisible men and women to some present-day scholars whose references to black criticism begin with Henry Louis Gates and bell hooks, despite the frequent allusions Gates and hooks make to their predecessors. In 1976, for example, Johnston himself had published a book entitled *Phenomenology of Space and Time: An Examination of Eugene Clay Holmes' Studies in the Philosophy of*

Time and Space, which, as its title indicates, explicates and reflects upon the work of the scholar who followed Alain Locke as chair of Howard's Department of Philosophy. Although it remains impossible to prove the motivations for an absence, I would propose that at least one reason for the absence of references to this 1976 publication in any critical study of recent American poets may be that contemporary critics are more likely to think of phenomenology as a useful approach to the study of black writing than as an overt subject matter to be found *in* the writing of black American poets. Johnston's essays and poems performed the sort of intertextual revisionist readings described by Houston Baker in *Afro-American Poetics: Revisions of Harlem and the Black Aesthetic* (1988). According to Baker, "one must take on the enemy by claiming that a legitimate line of succession runs through one's own, as opposed to his, vein of reasoning" (148). Baker, who also attended Howard University as an undergraduate, has thus offered a cogent summary of the philosophical tactics of the Dasein group, as well as a reason why many white scholars, even revisionist white scholars, cannot seem to find these poets when constructing their historical surveys of black thought.

Winston Napier has argued against the tendency in some quarters to speak of the Howard poets and the Dasein poets synonymously, yet it remains difficult to speak consistently of two moments or movements, since these groups were essentially overlapping sets, with one, as Napier rightly notes, "necessarily growing out of the other" (57). It is the area of overlap that is most significant to the present discussion. The Howard poets – those poets who began to meet and read together around the Howard campus in the late 1950s and who were also associated with various iterations of the arts journal *Dasein* – although they did not consistently share a disciplining poetics, were the most exploratory in their poetics of the larger, later group Napier covers with the encompassing term "Dasein poets." This latter term includes, in addition to the Howard poets, all writers who appeared in *Dasein,* including two, now probably better known than the Howard group: Dolores Kendrick, who attended college next door to Howard, and the much anthologized Lance Jeffers.

LeRoy Stone and Percy Johnston were already involved in publications when the Howard poets group began to draw together; both were on the staff of the university's student newspaper, the *Hilltop.* Oswald Govan, a mathematics major with an interest in Eastern philosophy as well as literature, joined Johnston in forming the group, along with his Cook Hall roommate Al Fraser, who had worked for Dizzy Gillespie before coming to Howard in 1958 (Napier 59). Stone and another Cook Hall resident, Joseph White, rounded out the initial group. In the spring semester of 1959 a new Howard student, Walter De Legall, who was already a poetry reader on the Philadelphia coffeehouse circuit, also joined the group (Napier 60). Though these student poets did meet for discussions and read their works to one another, this was not a workshop like that of the Free Lance group in Cleveland, let alone like the university workshops familiar to students on today's campuses. The term "Howard Poets" was put into play in *Hilltop* in a column written by Stone as a means of recognizing the existence of something beyond the usual coming and going of poetically inclined students. Stone pronounced the group a "school" of poets, and in so doing gave the movement for new writing in Washington, D.C., or at least along Georgia Avenue, a name and a public reality. As Napier describes the brief but frenetic period of the "school's" public appearance;

> In the short period between February 1959 and May 1960, their popularity as campus poets was meteoric. They were constantly in demand to read at various social functions on and off campus. They were invited to other universities in the Washington area . . . and were celebrated by the noted Dutch anthologist of Black American poetry and former teacher of Anne Frank, Rosey Pool, who would later publish some of their work in the seminal anthology, *Beyond the Blues.* (60)

The contact with Rosey Pool also later afforded the Dasein group an opportunity to pursue its interest in black literary internationalism. In a letter to Pool written on May 3, 1962, Johnston inquired, "By the way, did you come across any poetry or prose during your trip to Africa which we might use in DASEIN[?] . . . We are anxious to build a bridge between Europe, Africa, America in a kind of triangle trade route of literary cargo" (Pool Papers 82). Two poets who belonged to the group in the early stages were featured in an evening of poetry hosted by the Alpha Kappa Alpha sorority (clearly things were different among Greeks in those years), and Richard Eberhart, who was then

Poetry Consultant to the Library of Congress and who would later publish in *Dasein*, invited the group to appear in the Library of Congress poetry series. This would be seen as a singular event in any case but takes on added significance in light of the more usual tendency of Poetry Consultants and Laureates to ignore District of Columbia poets in general and Howard poets in particular, the exceptions being William Meredith, Gwendolyn Brooks, and Rita Dove. By the spring of 1960, however, the group had broken apart, and Stone and White had moved on from the university.

It was in the following fall semester that Johnston began the publication of *Dasein*, taking the name from a suggestion of Govan's, and the first issue, paid for largely by Johnston himself (the lack of university sponsorship should also demonstrate that this was not in fact a college review), appeared in March of 1961. This was followed by a double issue, but by the time the next *Dasein* appeared, De Legall was the only original group member remaining at Howard, and Johnston had relocated to New York (Napier 61–2). Johnston resumed publishing activities with his own press, Jupiter Hammon Press, and future projects of his generally bore either the imprint of Hammon Press or were credited to the Dasein Literary Society, though there was no longer a functioning Dasein group beyond non-Howard associates whom Johnston brought together for his varied ventures in publishing and play production.

The last publication in which all the original Howard group appeared together was a sixty-page book published in Washington under Johnston's Jupiter Hammon imprint in 1963 entitled *Burning Spear: An Anthology of Afro-Saxon Poetry*. That title may appear curious to new readers unfamiliar with earlier periods of African-American public nomenclature, but its subtitle does not signal any form of assimilationism in the book. To the contrary, the title and subtitle are meant to link two moments of black publishing and political history with a nationalist ethos. The oppositional stance with regard to mainstream "white" assumptions was rendered explicitly in the much quoted back cover blurb: "These eight Afro-Saxon poets are not members of a literary movement in the traditional sense of the word, because they do not have in common any monist view about creativity or aesthetics. Collectively, however, they are indifferent to most critics and reviewers – since criticism in America is controlled and written in the main by Euro-Americans." Public reception of the book, which identified itself as an anthology of "the Howard Poets," was all that the blurb writer seems to have anticipated. Mainstream critics apparently did not share Eberhart's enthusiasm for the Howard phenomenon and were as indifferent to these poets as the poets promised to be indifferent to their critical reception. *Burning Spear* presents the group as a self-conscious avant-garde who root their sense of their own novelty in their sense of the Be Bop avant-garde that had preceded them in music. The book's back cover announces the eight poets anthologized as "a new breed of young poets who are to American poetry what Charlie Parker, Dizzie Gillespie, Thelonious Monk and Miles Davis are to American jazz." If we think about the relationship that Parker's music bears to a song like "Cherokee," we can see how to read this advertisement. It is not that the "new breed" of Howard poets has rejected all the structures of existing American verse, but that they have set themselves to do something new with, or to, those structures. Despite the fact that Parker's performance, with its new melody and improvisations, rightly bore a different name, practicing musicians could hear the chord changes of "Cherokee" bristling beneath Parker's brilliant music. Readers of *Burning Spear* will not find the radically experimental forms of an Atkins (nor, it must be said, anything quite as formally adventurous as Parker's inventions). What they will find instead is a powerfully racialized improvisation within existing forms, or perhaps it may be more accurate to say that the Howard poets had reread the racial markings that had been present but not always remarked throughout the critical history of American verse. Oswald Govan's poem "The Angry Skies Are Calling" reads Whitman through the reinscriptions of Sandburg and Ginsberg:

> Oh Walt, Walt Whitman, old man of sorrow and aging
>   thighs
> burnt white and fragile,
> still hungry in the rain swept fields of nights
> for the germinal seed,
> the rocking of the cradle in the womb of the earth.
>
> (22–3)

Like the Beats, Govan repositions the Romanticism of Whitman within the "rhythmic dance of anguished sparks / in the hearths

of industry," but at the same time Govan's reading of the white-
ness of Whitman throws into relief both Whitman's absorptive
identifications with other races and nationalities and the Beats'
reenactments of that absorptive identification with their own
appropriations of jazz and blackness.

Likewise, Percy Johnston's "Variations on a Theme by Johnston," with its title's characteristic Johnstonian whimsy, recon-
figures the now familiar Beat alienation from the emerging con-
sumer culture, and from the Cold War political apparatus put in
place to guarantee its proliferation, against the most material
consequences of America's racial past, a past of confiscatory eco-
nomics that enabled the advent of the twentieth-century con-
sumer culture:

> To you, Eileen, and to New England's
> slaveship owners' sons, I confess:
>> I have a library card,
>> I wasted the GI bill on poetry,
>> I read the Bill of Rights,
>> I don't worship the white man's God,
>> I sleep where my caramel body is unwelcome,
>> I don't salute old glory!
>> I wept for Patrice Lumumba,
>> I respect Jomo Kenyatta!
>
> (46)

Another Johnston poem included in *Burning Spear,* "Dewey
Square, 1956," again makes use of the Whitman–Sandburg–
Hughes–Ginsberg free verse litany form, but the poem also begins to move in the direction of Baraka's syntactic compression.
Like Baraka and the other Beats, Johnston uses his poem to
measure his distance from the American dream that popular
culture icons had inculcated in his generation. "I / Cannot re-
live Brick Bradford / Flash Gordon Jack Armstrong days," he
concludes from his observations, but, as the poet revisits the
scene of his consciousness just a few years earlier, the signs of
shifting racial and ethnic territoriality are delineated in an also
shifting regard for the written markings of the territory:

> Scrawny-necked black girls
> In slingshot shoes, grimy
> Hotdog and sauerkraut vendors,

Broken windows where I once wore
The green letter "T" –
And something revolutionary for
Unkinking hair (written in Spanish)
Where the Breyer's ice cream sign
Had been.

(42–3)

The compression and the eye for the politics of inscription at work in this poem were to become increasingly prominent in Johnston's evolving poetics. In *Dasein/Muntu*'s 1988 quadruple issue, Johnston included his poem "BLAUPUNKT," in which the sonic effects of scat provide an ironic context for thinking about whites and black aesthetics. The poem's subtitle is "choruses Pepper Adams never took:"

Make your eyes go white on a
Saturday nite   like Leo Parker
at Club Bali for Paul Mann
'fore Korea –
Pound, Pound – unhuh-huh
Let Gerry Mulligan
make money
while you & Zoot
make music.
A bahtt for Zoot
tsit, tsit cymballlll
Boo dahh zummm

(151)

This poem allows us to hear anew the percussive qualities of names like "Ezra Pound" and "Zoot Sims." It also, perhaps unintentionally, calls to mind the peculiar percussion effects with which Pound accompanies himself on some recordings of his poetry. The poem's rhythmic play affords an attention-grabbing background for a sociopolitical critique joining realms of poetry and jazz (and seemingly making a sonic link between Buddha and Zaumist poetics), but joining them in a way that highlights the problematics of the act in a fashion far more akin to the poetry of the Black Arts movement than to that of the Beats.

If there is one element linking the works of the core group

of Howard poets who began *Dasein,* beyond their shared determination to celebrate an outsider's poetic stance, it is their dedication to the works of the generation of jazz innovators they listened to as they came of age. For the Dasein poets, those musicians offered a political as well as an aesthetic model. Like Baraka, the Howard group heard in the constantly varying choruses of hard Bop a score of praise songs and sympathetic magic. In their turn, the poets attempted to write stanzas not only memorializing the music but performing what they took to be its political imperatives. This was truly the calligraphy of black chant. Where Whitman had found inspiration for his free verse chants in the recitative and arias of the then newly fashionable (in America) Grand Opera and in the biblical model of the Psalms, molding these forms around the American idioms he heard as the call in the midst of a crowd, the Dasein poets found Whitman's free verse line jazzed by Langston Hughes and shaped it to the formative impulse they found in Coltrane's sheets of sound, or Monk's tripping meters and odd chords, or Miles Davis's eggshell fragility and muted modal ironies, or Ornette Coleman's Free Jazz. Always the sound of race rang in the changes. Walter De Legall's "Psalm for Sonny Rollins," which appeared in the sixth number of *Dasein* in 1966, is characteristic of the Whitman–Hughes legacy wedded to the newer formalisms of hard Bop:

> Blow down thunder and lightning
> And White People! Blow down moons
> And stars and Christs! Blow down
> Shirleys and stareyes and West Coasts!
>
> Walk naked into a 52nd street basement
> And show them the "Bird" in your thighs.
> Open your Prestige mouth and let them see
> The "Hawk" in your voice. Recite ten
> Stanzas of blackeyed-pead *Bluing.*

(76–7)

There are at least two major formal analogues to Rollins's music in De Legall's poem. His rolling free verse lines mimic the spiraling cadenzas of Rollins's solos. Additionally, just as Rollins playfully cites innumerable recognizable melodies in the progress of his solos, De Legall cites other tunes ("Bluing"), major musical influences on the saxophone style of Rollins ("Bird" and

"Hawk"), and even the record label on which some of Rollins's best works are heard, Prestige.

The efforts of the Dasein poets to suit their structures to the music of their models is further evidenced in LeRoy Stone's quite different poem, "Flamenco Sketches." Whereas De Legall's poem stretches out in time like the serpentine choruses of Rollins, Stone matches his stanzas to the spacious forms of Miles Davis, making stanzas in which rests count for as much as utterances: "Comment / blue utterance / uttering in mutes a passion" (194). Stone's "Flamenco Sketches" is divided into five sections, entitled "ouvert," "selim," "cannons," "enart," and "bill." Each is measured as if to the "Davis durations" that appear in the poem, and each names a relationship to Davis. "Selim," for example, is Miles's name spelled backward and was later used as the title of a Davis recording. Like the *Sketches of Spain* recording sessions that inspired the poem, Stone's "Flamenco Sketches" find in the modernist aesthetic of Miles's music, and the Gil Evans compositions and orchestrations, a meeting place of Europe and Africa. In the Gypsy music of Spain (as in Lorca's poems) Miles could hear the living vestiges of the Moorish epoch, and in the arrangements of *Sketches of Spain* we can hear recorded the blues meeting the modernist concert music aesthetic to a background of Iberian syncretism. It is at least partly in response to the improvisatory formalism of these arrangements that Stone uses occasional rhyming and sibilant tones in his tribute to Miles:

> Dissonant nostalgia of one kiss
> Penance to a Spanish maid
> She was his Flamenco cadence –
> three-four time
>
> Leave him pay those awesome dues
> In splashes of Flamenco blues
> Should one make a full confession? –
> still in three-four
>
> Need he confess necessary slavery
> to hot breath "en extase"
>
> (194–5)

Joseph White, like Stone and De Legall, finds a grounding for his political stance in the history that saturates his listening. When White hears the blues,

In these moments when the sun is blue
When the rivers flow with wine
When the neck bone tree is in blossom
I raise my down bent kinky head to charlie
    & shout
I'm black. I'm black
& I'm from Look Back

(262)

White's blossoming "neck bone tree," one of the most memorable images to find print by a Dasein poet, again makes the case for a black vernacular base for African-American surrealism, a jazz- and blues-based surrealism that would find its culmination in such works as the densely compacted writings of Los Angeles poet Will Alexander two decades later. The technique of embedding surreal imagery in a familiar, vernacular mode of expression (and what else was Magritte doing with his raining businessmen?) has the effect, as here in White's poem, of naturalizing the psychology of the poem. Thus a methodology of the avant-garde is provided with a traditional genealogy, and surrealism becomes the working means of black poetic saturation.

Yet another setting of the same methodology is found in Al Fraser's "To The 'JFK' Quintet," a poem that originally appeared in the second and third issues of *Dasein* and was later anthologized in more widely circulated collections, including Baraka and Neal's *Black Fire*. Once more there is a substantive shift in form to correspond to the very different form of music produced by the JFK Quintet. In these musicians Fraser finds "off red and brown / in the light behind, / five bundles of controlled panic" (272). Fraser sees similarity between himself and these young "screaming bitter blue boys / deep underground," and, as if signaling his agreement with Robert Creeley's adage that form is never more than an extension of content, each of Fraser's stanzas in tribute to this quintet is composed of a quintet of lines – until the last stanza is reached, the stanza in which Fraser establishes his likeness to the quintet, when the stanza is expanded to take in a sixth member.

As so often, it was Johnston, the son of a jazz drummer and a classical harpist, who worked the most changes on these modes of musical tribute. His "Round about Midnight" poems pay simultaneous homage to Monk, who wrote the piece named in the title, and Davis, whose recording of the song may be the best known. "Opus 6" of the series, first published in issues 4 and 5 of *Dasein* in 1966, describes a "coal-oil driven wind" that rushes through the silent places of the song. "I rest on a concrete apron," Johnston writes, "In onyx night, / 'Round about midnight, with / Navigation lamps inactive" (232). Johnston's lines prefigure Clark Coolidge's later poem "The Great," in which Coolidge writes,

> I only want to make midnight mast to my song
> > in shivered and tracing words in other words
> > > the Miles off further from the phantom he is
> > > > blow back
>
> (13)

Johnston was not a source for Coolidge. What was at work here is that two poets just a few years apart in age, sharing an interest in late twentieth-century aesthetic revolutions, have both improvised in antiphonal response to the openings made for them by the black music of Monk and Davis. But whereas Coolidge, as outside as he may remain in terms of mainstream academic canons, has been the recipient of much critical attention and continues to be widely anthologized, Johnston has received almost no critical attention and has been left out of most anthologies of the last two decades. Further, because of the disinclination on the part of most critics to discover African-American *literary* precedents for white avant-garde writing, even in the case of a poet as deeply involved with black music as Coolidge, no criticism has adduced early black experimentalists such as Johnston as formal precursors of Coolidge's aesthetics. Clearly, though, the compressed imagery and syntax of Johnston lines like "Chilling chockwheel, monoplane me" are choruses to the same chart that gives us "make midnight mast to my song."

In "Opus 17" of Johnston's "Round about Midnight" poems, the poet again roots the surrealism of his imagery in the quotidian language practices of black people. Hence, we get images of nights and nightclubs in which "dues are piled up / Barstool high" (192). Also, this section of Johnston's Monk–Davis project makes an identification common to avant-garde black poets between writing and soloing, between inscription and song, singing and signing:

Let's blow
A chorus all 'bout
Cabbage and yams,
Let's blow
A chorus all 'bout
Cornbread and fish,
With brush or pen or horn or
Just your voice
Just as long as someone's
Blowing blues.

(193)

Across the arc of Johnston's development as a poet there is a
steady movement in the direction of such compression, always
formed from vernacular detail, always wrapped around an insistent politics of race. In the early poem "Pax Romana," which
appeared in the very first issue of *Dasein*, the racial objective
correlative or material of saturation is provided by the poem's
invocation of the history of slavery:

Rising
With the parabellum sun like our ancestors who built the
New World (*de facto*), we olive-drab armored knights
Bring Pax Romana via Arlington and the Foggy Bottom.
With *asientos* (made in Hershey, Pennsylvania) we enslave
The weavers of khaki belts (scouts in, medics out)
Until we restage our ancestors' conquest – and Merovingian
Brass is silent (medics in, chaplains out).

(43)

In this instance it is not the language of the poem that is staged
in the vernacular but the historical experience. Possessed of a
domestic *asiento*, the once-slaves enslave the enslavers. The poem
becomes a militant antimilitarism poem. A new group of reserves
turns aside the New World mission of dominance enacted as the
Pax Americana. Some of the diction of these early poems is
clichéd, as when Johnston's armored vehicles are described as
"Petrol gulping chargers," but the rewriting of history as a
righting of history in "Pax Romana" is handled in a highly original manner well worth recovering for contemporary readings
and studies of political poetry. Soon Johnston would learn to
combine vernacular experience with vernacular diction while

at the same time continuing to work by a poetics of syntactic compression and surreal imagery. Poem "#4," from his 1964 book *Six Cylinder Olympus,* indicates the direction that would lead him to such later poems as "BLAUPUNKT." Poem "#4" is a mythic bit of bragging:

I, Bos Taurus spatha,
Spading the pinto bean earth
Like a wintergreen rubbed down
Sprinter before the gun,
Have repulsed the picadores
Under the E-flat trumpet sun.

(8)

Johnston has been both the most prolific of the Howard poets and the most consistent in his application to the philosophical, political, and aesthetic issues of his times. In addition to the separately published prose works he authored, he filled the pages of *Dasein* with a steady stream of meditation and comment. (He also contributed a translation of Goethe's "Prometheus.") Johnston regularly published essays in philosophy in his journal, as Atkins did in *Free Lance,* and, resembling Atkins in this respect as well, Johnston often poked fun at his own philosophical interests. A poem he included in a small volume of pieces by Stone and himself is entitled "Lines on the Practical and Theoretical Results of the Impact of Urban Industrial Conditioned Social Philosophy on Aesthetic Delight and or Psychological Well Being, With Special Reference to the Deterioration of Beneficial Hedonism." The small poem nestled in the shadow of this unwieldy title appears to be a vernacular translation of the title. The entire poem consists of the two lines: "They don't get high for joy / In America no more!" (7) But Johnston took his philosophy and its history most seriously. He wrote on Benjamin Peirce's description of mathematics in the sixth issue of *Dasein,* and in an unpublished manuscript Johnston "attempted to clarify Descartes' rejection of Democritus as not solely explainable in terms of dualistic epistemology and metaphysics" (*Phenomenology* 9–10n). Later, while working at Montclair State College, he assembled an anthology entitled *Afro-American Philosophies: Selected Readings from Jupiter Hammon to Eugene C. Holmes.* Johnston was unwilling to observe the academic separation between the work of the poet and the scholarship of philosophy. In one of his footnotes to *Phenomenology of Space and Time,* in fact, he refers readers to a poem he published in his 1960 *Concerto for Girl and Convertible and Other Poems* as a source for his thesis concerning cosmology (*Phenomenology* 31n).

Johnston was *Dasein*'s principal critic and historian, in addition to being its publisher. His numerous reviews and essays included important pieces on film criticism and on black historiography. On every occasion, Johnston continued as a proponent of new writing, as a sharp observer of movements in black aesthetics, and as an unrelenting critic of the racial politics of America's literature industry. His review of the Broadside recording *New Jazz Poets* is a good example of his propagandizing for the new (he calls the album a "prosody shattering disc anthology" [44]) and of his promoting, in the Whitman–Pound tradition, his own works. (He was one of the poets who performed their works on the record. In his review he termed his own performance "broadsnatching made sophisticated" [46].) Entitled "Minton's Midtown, Baby!", the review argued for tribal chant as a frame of reference and applauded poems by David Henderson, Paul Blackburn, Ronald Stone, and Calvin Hernton for "restructuring the lyrical line on the foundation built" by jazz musicians' restructuring of the melody line (45). He singled out Norman Pritchard's poem "Gyre's Galax" as one of the "most stirring performances the album has to offer." In discussing Pritchard's recording, Johnston noted the impossibility of tying the recited piece to the printed page. William Carlos Williams inscribed a visual text to be read in a manner quite different, generally, from his own oral presentations of his poems; in the same way, Pritchard's texts are at once concrete, graphic text imagery and sound texts. Indeed, according to Johnston, "No one on earth at all can ever aloud, in silence, or any [other] method, approximate the poem Pritchard performs" (46). Each reading, each reiteration of Pritchard's text, must be a renewed improvisation. As for Pritchard's own realization of the poem, in Johnston's description, "he whails [wails] & scuttles fast & clean & nittygritty like Coltrane with Sonny in the audience" (46).

Another mood entirely is represented by Johnston's notice of William Styron's novel *The Confessions of Nat Turner,* a review Johnston entitled "Confessions of Whitey." Johnston wasted no time in getting to his point. The first sentence states, "Styron is a conscious propagandist & an unconscious bigot" (39). Bringing his poet's gift for language to the fray, Johnston wrote that *Confessions* "re-enforces the priapismic/phallic myth of sexualis inkcolour, of holy sweating fornicatress negritude goodness needing the puny orgasm of hominy grits Celtic Odin to replace the tranquil embrace of Edshu. & out of such false copulation would springforth a chocolate coloured Jesus/Madhi/Messiah/Davidic Chiruwi cat who would pick up his hammer like Lionel Hampton & we'd be Flying Home" (39). Additionally, Johnston takes the novel's success as yet one more sign of commodification replacing artistic invention, another sign that "an establishment publisher can market successfully a nonbook with the sheer weight & bulk of its massive Brontosauric budget." To Johnston's eye, though, an equally troubling phenomenon underscored by the appearance of Styron's *Confessions* was what he took to be the failure of black novelists to make viable contemporary art out of the revised histories made available by scholars like W. E. B. DuBois, J. A. Rogers, Carter G. Woodson, Rayford Logan, and E. Franklin Frazier. As Johnston gauged the situation in 1968, black fiction writers had a good distance to cover in this regard if they were to reach the level of art grounded in history to be found in the poetry of Melvin B. Tolson, Robert Hayden, Sterling Brown, LeRoi Jones, and Walt De Legall (39). What Johnston hoped for in fiction, and what he hoped anger over Styron's book might hurry along, was that black novelists would use historical materials artistically to "destroy the air castles" of history constructed by popularly accepted white novelists, in the same way that Ralph Ellison, LeRoi Jones, and A. B. Spellman had demolished the standard interpretive models of jazz history propounded by white critics. In the end Johnston came, by a peculiarly unlikely route, to a call for white authors to redirect their energies: "Styron might redeem his artistic soul (if any) by following the suggestion that William F. Buckley & Godfrey Cambridge agreed on in a recent telecast, study white America. Then perhaps we can look forward to the 'Confessions of the Grand Whatsis of the Ku Klux Klan,' or the 'Confessions of Quantrell,' or 'The Authorised Confessions of Thomas Jefferson' " (39).

Johnston has made a lengthy voyage along the uncharted borders of American publishing since the days when he and the other Howard poets read at Coffee and Confusion in Washington, D.C., and were invited to read at the Library of Congress.

This was about as close to critical acknowledgment as the Dasein group was ever to come. The Dasein poets have remained a mostly unknown site of black poetic invention, despite Johnston's positive genius for self-promotion. (Reprising a Whitmanian moment, Johnston sent the manuscript of his poetic tribute in memory of the late John F. Kennedy to then Attorney General Robert Kennedy and subsequently published the attorney general's thank-you note, on official stationery, as an addendum to the book version of *Sean Pendragon Requiem* [27].) The Dasein group began by publishing their lack of concern for establishment acceptance, and Johnston began his publishing ventures out of a conviction that there was little hope that black writing so "outside" would ever be taken on by the establishment press. Had he not made that decision, the texts of the group might have remained wholly unavailable, and an important moment in the history of African-American verse culture might have gone unrecorded. Johnston has continued to find ways to reach a large public without subjecting himself to critical mediations. For some years he operated a theater in Greenwich Village, Studio Tangerine, where, in addition to plays by Sartre and Shakespeare, he was able to stage his own writings for a wider audience. It was here that he developed *Dessalines: A Jazz Tragedy,* inspired in part by C. L. R. James's *Black Jacobins.* He later published his play in book form, and it enjoyed several productions during the 1980s, including a Soho gallery production presented by Johnston's old collaborator De Legall.

In hindsight, much of the work that appeared in *Dasein* seems rather tame, and, as is so often the case, it was Dasein poets like Lance Jeffers and Dolores Kendrick, poets whose works, granting their various virtues, were clearly rather normative language constructions, who were later more likely to be mentioned favorably by critics and historians than were the *Dasein* founders themselves. It is thanks to literary histories like Napier's that we are able to reconstruct the network of new writing in Washington, D.C., at the beginning of the postmodern era. As Johnston's work on *New Jazz Poets* and De Legall's work at the Soho gallery demonstrate, those Dasein poets who continued actively in the arts were directly engaged with other vortices of black creativity in America. The Dasein poets may have yet to attract the level of attention afforded to black Village poets or the Umbra group (which is little attention indeed compared with the literary industries like that surrounding the Beats, with its ancillary production of memoirs, recordings, films, academic conferences, and a new generation of imitators), but across three decades the Dasein group appeared and reappeared as a vocal instigator of the new black arts.

3

"A NEW YORK STATE OF MIND"

We liked the idea of sitting around being young poets, young
black dudes trying to find a way in the world.

Amiri Baraka, *Autobiography*

new york
won't you confess
your private affairs
inside both ears
of a leather uterus

Jayne Cortez, "Bowery Street"

The venomous ambiance of New York in the early 1960s was the
thump on the rump that forced the new black poetry into breath.

Lorenzo Thomas, "The Shadow World"

amerikkk amerikkka reach out
and touch your tv sets high
school graduation is just around
the conor

Elouise Loftin, "April '68"

A year later, I finished library school. The first summer of a new
decade was waning as I walked away from Seventh Street for the
last time, leaving that door unlocked for whatever person came
after me who needed shelter. There were four half-finished poems
scribbled on the bathroom wall between the toilet and the bath-
tub, others in the window jambs and the floorboards under the
flowered linoleum, mixed up with the ghosts of rich food smells.

Audre Lorde, *Zami*

Cleveland's Free Lancers and Howard University's Dasein poets were not the only folk flowing to New York City. From the end of World War II through the 1950s and 1960s, it seemed that all the communities of black experiment, and the lone writers from the outlands of black American literature as well, were converging upon New York. Eugene Redmond's critical history of Afro-American poetry, *Drumvoices,* records the fact that "From the variegated atmosphere of New York gushed forth a tide of black poets" (350). And the movements for new poetries of blackness had spread well beyond Harlem. Even during the Harlem Renaissance, the name of America's largest black neighborhood had been applied, as much as a convenience of nomenclature as anything else, to writers who often did not live there. In the ten years leading up to the Black Arts movement, when a number of black poets made a point of moving their base of operations home to Harlem, Harlem had remained a major center of artistic activity, if not always the intellectual capitol of black America it had once been considered. But although groups such as the Harlem Writers Guild, directed by John Oliver Killens, provided a locus and an impetus for many talented writers, poets moving to the different drummers of avant-garde aesthetics were just as likely to be found in the city's other boroughs, and Greenwich Village, followed by the Lower East Side, rapidly emerged as exciting crossroads for the new black American poetries. It was a period of great transitions, a time when it seemed possible to attempt anything. "Intellectual paperbacks were just coming out about that period," remembers Amiri Baraka of the days when he first moved into the Village, "And people could be seen with the intriguingly packaged soft pocket books, folding and unfolding them out of bags and pockets" (*Autobiography* 126). All over New York young black writers were exploring the newer poetics that had begun to appear and to be discussed almost furtively in little magazines here and there, exploring them with the same fervor, and sometimes confusion, with which they explored the meanings of their own lives. Audre Lorde remembers 1955 as a year of turning points: "That fall, . . . I took a course at the New School in contemporary american [sic] poetry, and I went into therapy" (*Zami* 214).

As readers may gather from the paucity of black writing in most anthologies of the period, the public face of poetic innovation in New York was white, masking once more the significant contributions of black writers to the gathering forces of the new. As recently as 1993, a major conference on the period, entitled "The Beat Generation: Legacy and Celebration," held on the campus of New York University, continued to marginalize black participation in and influence over radical movements in post–World War II writing. In his *Village Voice* summation of the conference activities, Richard Gehr noted that "the panel on the Beat–African American nexus proposed early on by Thomas Gayton never happened, [though] the influence of African American culture on the Beats ought to provide dissertation topics for generations to come" (18). Similarly, just a year previously, San Jose State University hosted a West Coast symposium on the Beats at which *only* white writers spoke. This resulted in the spectacle of speaker after speaker (most notably Allen Ginsberg and Diane di Prima) addressing the central importance of Amiri Baraka to their work and the even more critical role of black music in the development of their aesthetics, all to an audience that included none of the black writers who might have had something even more direct to say about the subject. This is an old pattern, of course. In June of 1958, Arna Bontemps, who had just been reading about a new anthology entitled *The Beat Generation and the Angry Young Men,* wrote an inquiry to Langston Hughes that comically mirrors their attempt to discern the true race of the pseudonymous poet Mason Jordan Mason. Bontemps asked if Hughes had ever met Anatole Broyard. "His picture in *Time* this week makes him look Negroid," opined Bontemps. "If so, he is the only spade among the Beat Generation" (*Letters* 373).

In fact, though it was a fact too often kept from public view (except for those occasions when somebody wanted to produce black Beats as evidence of the decadence of the white Beats), the Village, with its emergent hip scene, was the meeting place for numerous black artists. Only Baraka and Ted Joans are remembered with any frequency in this context by most mainstream literary histories. Even a *Heath* anthology will omit mention of such writers as Tom Postell, Harold Carrington, A. B. Spellman, or later black poets from New York such as Elouise Loftin. The Village was the bohemian magnet, and, as Baraka recollects, Romero's on Minetta Lane was "the maximum hangout spot for many blacks in the Village" (*Autobiography* 126). The coffeehouse scene was already going strong and quickly exercised a powerful attraction over the new generation of black bohemians: "Coffeehouses, at that time, were very popular. The post-WW II decade of American visitors to Europe had brought back the coffee-house as one evidence of a new reacquaintanceship with Continental cool. Certainly, for me, the coffeehouse was something totally new. Downtown New York coffee smells I associate with this period of my first permanent residence in the city" (Baraka, *Autobiography* 126). In the coffeehouses, cafés, bars, and streets of the Village the young intellectual African Americans met one another and were part of a revolution in the making. Here Baraka met artists like Virginia Cox and Vincent Smith (Baraka's *Autobiography* often employs both pseudonyms and real names for the same individuals; for example, I suspect that his "Tim Poston" and "Tom Postell" are both Tom Postell), and he would soon meet other black innovators migrating to Manhattan, such as Cecil Taylor, Ornette Coleman, and Archie Shepp. "I was blotting paper for all sensation, all perception," Baraka says of himself at this time, "walking and looking, listening, trying to emulate and understand" (*Autobiography* 129). Quickly, Baraka, who was orthographically transforming himself from Leroy to Le*R*oi Jones (perhaps as much a mark of Continental cool to remove some of the Newark air as a revision of his father's act of naming), became not just an emulator but a leader among the new generation of artists, black and white. With his first wife, Hettie, he began the highly influential magazine *Yugen* and started Totem Press. With Diane di Prima he started the mimeo-graphed magazine *Floating Bear*, one of the most consistently challenging of America's underground publications. He was also associated during its early days with Kulchur Press. Baraka's homes became a series of salons. When he lived on West Twenti-eth Street his regular circle of visitors included Gilbert Sorren-tino, Joel Oppenheimer, Hugh Selby, A. B. Spellman, Fielding Dawson, C. D. Transan, Joe Early, Larry Hellenberg, Mark Fine, and Sam Abrams. Such a center of the new arts had Baraka's home grown to be that many artists listed their mailing address as "c/o L. Jones, West 20th Street" (*Autobiography* 163). When Baraka later moved to Cooper Square, the salon moved with him, and it was common to find Archie Shepp (who lived in the same building), Marion Brown, Bob Thompson, Spellman, Joe Overstreet, and Sonny Murray dropping by to hang out with the other writers, musicians, painters, and assorted spouses gathered around the LeRoi Jones household vortex.

Although substantial preliminary historical work has been done documenting the developments in African-American poetry that followed this postwar surge of innovators, there is still much work to be done before we will have a clear conception of the forces in motion among the new black poets of the 1950s and early 1960s in New York, the generation that laid the formal groundwork for the Black Arts movement that was to come. A first step toward that fuller comprehension will have to be a project of reclamation, perhaps as daunting and rewarding a project as recent rediscoveries of nineteenth-century African-American texts, because the texts of this early period of black postmodernity are mostly fugitive, having passed out of print or never having been printed in the first place.

One little-known poet whose work needs to be recovered is Tom Postell. Postell was one of the writers Baraka met early in his Village period, and his death at an early age prompted one of Baraka's angriest and most infamous poems. When Baraka wrote of Postell's death in the 1960s, he felt,

> I should have screamed
> for you brother. I should have climbed to the tops of
>   buildings and
> screamed and dropped niggerbombs on their heads. For my
>   dead. For my
> dead brother. Who told me. A thousand years ago.
>
> (*Black Magic* 153)

It is no doubt because of Postell's early death that he is so little known among literary scholars. He is not mentioned, for example, in Redmond's *Drumvoices* (which seems to name almost everybody), nor did his poetry appear in any of the widely circulated black poetry anthologies of the period, despite his influence on other black writers in the 1950s. Further, unlike Henry Dumas, Postell had not published a considerable body of work at the time of his death and has not been posthumously republished, as Dumas has been. The small set of Postell's poems that appeared in the first two issues of Baraka's *Yugen*, both published in 1958, indicate that he was a poet of considerable interest, poised to make a significant contribution to the aesthetics of black verse. His poems in the first issue of *Yugen* are long-lined, stately, psalmlike surrealist lyrics. The first piece is, like Stephen Jonas's works, a poem that locates the departure point for a postmodernism in the then somewhat neglected experiments of Gertrude Stein. Postell's poems sound nothing at all like Stein's, and their surreal imagery contrasts with the regularity of their syntactic arrangements. But there is a Steinian departure from referentiality that never quite entirely leaves the referents behind, as though the ghost of Stein were haunting a more traditionally constructed, but slightly out of kilter, lyric. The long lines stringing together slightly maudlin imagery reconfigured in a quirky context seem of a piece with the poems that John Ashbery was writing at the time. Ashbery's "The New Realism" tells us, "The child skipped happily over / the western pages" (59). Postell, a New York poet of a blacker school, envisions a world where "blighted riff-raff children skate and / laughingly dig the hole for the mid-western bonfire" ("Stein" 9). At the poem's end, Postell announces what might, in retrospect, be seen as an annunciation of the postmodern from the blighted wreckage of modernity: "Gertrude Stein is long dead but under cover rides the torn down El" (9). It is a fitting vision for a post-Steinian universe, Stein riding a deconstructed train.

The second of Postell's poems to appear in that initial issue of *Yugen* follows the same aesthetic principles. It offers a dreamscape in which we "see the Brooklyn Dodgers on Times Square with their bats and balls practicing" and we are asked to "enter the redundant oasis which rips of jungle beats on glasses of gin" ("I Want" 10). Though the poem is not overtly political, its penultimate line registers a claim that, for all the surreal imagery of its expression, has to be read against the backdrop of the growing Civil Rights movement and the gathering focus of American protest: "O give me a solid piece of sunlight and a yardstick of my own and the right to holler" (10). Postell's final contribution to *Yugen* was a prose poem entitled "harmony," which appeared in the second issue. Here the influence of Stein's *Tender Buttons* clearly joins that of the Continental prose poem and, quite possibly, also that of Aimé Césaire. Like Césaire, Postell's surrealism was populist and Afrocentric and avowedly political. Although some of Postell's more nearly lily-white readers may not have glossed his reference to "ash" in the first line of the piece, it would have required a head of a certain thickness, even in the pre–Black Power era of 1958, to miss the political and historical directions of a poem that begins, "We who stung stone know how our toil bathed us in ash, while the lilies of the land covered their heads and shuddered" (8). It is difficult to imagine, with the scant evidence of these texts, what Postell's future direction might have been, but it is not at all difficult to see that this poet who had so many conversations with the young Baraka was working toward a similar ideology to that which produced later Baraka poems like "Black Art." Baraka's "For Tom Postell, Dead Black Poet" overstates the case, in Baraka's rage and grief, but his testament to Postell's influence is not to be ignored:

> I wallowed in your intestines,
> brother, stole, and changed, your poems. And rode was rode
> by the cows and intelligent snakes of the age. While they
> killed you, while they ran you down third avenue.
>
> (*Black Magic* 153)

Like Tom Postell, Harold Carrington died young, before he had had much opportunity to publish any of his memorable and voluminous writings. Indeed, the first chapbook bearing his name did not appear until seven years after his death, when *Drive suite* was included in Paul Bremen's Heritage series of pamphlets published in London. Carrington is probably much better known to students of literary history for the role he inadevertently played in Baraka's first obscenity trial than for his own work as a poet. Carrington had been in prison most of the time since his sixteenth birthday. He subscribed to *Floating Bear,* which was delivered to him at the jail. Since his jail-house censors read all of his incoming as well as his outgoing mail, they read his copy of the ninth issue of *Floating Bear* before he did, and shortly thereafter Baraka and Diane di Prima were arrested as the editors and publishers of an obscene literary magazine.

Carrington was never able to visit in person with the other writers on the Beat Village scene, but he was an intimate member of Baraka's circle nonetheless, via his extensive correspondence from jail. In addition to Baraka, Carrington wrote frequently to Jonathan Williams, Robert Creeley, Walter Lowenfels, and Diane di Prima, often enclosing poems and other writings for their comment. Di Prima, recalling her early days as an editor of *Floating Bear,* says, "I had a lot of poems and letters from him and they were pretty far out" (di Prima and Jones, *Bear* xiii). The poems scattered among the correspondence Carrington carried

on with his friends on the outside evidence an unusual range of
poetic forms and interests for one so young. Although many of
his poems seem characteristically Beat in tone and shape, he had
already developed a highly individual approach to lineation and
to the organization of sounds. His unpublished poem "Woo's
People," which he mailed to Jonathan Williams from jail when
he was just twenty-two years old, is unlikely to be mistaken for the
work of any of his corresponding collaborators:

SOME ANTI-
BLASPHEMY
OR LARK

(DENIAL)

CHALLENGE
TO THE CHALLANG-
ABLE

(DENIAL)

CUNNING FANGS
OF
AGE

(DE_____?)

O
SWEET & VIRGINED
MOTHER

(Buffalo B27F30)

Just four years later Carrington was dead. He had finally been
released from jail on July 27, 1964, and returned to his hometown, Atlantic City. Within days of his release he died from a
drug overdose. It was a tragic end to a promising talent. Carrington had been looking forward to, and joking about, the work he
would do when he got out. In a postscript to a letter he wrote to
Baraka from Rahway State Prison, where he was inmate number
37975, in April of 1961, Carrington had made a wry comment
on Baraka's growing activism: "don't destroy country, wait till i
get out, i find lumumba & we do it for you" (Baraka Papers).

An indication of what most of Carrington's short adult life had
been like may be gleaned from a "Notice" that is stamped on the

letter he sent Jonathan Williams from the Atlantic County Jail
when he sent his poem "Woo's People" for Williams to read: "No
food, articles of wearing Apparel, Candy, Tobacco, Cigarettes,
Books, Magazines, Papers, Etc., will be permitted sent to inmates
by mail or otherwise" (Buffalo B27F30). As he was moved from
reformatory to county jail to state prison, he was, like most inmates, confronted with an ever shifting array of such restrictions
and prohibitions. Not only did this lead to Baraka and di Prima's
arrest; it also left us a record of Carrington's reading and largely
determined the course of his correspondence. One of the reasons that his exchange with Jonathan Williams and Baraka was
so crucial to his evolution as an artist, in addition to their obvious value as critical readers of his early texts, was that they could,
in their capacity as publishers, ship books and magazines directly
to him. Since Carrington was only allowed to receive books
shipped directly from the "Source of Sale" (and he was often
restricted to no more than twelve books in his cell at a time),
Baraka and Williams became his intellectual lifeline. The importance to Carrington of his book orders from Williams's Jargon
Press and Baraka's Totem Press may be gauged from the portion
of his small income they consumed. In a letter to Walter Lowenfels, Carrington explained why it was so difficult for him to keep
up with developments in the literary world outside the walls of
his prison. It was exceedingly unlikely that any jail library available to Carrington would have subscribed to radical small-press
magazines or maintained standing orders for the latest chapbooks of the New American Poetries. Meanwhile, as he told
Lowenfels, "We have jobs and I make 17 cents a day, which gives
me about $3.50 a month to spend. Out of this I have to get all
the necessities and then try to save something each month towards a book; but I don't want to burden you with my troubles
of jail, as had I stayed on the street this would have been
avoided" (Baraka Papers). Even at a time when a typical chapbook might only cost a dollar and a subscription to *Yugen* could
be had for only two dollars and fifty cents, three fifty a month
did not allow for much library building in Carrington's cell. Still,
he ordered copies of works by Mina Loy, Robert Creeley, Jonathan Williams, Kenneth Rexroth, Michael McClure, Charles
Olson, Louis Zukofsky, Barbara Moraff, and others. Contending
with the jail restrictions was a problem both in receiving and in
sending materials. One of the poems that he attempted to send

out to Lowenfels was returned to his cell on the grounds of its purported obscenity. Another time he was moved to a county jail where the newly popular paperback format was sufficiently suspect in the eyes of the wardens to be banned entirely. Apparently certain that the content of such an insubstantial format must be questionable, the authorities of that institution only allowed the more respectable hardback format inside their walls. That policy resulted in a plaintive handwritten note to Baraka: "If there are any hardbacks available by yourself or any of the people who've appeared in *Yugen* I hope you will let me know about them, as we are allowed to have them here" (Baraka Papers).

Ray Bremser was an invaluable, if unsteady, ally of Carrington's. The two young poets met in jail and became a prison-house workshop of two, finding their way to the most exciting new poetries together and reading each other their own works. When Bremser was released, Baraka was his custodian, on paper at least, and Carrington would write to Bremser at the *Yugen* address, even though Baraka often did not know where Bremser was. Bremser and Carrington's cellblock salon carried over into Bremser's outside life, often with Baraka as go-between. In one 1959 letter to Baraka, Carrington remembered a day when he and Bremser had wracked their memories trying to think of a "Negro Lady Poet." After Bremser's release Carrington discovered Margaret Walker's by then quite old Yale Younger Poets series book, *For My People*, and sent word of it to Bremser via Baraka. Bremser's departure brought about other disruptions in Carrington's intellectual life. In that same letter of February 17, 1959, Carrington ordered back issues of *Yugen* that he planned to share with other inmates. He explained to Baraka, "I've absolutely nothing to read, Ray having taken nearly all with him. We've (Nick & I, my tenor playing friend) read YUGEN enough to recite the entire issue by heart, to give an example of the situation" (Baraka Papers). (Today, when nearly every prison and county jail has its own visiting poets from the local college offering therapeutic, publicly funded creative writing workshops, many Americans might still be taken off-guard by the prospect of two inmates reciting the most avant-garde of postmodern verse together.) Following Carrington's death in July of 1964, Bremser wrote a memorial "blues for Harold," which begins,

you took

```
all the solos
& now yr/ax is in hock
somewhere in Trenton,
New Jersey State Prison
                    ,2-wing, down
an abolished corridor . . .
                    some white man blows yr/horn . . .
you were born enslaved
& died free
```

(54)

Bremser's poem is a memorial to the long nights in lockup when the two jailed poets sat up talking of music and poetry, of Jimmy Smith, Miles Davis, and the "first stirrings of Coltrane." Bremser reads in Carrington's death a systematic murder, reads Carrington's death by drugs as a playing out of racist forces determined long before Carrington's birth. Bremser declares, "those who hate you have slain you," and then yet more sadly, "the pure sounds of your own spheres / in yr/own head cldnt keep you out of it – " (56).

Much of Carrington's apprentice work bears the familiar stamp of the Kerouacian Beat ethos. In "Lament" the poet imagines himself

```
on the way up to Harlem
to have a ball,
(funky)
cultivate a wine habit
so I can comprehend
& shout
THUNDERBIRD SUITE
split to the far coast
blow in the cellar,
down to Mexico for bull fights
mushrooms
& crazy visions
then in a blaze of violence
we'll quit-it out the back door
on some crowded city street
coming to a screeching
halt –
```

(Baraka Papers)

Carrington, though, was more likely than his white counterparts to invoke as muse the most obvious precursor for his jazz-oriented poetry, Langston Hughes. "Lament" takes place against the backdrop of a sleeping city where

> the lonely moan a weary blues
> reflecting
> on the poet's silent, unobserved departure
> contemplating the poet shoes he left behind
> & are as yet
> unfilled –

The next section of the poem is addressed specifically to "Ray," and it would seem that this transition is an overt effort by Carrington to make the link between Hughes and the subsequent generations of jazz-influenced prosodists that mainstream critics of the time seldom noted.

It was the hope to bring jazz techniques into the new verse forms of the American idiom in the years after World War II that most clearly joined the projects of Carrington to those of the Beats and to Black Mountain poets such as Charles Olson and Robert Creeley. What all had most in common was the poetry of Ezra Pound and William Carlos Williams and the music of Charlie Parker. Carrington's own search for writerly analogues of the black chant of jazz was insistent and continual. He felt, as so many people his age in or out of jail do, the hard press of time against his ambitions. He worried that he was losing time that he needed for the completion of his experiments. He told Baraka, "waste lotsa time / which i got plenty of / but none for wastin'." In letter after letter we see him trying out ideas about this effort on his many poet-correspondents. He genuinely wanted to know if they thought it possible, let alone likely, to achieve on the page effects parallel to those of black instrumental music. It seems clear from some of his examples that he sensed that if the instruments seized upon by African musicians in the New World could be induced to make sounds that are like the human voice, without attempting to mask their very instrumentality, their individuated properties as instruments, then it might be possible to write jazzlike effects without in so doing attempting to make the writing itself disappear as writing; it might be possible to inscribe a calligraphy that carries its material substance along with it as it rises into song. In 1960 he wrote to Jonathan Williams,

Would like to ask you if you think it possible to convey
funk in writing say as Milt Jackson, Horace Silver or Bobby
Timmons do in music, I mean as like it is conveyed in
figures like *"Bag's Groove"* by Modern Jazz Quartet or Bobby
Timmons' *"Moanin'."* (Buffalo B146F37)

That following April, Carrington wrote again from Rahway State
Prison, describing metaphorically the effect he strove after:

Still haven't produced the complete jazz thing yet, but the
intent is there . . . like creeley [sic] says: i recognize a frog
by its structure . . . well like, i want to recognize *my* jazz
poem by its structure plus get the same or similar impression i get on hearing jazz plus originality plus swingin' plus
the great god FUNK plus which all in all is a large order
plus which after reading the poem you can see the need for
study. (Buffalo B146F38)

(Carrington's commitment to his fellow New Jersey poet William
Carlos Williams's insistence upon the American idiom as the
structuring principle of American poetics is humorously dis-
played here by Carrington's use of "plus which" as a punctuating
figure in his discourse. "Plus which" was an element of the New
Jersey lingua franca Williams could have appreciated.) It is in a
letter dated just eighteen days later, however, that we can read
Carrington's fullest statement of his desired aesthetic:

(1) people shd be able to feed theirselves & this w/out nobodies foot in their neck, that is me for the most part
(sometimes maybe i find something else to celebrate) &/or
(2) for the thing to be jazz & this is where the clouds come
from . . . e.g. *4*our bar blue*s*, 1st i got melody, then solo, am
hopeful to eventually get the thing to complete jazz figure
structure-wise, in 4/bar here is trouble: the melody i write
lotsa times which makes for repetition, what happens is i
have never been able to read something of mine to anyone & have it sound right, so have come, for the most part,
to think of poems for reading rather than the recite thing.
if it was read aloud instead of the repetition you cd have
one instrument play the 1st few bars of "bluesology" (tune
which that part of poem is based on) & just read the solo

parts/think this wd work best w/ a bass or congo or some such type drum ... now, other problems like something comes & is only solo, i mean, no jazz structure in that there is no figure &c. so i get a thing like *front line* poem/i got blowin of a sort & like this particular one 'cause it did'nt get away from me or i stayed in control & even changed tempo w/ no hassel. was you cd say standard changes & did'nt try to *make* melody line or such cause i figure i'd blow what i had, like you take in 3-days-9, discard the melody line or figure part & w/ little more work on solo i'd maybe have somethin' ... so when this happens i get a poem but not one from jazz structure state of see, & the results (?) well you like *swing* all which is more of a jazz structure and less solo, & on the other you also like *riff* which is all solo & no structure ... to get at the structure from other state of see: mostly people feeding themselves &c. now i get clarity problems. (Baraka Papers)

The letter itself is practically an instance of the aesthetic Carrington seeks, with its return to the opening theme at the close of an extended riffing.

Only one book bearing the name of Harold Carrington as author has ever been published, *Drive suite*, distributed in 1972 as the fourteenth volume in Paul Bremen's Heritage series. The copyright for the suite was registered to "the estate of Harold Carrington," since Carrington himself was dead. The jacket copy makes tantalizing reference to other unpublished works of Carrington's, including the prose sketches "3 days 9," which Carrington had written about in his letters, and a novel. The series editors remark that they had finally chosen *Drive suite* "both for its sheer virtuosity and as a tribute to the one interest we shared: Cecil Taylor's music." There is no mention in the jacket copy, no doubt because the editors were unaware of the fact, that different versions of the suite had already appeared attributed to Carrington's former cell-mate Ray Bremser. In 1960, while Carrington was still incarcerated, Stanley Fisher had included a version of the suite's first section in the widely circulated anthology *beat coast east: AN ANTHOLOGY OF REBELLION*. In 1968, after Carrington's death, Ray Bremser had published a longer version of the suite entitled *Drive Suite: An Essay on Composition, Materials,*

References, etc. . . . (the volume contains no prose), as the first in
the Nova Broadcast Series of chapbooks edited by J. Jacob Her-
man and distributed by City Lights Books. In this 1968 edition,
Bremser adds dates and places of composition to the end of the
suite's sections, and those dates and places coincide with his
imprisonment in New Jersey, a portion of which time he spent
with Carrington. I have attempted to contact Bremser with questions about the composition of *Drive suite* but have not yet received a response. Bremser is probably the only living person
who knows the truth of this poem's authorship, but it seems
safe to say, following a careful examination of the poetry and
correspondence of both writers, that the poem was the product
of their lengthy discussions in the jails of New Jersey. Whether
Carrington, Bremser, or both ultimately prove to have authored
the suite, its form and content appear to proceed from a close
collaboration between the two young poets. In another work
composed in the New Jersey State Prison at Trenton, *Angel,* a
piece written during one night of solitary confinement, Bremser
wrote, "I have discovered some beautiful people . . . That makes
it worth it" (50–1). One of the beautiful people he lists is the late
Harold Carrington.

A reading of *Drive suite* reveals affinities to such extended
Langston Hughes works as *Montage of a Dream Deferred,* but it is
equally evident from this poem that both jazz and poetics had
altered substantially from the state represented by Hughes's jazz
and blues poems. *Drive suite* is subtitled "an idiom of Cecil Taylor," simultaneously evoking William Carlos Williams's poetics
and the musician's sense of idiomatic forms of expression.
Throughout, the suite takes Taylor's modes of composition as
its formal model, attempting verbal analogues for the highly
percussive effects of Taylor's piano work and creating an arrangement of three lyrical sections that parallels the "unit structures"
of Taylor's performance. The first part of the suite is entitled "a
thousand pounds of ponder," a title that might well describe the
effect of a first listening to Taylor's music. Like so many of
Taylor's solos, this opening section begins with oddly balanced
small clusters of sounds that will later be repeated at greater
volume, speed, and intensity in ponderous combination with
additional sound clusters. The thematic materials of the opening
phrases may be read as commentary on the social and political
climate of the time and as descriptive of Taylor's eruption in the

1950s within a jazz world that seemed in danger of stultification. The birth of the "cool" was, unfortunately, linked to the critical death of much else in jazz:

```
                            icy regimentation
    it is a cold year          /      historic trompings . . .
    icy regimentation    wham    /   cymbal   cymbal
       cymbal
    cymbal      /     wham
                . . . icy . . . cold . . . blue . . . hard
```

                                                                    (4)

From this opening set of statements the section builds into longer, more densely compacted segments matching surreal imagery to sonic intensity, always within a racially specific reading of the jazz text ("a negroid spirit haunts the cave" [4]). As the poem increases its percussive attack, the typeface moves into majuscules, and signifies within Marianne Moore's imaginary gardens (his real frogs and toads may also be playful allusion to Creeley's remarks about the structural recognizability of the frog or poem):

```
    GOD SAY TADPOLE!
    GOD SAY FROG!
    GOD SAY goddam TOAD / cymbal
    WHAM
```

                                                                    (5)

We may also discern James Weldon Johnson's "The Creation" in the deeper background *mixage* of these improvisations. As the poem works its way through the construction of the "indestructable hot fort" of its tribute to Taylor, it launches a breathless scatting phrase that relies as much upon the graphic presentation of its cacophonous spiral as upon the clashing sounds of its consonant-rich chant. That the poet is not simply riffing through his dictionary here is evident from the neologism of the third line as well as from the direct reference to a Charlie Parker tune in the jamming syllables of the next-to-last line:

```
        (   QUICKLY NOW    all  the  big  words  I  can
                think of!)
    incomprehensible
        callaesthetics
```

        conundrum
           brachycephalic
              augmentation
(more)

              casowary (ZONKS)
           kangaroo (Wham)
         vibraharp (Wham)
      dissimulate (Wham)
precipitous
(cymbal/wham)
tempestuous   dromedary   lackadaisical   rotundity
   (Wham)
protoplasmic-fellaheen-unconditional-proboscous-ontology-
   minuscular
        (Wham) . . .
phenomenological/klackdoveedestine/amapola-poppy/
   phonetic-syzygy
           Wham . . .

                             (6)

The second part of *Drive suite,* entitled "sweet funk, the im-
probability," is more meditative in tone and includes statements
of the aesthetics that govern the composition of the first part.
Longtime followers of Taylor's career will have noticed the striking similarity of tone and shape in the first part of *Drive suite* to
those of Taylor's own poems that he has published as liner notes
to some of his recordings over the years, and may also gloss
"sweet funk's" declarations as a commentary on the poetics of
Taylor's approach to composition. In *Drive suite* the freedom
of Free Jazz comes at great expense and is, if anything, more
demanding than the practice of traditional forms. In the poet's
view, "FREEDOM'S a rack and growth / of torturous sweat!",
and, in what might easily have been taken as an aphorism to live
by among various poets of the New American Poetries, he declares that "only FORM & ARREST / is freeflight!" (7), a declara-
tion whose pun upon his own arrest is unmistakable. This second
section ends in ellipses, following an observation on the state of
the artist with an opening out onto the poem's concluding segments. The poem appears to follow the poetics of serial forms
and "open field" composition made more familiar by Olson and
Duncan and Spicer, but the role of the poet here envisioned is

yet more problematic even than the positions assumed by those writers. Art, in this view, is an inescapable burden of beauty. We "wept for the beauty of light," the poet wrote from his prison-house in the language of free improvisation, "and i tried to avoid this poem . . ." (8).

Drive suite's concluding segment, "Le Mans," returns us to the reptilian, amphibious modern landscape of the first section, a landscape across which lizards race against sports cars, in which buzzards coexist with the brontosaurus, and the primordial im-pels the space age. Like Olson's, this poem records the discovery of a thought-to-be-extinct species swimming about in the waters of postmodernity and puns terribly upon the collapsing human-ist cosmos:

> the state crumbles
> fish are fish and coalacanth out of New Zealand
> , O the Neanderthal of it all . . . tumultuous, . . .
> the Ganges . . . rape of the whole western
> mind! cacaphony! spontaneity! obscenity!
> wham.
>
> (10)

It is in these passages that the critique of modernity becomes most typically Beat in tone, but even here the use of sound scored in imagery that reifies the abstract is an unusually per-sonal accent. Like Emily Dickinson's "zero at the bone," "scanned-once scene of scream" effectively concretizes the ephemeral. It is a thickening-into-materiality of the abstract achievable only *in* writing that seals the condemnation of a rei-fied commodity culture:

> man, the consumer
> , man, the malignapoid . . . anthropo-
> itic-itious, fool after fool the
> foolhardy, blob on a scanned-once scene of
> scream – the screened spleen
> man
>
> (11)

As if to enact Carrington and Bremser's search for funk ana-logues, the poem then returns at its end to the percussive ono-matopoeia of its opening lines: "Wham (viz.; wham wham wham

wham / wham / cymbal / wham/ cymbal cymbal wham . . ."
(11).

That use of sound imagery in the concretizing of the abstract
is a technique also employed to great advantage in the poetry of
A. B. Spellman. In "the beautiful day, V" Spellman wrote that
"quietly, and without warning / them, night leaked into the /
room, into the 'idea' of the group" (*Beautiful* n. pag.). Spellman
would have agreed with William Carlos Williams's oft repeated
dictum "no ideas but in things," so long as it was agreed that
ideas can be things. Spellman's poem is not a "poetry of ideas,"
but neither does he fear that an idea might violate the poetic
vocation, and his poem flies in the face of many current-day
creative writing class commonsense dicta about preferring the
concrete to the abstract. For Spellman, the "idea" of a group is
palpable among the group and within the inscribed lines of
the poem, but it is also subject to the material interventions of
temporality, of day's passing. As the beautiful day wanes, the
identity of the group gathered into the idea of itself is interrupted, just as the line of the poem is interrupted in caesura
when a comma interposes itself between the room and the group
that inhabits it.

Spellman is much more widely known than either Carrington
or Postell, but his poetry is nearly as rarely read and discussed as
theirs. He is in fact probably best known as the author of *Four
Lives in the Bebop Business* (1966), a seminal collection of essays
based on his interviews with Cecil Taylor, Ornette Coleman, Her-
bie Nichols, and Jackie McLean. In the introduction he added
to that book in 1985, Spellman predicted that "you could empty
a room of American cultural policy makers by requiring them to
distinguish a solo by Coleman Hawkins from one of Lester
Young's" (ix). A room full of cultural policymakers might be far
more familiar with Spellman himself; he has for many years been
a cultural policymaker by virtue of his position on the staff of the
Expansion Arts program of the National Endowment for the
Arts. It would, however, probably be possible to clear a considerable space by requiring a crowded room of American poetry
scholars to name a poem by Spellman. Whereas *Four Lives* was
produced by one commercial publishing house and later reprinted by another, Spellman's sole chapbook of poetry, *The
Beautiful Days* (1965), is little known and has not reappeared.

For over a decade Spellman seemed a ubiquitous poet, appearing in magazines such as *Yugen, Cricket, Floating Bear,* and the *Journal of Black Poetry,* while also publishing notes and essays, particularly on jazz, in *Ebony, Nation, Liberator,* and *Metronome.* His poetry was, of course, selected by Hughes for inclusion in *New Negro Poets U.S.A.* in 1964, and he was also represented in the anthologies *Beyond the Blues, Dices or Black Bones, Black Fire, Negro Verse, The New Black Poetry, The Poetry of Black America, Understanding the New Black Poetry,* and *The Black Poets.* Still, following that prodigious burst of publishing, Spellman simply vanished from most anthologies that appeared after the mid-1970s. As a poet, critic, editor, and teacher he has exercised considerable influence on the directions taken by black writing and critique, and yet he remains a veritable invisible man of critical history. In *Drumvoices,* Eugene Redmond grouped Spellman together with Baraka and Joans as a constellation of poets centered in the New York bohemian scene and comparable to the *Dasein/Howard* group (324), but few literary histories have evinced much interest in following up on Redmond's suggestive linking. Spellman has merited an extensive entry, written by Carmen Subryan, in the *Dictionary of Literary Biography*'s volume of black poets after World War II, but it is significant that Subryan, writing in 1985, was unable to cite any substantive published criticism of Spellman's poetry.

Many recognized *The Beautiful Days* as the herald of a significant new talent when it was published in 1965. Spellman's poems had been appearing here and there since the late 1950s, and his first book of poetry had been eagerly awaited by his many friends and admirers. Diane di Prima recalled that Spellman's chapbook was the first one that she ever printed at the Poets Press (di Prima and Jones, *Bear* n567), and the book bears a short introductory note by Frank O'Hara, who wrote, "His poems speak about an existence happening between extreme heat and extreme cold, between black and white, fire and snow, and what a poet's sensibility must ask of him" (n. pag.).

The son of two schoolteachers, Spellman had first met Baraka when both of them were enrolled at Howard University. While at Howard, Spellman (who at different times early on signed his poems as "Alfred" or "Ben") took writing, theater, and literature courses from such legendary figures as Owen Dodson, Arthur Davis, and Sterling Brown (Subryan 311), each of whom was soon to assist the Dasein group. Spellman was reunited with

Baraka in New York in 1958, often staying at his home, at a time when, as Spellman remembered it, " 'abstract, expressionist art was hot, jazz was going into a new avant garde' and poetry was at its most popular point. 'Then Malcolm X appeared on the scene; the civil rights movement heated up' and 'black consciousness swept down from Harlem' " (qtd. in Subryan 312).

Spellman's poems mark a site of convergence for all the tendencies linking the various black practitioners of the newer poetics who formed the generation that first began publishing after World War II and established the formal structures that would subsequently be taken up as a vocabulary of black aesthetics during the Black Arts movement. Only in the multiplying texts of Baraka himself will we find a still more extensive working through of these modes. In both poets we can read a critical juncture between the modernist forms of Pound and Williams, the alteration of those forms at the hands of the authors of the New American Poetries (especially Olson's projective verse), and the historicized particularities of black vernacular expressive forms graphed in black writing. Just as Olson represented a transmutation of the poetics of Pound (but merciless rejection of his bigotry), Spellman, Baraka, Postell, and Carrington each played changes upon the "changing same" by reworking Hughes's modernist experiment with blues and jazz forms in a postmodernist restructuring that paralleled the revolutions of hard Bop and Free Jazz. Further, under the powerful influence of their readings in Lorca and Césaire (and Hughes's translations of Negritude writers), this new generation of poets created novel forms of blues imagery, less determined in its connotative values, perhaps, than the imagist ethos, and taking the concretized abstractions of the blues as its point of departure. ("There's nothing wrong with your engine," sing Sonny Terry and Brownie McGhee, "you've just been using bad gasoline.") Lastly, these poets, some of whom had studied with Sterling Brown, wrote a yet more politicized verse than their immediate predecessors. As the poetry of the 1930s and 1940s written by poets like Brown and Melvin B. Tolson clearly demonstrates, there had been no real dilution of political statement between the period of the New Negro and the 1950s, but as the difficulty those two poets faced in their attempts to publish also demonstrates, the willingness of establishment publishers to support radical statements by black poets, as well as the willingness of establishment critics to read them, had nearly reached a vanishing point before the rising Civil Rights movement again caught the attention of the national press. Brown's *Southern Road* had been released by a commercial publisher, but the firm expressed no interest in publishing his second collection, and by the time Baraka and Spellman came on the scene it was clear to them that they would have to create their own means of literary production and dissemination. There was, it is true, a generational and class-based antagonism that often found its way into print in the 1950s and 1960s, sometimes producing the ludicrous spectacle of one comfortable bourgeois writer denouncing other comfortable bourgeois writers for being comfortably bourgeois. There was a specifically African-American variant of the traditionally bohemian desire to stick it to the bourgeoisie. Ted Joans's poem "The Pit of Cold Brother Bullshit" is a particularly localized version of the genre, recalling Leadbelly's song about Washington, D.C., with its chorus: "It's a bourgeois town." Joans's version of "The Bourgeois Blues" expresses a missionary zeal:

> They of Wash. D. C. nigger high ass
> They think they've made it
> up white imitation ladder at last
> Those cold brothers down in D. C.
> We gotta pull their coatails/and FAST!
>
> (*Black Pow-wow* 15)

But those who, like Spellman and Baraka, had experienced firsthand both the class antagonisms among African-American communities of the nation's capital and the radical, blues-based poetics of Brown knew that there were available models for their own rebellions "in the house."

This did not make political differences disappear. When Spellman's poem "Zapata & the Landlord" was published in the eighth issue of *Floating Bear* in 1961, it bore an ironic dedication, "for allen dulles." When the poem was reprinted three years later in Hughes's *New Negro Poets U.S.A.*, it had, for whatever reason, been sanitized to the extent that the ironic dedication had vanished, and with it at least some of the poem's critique of America's postwar empire building.

All the same, Spellman's generation, whether they were social activists or not, tended to view the political as suitable material for poetic composition. Whether or not they agreed with Auden that poetry "makes nothing happen," they viewed the poem as a place where politics could happen, and this may have prepared the way for the dominant view during the Black Arts movement that the chief role of a poem *is* to make something happen. There were also intervening events that made many black artists sure that there was little to choose between a poetry of quietism and a poetry that at least tried to provoke its audience to action. In Spellman's later untitled poem beginning "when black people are," which appeared in the fall 1968 issue of the *Journal of Black Poetry,* the poet remembers

> driving from atlanta
> to the city with stone and featherstone
> & cleve & on the way feather talked
> about ambushing a pair of klansmen
> & cleve told how they hunted
> chaney's body in the white night
> of the haunted house in the mississippi
> swamp while a runaway survivor
> from orangeburg slept between wars
> on the back seat.
>
>   (19)

As if this were not enough motivation for the move to a revolutionary poetics, Student Nonviolent Coordinating Committee (SNCC) activist Ralph Featherstone died in an explosion on March 9, 1970, during a drive in the Bel Air, Maryland, area, underscoring the tragic accuracy in the concluding lines of the poem:

> times like this
> are times when black people
> are with each other & the strength flows
> back & forth between us like
> borrowed breath.

Even in his earliest works Spellman used a poetic vocabulary that added a racial politics to the epistemological questioning his poems shared with those of Olson, Creeley, and William Bronk. A poem published in the second issue of *Yugen* in 1958 reads at moments very much like a Bronk or a Creeley poem.

The link is, more than likely, the philosophical lyrics of Wallace Stevens. In a section entitled "THE TRUTH YOU CARRY IS VERY DARK," Spellman writes;

it is not spoken to him
who has bled salt
but to him who lives within
the Penumbra of the Silent Mind
upon this shadow
cast the shadow of the wind

(22–3)

There is an intertextual music at play among these lines that comes in range of our hearing when we place the poem in a wider context of African-American poets. Two years after the appearance of "THE TRUTH," on the other side of the continent, the black Beat poet Bob Kaufman published in San Francisco an extended prose piece, seldom studied today, entitled *Does the Secret Mind Whisper?*, a jazzy fantasia that details the life lived "within / the Penumbra of the Silent Mind." Just two years after that, back in New York City, a predominantly black group of writers began meeting on the Lower East Side, committed to producing, as David Henderson later described it, "Blackworks from the black galaxy" (*Blackworks* n. pag.), and though they took their name, Society of Umbra, from a poem by member Lloyd Addison, the name of the "Umbra group" and the title of Addison's poem both clearly marked a celebratory return to the shadowy poetics of blackness forecast by Spellman's poem. According to Carmen Subryan, Spellman was an early promoter of the Umbra group and its works (312). The epistemology in his poem is every bit as severe and demanding as that of the earlier Objectivists. He writes that "truth is what we touch," and then, obviously alluding to Stevens and his snowman, adds, "if it is there / if it is not there." When viewed in the modernist/ Objectivist lineage, Spellman's limning of the truth that we touch when it is there and the truth that we touch when it is not there may be seen as a furthering of a poetics of phenomenology that forms a major thematic project of twentieth-century literature in the West. When viewed in the context of African-American literary history, the poem may also be seen to further the problematics of double consciousness and racialized epistemologies that forms a major thematic strand that precedes even Paul Laurence Dunbar and stretches through the texts of W. E. B. DuBois into the postmodern present. (People living inside the veil of double consciousness may always have been suspicious of metanarratives.) It is probably safe to say, without fear of essentializing, that persons whose social identities have been constructed as black in America inhabit a redoubled "penumbra" of reifications and veilings, a penumbra in which, when the "truth" is constructed by the white hegemony, the truth is the "not there" that "we touch."

In like manner, poems such as "I Looked & Saw History Caught" participate in versions of that questioning of the teleological humanist metanarrative so evident in Olson, Creeley, and Burroughs. For Spellman, the available narratives of history always had been two-faced: "I looked & saw history caught / on a hinge, its two heads / like a seesaw rocking" (126). In these ominous lines we can read the hinge that produces double consciousness, the hinge of Atlantic Middle Passage linking African and European narratives permanently in a motion of history that is constantly disruptive, constantly teetering between its teleological poles of black and white cosmologies, constantly creaking at the balancing point of its intertextual and interracial joint. It is the violence and indeterminacy of this hinged history that placed black American consciousness also at the hinge point of modernity and its possible "posts-." In the view of C. L. R. James, the Middle Passage and the creation of a diaspora in which masses of toiling Africans formed a new class of revolutionary workers had created the New World black, the African American, whose new identifications and subjectivities can be read, out of the textual gap linking the names of two continents, as the first truly modern peoples. In *The Black Jacobins,* James describes the manner in which the Western discourses of slavery and race incapacitated the rulers for the task of recognizing the very revolutionary forces they had helped to bring into being. Not the "furthest imagination" among them, James believes, could "have envisaged the entry of the chorus, of the ex-slaves themselves, as the arbiters of their own fate" (292).

Nearly three decades after James's book appeared, the Black Power movement was still insisting to a recalcitrant, white-dominated political structure that "the ex-slaves themselves" would finally be the arbiters of their own fates. What had changed in the interim was the faith in a Western telos of the inevitability of revolution. Spellman, though he hoped steadfastly for forms of revolution in American culture and politics, no longer rested those hopes in James's Marxist narratives of emancipation. But neither did Spellman's poem simply counter a linear view of Western progress with a "Third World" faith in historical cycles. What is seemingly sure in "I Looked & Saw History Caught" is an apocalyptic vision of the death, in an "Inner / College of Murder," of the reigning ethos:

> *that* head swings down to
>
> ward what has been western, up
> with pocketsful of shit to spread
> on hectares of earth, earth
> warm with the voicings of minnow
> eucalyptus & cowrie.

> (126)

Spellman had no predictive metanarrative he could rely upon to tell him what would follow. He believed, as did James, that the hegemony of the present order was "rotting of their own / interior commerce," but he could only pray that the other head of his historical vision would "swing / down to root."

Black music serves as the steady point of reference in all of Spellman's works. Poems like "Jelly Wrote" and "John Coltrane: An Impartial Review" testify to Spellman's enduring love of the musical traditions and of the spirited new innovations that moved the traditions into novel spaces. "The Joel Blues" shows Spellman looking back to the powerful influence of Hughes and bringing that influence to bear within the context of the New American Poetry. As effective as the poem may be, both as tribute to Hughes (and to the blues) and as tribute to Spellman's Village friend, the poem remains obviously a look backward, in contrast to poems like "Jelly Wrote," which gave new conceptual and formal direction to the blues-based lyric poem. The critic Stanley Crouch, who for some years appears to have made a part-time job out of attacking Spellman, revealed his essentially conservative critical aesthetic early on by singling out "The Joel Blues" as virtually the only poem of Spellman's worth attending to at all. In a 1968 review of Spellman's *The Beautiful Days*, Crouch called "The Joel Blues" the only piece in that slender

volume "that's not as horrible as the rest of the things" ("Books"
91), then went on to say that "it is still not an actual poem." In
fact, "The Joel Blues" is simply and straightforwardly a blues
lyric, borrowing many of its lines from earlier songs, and as
regular in its rhythms as the blues lyric that Hughes once dashed
off while listening to music at the Newport Folk Festival and
passed to Muddy Waters, who promptly sang it. The difference
between "The Joel Blues," which was first published in 1961
(probably as a tribute to Joel Oppenheimer) in *Floating Bear*
and a poem like "Jelly Wrote" is the difference between simply
improvising upon a standard form and improvising new lyric
forms out of the blues, something that Crouch was as set against
then as he has been set against most forms of formal innovation
in literature and music in recent years. Crouch found nothing
"actually worthy of note" in Spellman's writing and, in his 1969
review of Baraka and Larry Neal's anthology *Black Fire*, went so
far as to discourage other writers from following the poet's lead,
predicting that poet Sam Cornish might one day amount to
something "if he leaves A. B. Spellman, who is a terrible influence, alone" (67).

Although there are some passages of purple sentiment in
Spellman's youthful lyrics, there is a great deal that is worthy of
note in his work, and he was considered a poet of note by such
astute critical voices as Neal and Henderson. One especially
notable aspect of Spellman's poetry is the fashion in which it
continually reinscribes a thematics of the materiality of vernacular signification. "Jelly Wrote" is a title that puns wildly upon the
name of "Jelly Roll" Morton while at the same time calling our
attention to the very physicality of Morton's compositions (not
to mention piano rolls), to the retrievable textuality of his music
(*Beautiful* n. pag.). Likewise, the poem "Baltimore Oriole," a
1960 composition that was first printed in the twenty-fifth issue
of *Floating Bear* and which appeared on the page facing "Jelly
Wrote" in *The Beautiful Days*, reprises from "THE TRUTH YOU
CARRY IS VERY DARK" the concretizing of "truth" as a palpable,
readable text in the world. "the lines in our faces / talk for us,"
Spellman wrote in the lines of his poem, giving a qualitatively
different sense to the entire notion of presence and orality, a
sense of the face as talking book. As the poem moves into its
final statements it again recalls an Objectivist epistemology, but
here a significant alteration was registered in the poem as it

moved from its initial appearance in the *Bear* in 1962 to its final version published in *The Beautiful Days* three years later. The earlier version is more certain in its conclusions, offering a physical answer to deep questions of perception:

> will night in any sense be
> bright to us ? anything living
> is visible   , can be held in our
> fingers or tasted on our tongues   .
>
> & vernacular's become a wineless habit.
>
> (di Prima and Jones, Bear 283)

In this version we read a lingering faith in the evidence of our senses and in the relationship between perceptions and quotidian language. However, the poem in its later form is considerably less sure of itself, willing only to advance tentatively into the world at the edge of the penumbra, only able to hope for a faith:

> will night in any light come
> bright to us?   anything living
> be visible, held in our fingers
> & tasted on our tongues?
>
> & vernacular become a loveless habit?
>
> (Beautiful, n. pag.)

It may be that Spellman maintained his belief that anything living is visible, readable, and can be held, but he was no longer certain that there would be anything living to read and taste. Part of this growing epistemological uncertainty must have been related to the growing political instability of the time. Spellman was willing to advance into the shadowy text of the world's future, but he could not know what he would find there. The anxiety this produced in certain of his poems is radically different from the social angst and alienation so often associated with Euro-American modernity. Spellman's anxiety was a product of his confrontation with that modernity:

> it is the fear of winter passing
> & summer coming & the killing
> i have called for coming
> to my door saying
> hit it a. b., you're in it too.
>
> ("when black people" 19)

Though Spellman has continued his involvement with literary communities (upon moving to Washington, D.C., for instance, he assisted a workshop for new black poets in the city), he appears to have ceased publishing new poems. Carmen Subryan, in the *Dictionary of Literary Biography*, simply says that "Spellman now devotes his creative energies to his administrative responsibilities" (315). Still, there is much in Spellman's earlier works that needs to be reread if there is to be a critical reopening of the questions raised by black postmodernity. The shifting final line of "Baltimore Oriole" should serve as both a caution and an impetus to discussions of black vernacular forms in African-American writing. Moreover, Spellman's frequent insistence upon the poem as a self-reflexive but still material space for the graphing of utterance serves as an effective locus for reconsidering the writerly in black writing. In "daniele's poem," he muses over the problem of fitting form to experience:

> those foot stampings
> & those interdigital hairdos
> your lovers know you by are too strange
> to the form & filling of the poem.
>
> (*Beautiful,* n. pag.)

What Spellman's "interdigital" writings give witness to is that the poem is the graph of its own experience, that form and "filling" arrive together, and that nothing is too strange for poetry to form itself around. Baraka, commenting in *Floating Bear* on Cecil Hemley's review of Allen's *New American Poetry* anthology, claimed that the book was "as much a chronology of a *process* as it is a yearbook. And . . . history, itself, can be measured by ideas (their cessation &/or resurgence) as well as events" ("Revue" 16). Spellman's lyric poems, few in number though they may be, register a process of the cessation and resurgence of ideas, and a history of the processional of African-American poetry must, if it is to be of use, chronicle the writing of A. B. Spellman.

Writing later in *Cricket,* the black music magazine that he coedited with Spellman and Larry Neal, Baraka once again reconfigured a primary slogan of American modernism as a derivation from African tradition. Like Tolson before him, Baraka was able to reterritorialize the shock of the new that was modernism upon the landscape of a continuing African heritage:

What is necessary is constant effort at achieving a total. At achieving something New. Make it New attributed to Ezra Pound is Eastern. It is the African (and Sufi) explanation of why life, even though contained by an endless cycle, or not contained, *is* an endless cycle can be, is worthwhile, i.e. make it new and lo and behold KARMA (digit???) ("Notes" 46)

Baraka's totalizing impulse, which led him first to Cultural Nationalism and then to Marxism, may be of a piece with an odd conservatism that has to see the new as both ancient and derived. But what may be far more important than the viability of Baraka's totalizing gestures, at least more important to our understandings of the recent past of black poetry, is Baraka's insistence that constant artistic innovation is at the heart of African traditions of expressivity, and that modernity, perhaps postmodernity, is not foreign to but constituent in African and African-American art forms. The strategy, then, was never to "catch up" with Euro-American modernism but rather to interrogate it, rupture it, and reclaim an unacknowledged black modern that had existed within and as enabling strata. For Baraka, the artist of the new was necessary to the very survival of the culture, since, as he put it in the poem "Lowdown," "We are in the era of imminent brake failure." It is important to our historicizing of similar moments in the 1950s texts of the white avant-garde that we reassert and reexamine the black presence that gave so much to both the form and the content of that avant-garde. At the same time, it is crucial that we see Baraka not as LeRoi Jones, the lone voice of African America in the midst of the New American Poetry, as Allen's and most subsequent university anthologies present him, but as one of several young artists, including Clarence Major, Bob Kaufman, Jay Wright, Tom Postell, Stephen Jonas, A. B. Spellman, and Harold Carrington, who had set out independently to find modes of remastering and disfiguring modernism in a poetics of black expression, and who had then found each other in the pages of little magazines and in the coffeehouses and streets of postwar American cities.

Baraka's energy provided leadership, encouragement, and a point of intersection for this disparate group as well as for those who came after them. The magazines and newsletters that he published and worked with carried the new poetries everywhere.

Writing to Baraka from the West Coast in 1959, the young poet
Ron Lowensohn, who would publish one of his first books with
Baraka's Totem/Corinth Press, reported; "Talking to everyone,
seems like YUGEN has suddenly become THE magazine, sort
of combination Dial, Poetry, BMR [*Black Mountain Review*] &
Evergreen! WHOOPEE!" (Baraka Papers). It is true that after its
first year *Yugen* published far fewer black writers than it did in its
first two issues. It is also true that in the course of its short life
(eight issues), *Yugen* published many more black poets than the
vast majority of longer-lived poetry magazines. (Sadly, this has
been true of avant-garde and mainstream magazines alike). The
seventh issue of *Yugen* carried a notice at the bottom of the
contents page that, well before deconstructive inversions had
become a critical commonplace, gave fair warning of what the
new countermodernity the black poet envisioned might be like:
"We the kinda cats like to turn Hegel upsidedown just to see the
pennies fall out" (3). There is no overestimating the importance
of correspondence, little magazines, and personal contacts to
these small groups of poets working against a seemingly indomi-
table mainstream in the years before universities had become
the watering holes of creative writing and the last poets had
disappeared into the campus. Oppenheimer's letter to Baraka
published in that same issue of *Yugen* testifies to what being in
Baraka's house and magazine meant to that earlier posse of
poets:

> my peers, talk to me, too. there is communication, take a
> tape of a saturday with you and me at your house, i would
> guess, broken down like this: 30% nostalgia (old movies,
> radio, school, sex) 30% sports (current and old) 20% gos-
> sip 10% jokes 5% the dozens 5% our business in life, writ-
> ing the poem. but that/s where the poems lay, in all that
> bullshit, and sometimes they come out, and that/s all i
> know about it now. (60)

Far more than during the period of the Harlem Renaissance, or
even the 1930s era of left-wing interracial writers' congresses and
clubs, this was a period when black American poets, Baraka more
than any other, assumed positions of leadership internationally
like that seized at the beginning of the century by Ezra Pound
among the modernists.

It was not long before Baraka would begin to meet writers his own age and younger for whom his published works had already been an influence. Baraka's first encounter with the members of the Society of Umbra, which was taking shape on the Lower East Side even as he was organizing in the Village, came when two strangers approached him at the Five Spot shortly after the publication of *Blues People.* "You LeRoi Jones?" they asked, following with a challenge from the one Baraka calls "the big headed" stranger. "I like your prose. I don't like your poetry." The big-headed challenger turned out to be Ishmael Reed, who had come to Manhattan from Buffalo. "And so I'd met Ishmael Reed and Calvin Hernton," Baraka recollects in his *Autobiography,* "but I didn't know them from Adam's house cat" (182).

Despite Stanley Crouch's public warnings about A. B. Spellman as a bad influence, Spellman was one of the poets the members of the Umbra group looked to, and they looked to him precisely because of his location of material signifying traditions in African-American language practices. Lorenzo Thomas, in his 1978 article about Umbra's "Shadow World," has written that "One might significantly begin to study the new Black Arts Movement by reading A. B. Spellman's profoundly interior landscapes of the far edge of Manhattan" (56). Thomas, who was one of the youngest and most precocious of the Umbra group, may have overstated matters when he claimed that "Spellman's feelings have no kinship to the Western appliances of psycho-temerity that we find in even the best (and supposedly 'revolutionary') white American poets . . . and many black ones," but it is readily apparent that among the things that drew Thomas to Spellman's example was an insistently African-American poetics of the materiality of language, a black form of objectivism rooted in the blues tradition. In Spellman's verses, Thomas stated, there are, "in some deep sense that remains unclear, African feelings. There is a totally physical aspect to these words" (57).

Lloyd Addison's poem "Umbra" is reputedly the source for the name of the Society of Umbra and of its magazine, and Addison's poetry often reads as if it is carrying on a deliberately contrapuntal relationship with Spellman's, as if the two were, like jazz musicians on a stage, trading eights. Though Addison was a few years older than Spellman, his first small pamphlet of poetry, *Rhythmic adventures beyond jazz into avowal sound streams,* did not appear until 1965, the same year that Spellman's *The Beautiful*

Days was published. It was not until Bremen included Addison's *The Aura and the Umbra* in his Heritage series in 1970 that this poet's work achieved anything resembling wide circulation. Addison's poem "All the reasons for the snows" offers in tribute a rhymed chorus to the lead supplied by Spellman's "THE TRUTH YOU CARRY IS VERY DARK." Addison wrote, "My sun has gone down in drum suite penumbra / The mood of this rhythm my body is umbra" (*Aura* 8). This was a redoubling of metaphorical double consciousness, and that redoubling may be one thing that marks Addison's and Spellman's work as "post-" to the modernity of DuBois and Hughes. As Thomas has more recently described the moment, "It was not your father's double-consciousness – not even James Baldwin's. Believe that!" ("Alea's" 576).

The Society of Umbra has received considerably more attention than the Free Lance or Dasein groups, more even than their immediate predecessors working in the penumbra of the Beat scene, and this is due at least in part to the publishing success several members of the group have had. Calvin Hernton's book *Sex and Racism in America* was published by Grove Press and has gone through numerous printings. His later book *The Sexual Mountain and Black Women Writers* has also been well circulated. David Henderson published an early collection of poems with a commercial press in New York, Dutton, and his biography of Jimi Hendrix was a best seller in both of its editions. Ishmael Reed, of course, is one of the most prominent novelists, poets, and essayists of his generation, and his works have been the subject of an ever expanding bibliography of critical studies. But the critical attention that has been directed at the Society of Umbra has certainly been shamefully scant when compared to the increasingly numerous examinations of the New York school or the Black Mountain poets. Indeed, if we were to eliminate from our count those histories written by Umbra group members themselves, the entire corpus of critical texts about the group *as* a group could probably be read at one sitting.

One critic who has produced a thorough history of Umbra, Michel Oren, in his essay "The Umbra Poets Workshop, 1962–1965," has described a "pre-Umbra" phase that began with readings held by Raymond Patterson and Calvin Hernton and extended into the summer of 1962 (180), readings that brought the new generation of experimentalists into direct contact with their modernist elders. Patterson recalls one reading attended by Melvin B. Tolson (though he arrived too late to hear the poetry read) a few years prior to the publication of Tolson's *Harlem Gallery*. "Melvin B. Tolson came to the last meeting of the series," Patterson writes. "He missed the reading but stayed late with an eager gathering to talk. He is a shrewd and engaging conversationalist – shoes off, tie loosened; sly and illusive [sic], but provocative. I understand he is having a new book of poems published soon" (Pool Papers 124). Oren dates the initiation of Umbra proper to a call sent out by Tom Dent for young black poets to meet at his apartment. By the winter of 1963, the first issue of *Umbra* magazine had appeared. Dent, who came to New York in 1959 after a two-year tour of duty in the army, had been attending readings organized by Raoul Abdul (then Langston Hughes's secretary) at an art gallery located at Seventh Avenue and 135th Street, where he had met Addison and Raymond Patterson and had heard actor Roscoe Lee Browne read Hernton's poems (Dent, "Umbra Days" 105). By the summer of 1962, Hernton, David Henderson (with whom Hernton was staying for a period), and Dent had become friends and were, as Dent later put it, looking for "a device that could deal with race, that could serve to bring us together, that could be a vehicle for the expression of the bitterness and the beauties of being Afro-American" (106). That device proved to be the Umbra workshops. Dent remembers,

> We called an organizing meeting and sent out a call to all the black writers in the area we knew. Our first workshops, on Friday nights at my apartment, were a way of becoming familiar with each other's work, airing obsessions, fears, and plodding, jerking toward some concept of what we were by measuring our concepts against the beliefs / expressions of brother writers. (106)

Around two in the morning the group would usually remove to Stanley Tolkin's bar at Thirteenth Street and Avenue B. Dent refers here only to "brother" writers, but there were women in the house as well. The group expanded rapidly as participants brought other friends into the workshops. By the time they published the second issue of *Umbra* in December of 1963, the official list of members printed in the magazine included Alvin Simon, Art Berger, Albert Haynes, Joe Johnson, Tom Feelings,

Norman Wilkerson, Oliver Pitcher, George Hayes, Ishmael Reed, Rolland Snellings (Askia Muhammed Touré), Jane Logan, Mildred Hernton, Lennox Raphael, Maryanne Raphael, Lorenzo Thomas, Ann Guilfoyle, Asaman Byron, Rashid d'Phrepaulezz, Charles Underdue, and Brenda Walcott. The editors had been listed on the masthead of the first issue of the magazine as Thomas Dent, Calvin Hernton, and David Henderson. That first issue carried a "Foreward" that resembled the Dasein group's rejection of commonplace critical criteria and that anticipated a negative public response:

> We do not exist for those seemingly selected perennial "best sellers" and "literary spokesmen of the race situation" who are currently popular in the commercial press and slick in-group journals. There are unpublished and infrequently published ethnic writers whose works are excellent, important and often far superior to those adopted few with which the standard press habitually and expediently affronts the public.

Though the first *Umbra* included a number of poems whose normative syntax and phrasal line breaks placed them safely within the range of formal expression that even the mass market readership had grown accustomed to reading, it also included the kind of "hardbound idiom" found in Leroy McLucas's "Graph":

> Armful bedwork carbonized
> delinquent ejaculation
> fornicated ghetto
> hardbound idiom
> jackass jackknife jackoff jackscrew
> jailbird jaywalker jazzer jeer jesse
> james jivejitterbug jobseeker john
> joiner joggler juggler junkman
> knotty knight leaseless lofer
> muddymale nughtnymphs
> outrooted pantaloon
> quarter rubber stamp
> tenderfootin umbrella
> vaginal woebegone
> x yesman zulu

(39)

Such a syncopated tour of the alphabet, with its jazzy detour through the neighborhood of the letter j (including a guided subtour of the vowel sounds), certainly is not the kind of poem readers of *Phylon* or *Negro Digest* were subscribing to, let alone readers of the *New Yorker*. The alphabetic and phonetic organizing principles of McLucas's poem are the kinds of techniques critics are, even today, more likely to look for from the Oulipo group or the $L = A = N = G = U = A = G = E$ poets than from contributors to predominantly black magazines. The Umbra poets, though, can be seen as unacknowledged forerunners to the $L = A = N = G = U = A = G = E$ poets in this regard too. As Oren reviews poems such as McLucas's, he argues that "In this typically avant-garde stance, the breaking of syntax and the disruption of oppressive social conditions spring from the same impulse and seem part of the same enterprise" (189). He does not mean that they are the sort of poets " 'who could confuse the fibonacci number system with class struggle,' " as one $L = A = N = -G = U = A = G = E$ poet was accused of doing, but that they are the sort of poets who, as Ron Silliman has said in answering that charge, understand that the common "underlying issue is one of representation" ("Wild Form" n. pag.). Contrary to what proponents of social realism and the New Criticism alike held, there is no inherent reason why experimental verse form should be thought to impede or imperil (or be imperiled by) the making or comprehending of political statements. Indeed, McLucas's "fornicated ghetto" is instantly recognizable as an apt description of American political realities by literary poets and illiterates alike.

Thomas, in an interview with Charles Rowell conducted in 1978, made a remark that typifies the attitude toward literary experimentation shared by the Umbra group and poets like Spellman, Carrington, and Baraka: "The Black World – home, where we live, where we suffer – is where most of the avant garde music and art come from" (Rowell 30). It was this attitude that brought such revolutionary black musicians as Shepp and Taylor to Umbra readings (where Taylor often read his own poems [Rowell 34]). Like Shepp and Taylor, the Umbra poets, including McLucas, brought a high degree of vernacular irony to their political verse. McLucas's poem "Negotiation," included in the first issue of *Umbra*, finds a curious route into the Booker T. Washington–W. E. B. DuBois debate:

imagine   dinin   car
union railways
boot servin
brandy
in
walk
booker t
"what u wan? – ed'kashun"

(38)

The magazine was produced by equally innovative and populist means. According to Dent, the money for the first two issues was raised at parties held in the headquarters of the Communist Youth Organization (which had seemingly overcome Stalinist resistance to avant-garde arts), where Shepp and Bill Dixon provided the music and David Henderson provided the black-eyed peas (108n).

That so much of Umbra work was formally, as well as politically, radical is something that needs to be considered when we think about this group's importance to the Black Arts movement, in which several Umbra writers were key figures. Political radicalism linked older members of the group like Lloyd Addison (born in 1931) and Oliver Pitcher (born in 1929) to younger writers like Lorenzo Thomas (born in 1944) and Norman H. Pritchard (born in 1939). It is not necessary here to rehearse the year-by-year history of Umbra; it has been outlined already by Dent, Thomas, and Oren. But although the writings of Reed, Hernton, and David Henderson have been frequently published, widely read, and occasionally studied, sometimes even in universities, the more experimental writings of Addison, Pitcher, and Pritchard have been allowed to go out of print, are only infrequently anthologized, and are seldom included in African-American literature curricula. Analyzing the unsettling effect that the music of Cecil Taylor had on musicians and critics alike in the 1950s, Spellman has written that "Cecil's music was an abrupt challenge to the hard bop music with its ready availability to both performer and listener. Unless Cecil would just go away, music would never be the same, and the musical scene would never be the same" (*Four Lives* 14). The radical poetics of Umbra writers like Pitcher and Pritchard were no more lacking in precedent in black writing than Sun Ra's transmutations of the vocabularies of the big band were unprecedented in the black orchestral traditions; in each genre the innovators and outsiders were working with materials they had gathered from *inside* the tradition, but were working them in new ways. It remained the case, though, that critical power was often committed to the unchanging same. Sun Ra, Taylor, Pitcher, and Addison represented a threat to a soliloquizing essentialist narrative of black identity and tradition, and that narrative could not continue its hegemony undisturbed unless they could be made to go away. Black artists were returning to the sites of African-American modernity to see what new forms it could yield or yield to, in much the same way that white avant-garde poets were challenging the "high" modernism of the New Critics by returning for novel materials to the texts of Williams, Stein, Zukofsky, and even Blake. Musicians such as Taylor never did go away (though his poems are probably not taught in any English Departments) and Coleman has been awarded one of the MacArthur Foundation's "genius" grants. The writings of Addison, Pitcher, Pritchard, and so many others have, however, nearly gone away for good, and this has allowed critical histories to tell narratives of authenticity and triumphal identity politics rather than tell the multiplying free stories of ever more complex black modernities.

Lloyd Addison, born in Boston, lived in Virginia and New Mexico and served an Air Force tour in the Pacific before settling for good in New York. The author of several unpublished novels and short stories as well as a large body of poetry, also mostly unpublished, Addison supported himself by working for the Harlem branch of the Welfare Department, only occasionally receiving such recognitions as his appointment to be poet in residence for Harlem's Afro Arts festival in the summer of 1967. For a time he published a magazine called *Beau-Cocoa,* copies of which are now exceedingly rare. Thomas has termed Addison a "frighteningly intellectual poet" and testifies to his considerable influence in the early days of Umbra. When we read Thomas's critical assessments of Addison it becomes apparent that the older poet has embarked upon an enterprise much like that registered in William Melvin Kelly's epigraphs to *Dunfords Travels Everywheres.* Thomas writes that "Addison's poems, though indebted to T. S. Eliot and Melvin B. Tolson, seemed to emerge from the black community without any foreign influences; his language and themes were those expected from a people who grew up reading

the Bible" ("Shadow" 66). One might posit that black traditions
of revolutionary and apocalyptic visionary prose – for example
the vision narratives of Nat Turner – have as much to do with the
flashing imagery of Addison's lines as does his reading in the
master texts of Euro-American modernism.

There is evidence that Addison had been in contact with some
of the same figures of the white avant-garde that Baraka and
Carrington were corresponding with. A 1959 letter to Jonathan
Williams acknowledging return of a manuscript indicates that
Addison had already been writing to Williams from New Mexico
prior to his settling in New York. The letter is as oblique as much
of Addison's poetry and is in fact written in lines like a poem.
The letter's close is an odd form of commiseration, perhaps
prompted by pique:

> Sorry your legend is of the past.
> Yes, I would like to make school my
> Continual Answering – it's all in the way of it
>   No, there is no "too" – just one.
>
> (Buffalo B97F46)

One would require, of course, the other side of the correspondence to contextualize the opacity of these lines, but they also
resonate interestingly with the opening of a poem by Addison
entitled "I by you put on:"

> knew you upon the one true time
>   two   to times   shifting
> being too badly moved in mood
> to come to see me born again to be something born of you
>
> (Aura 4)

This mid-1950s poem owes an evident debt to the syntactic re-
arrangements of e. e. cummings's love poems, but it also clearly
joins in an African-American ethos of the secularized sacred. As
Thomas Dorsey could move from accompanying Ma Rainey into
the church, creating a blues-based Gospel sound, and as Sam
Cooke could move from Gospel to a pop-oriented Rhythm and
Blues, Addison's poem brings a Baptist's sense of thwarted rebirth to a blues ballad. What we would not usually find in a
similar moment in the works of someone like B. B. King, say in a
song such as his rendition of Percy Mayfield's "Please Send Me
Someone to Love," is the deliberate slippage of signifiers along

phonetic and orthographic axes. The ear cannot hear the move from "two" to "too" to "to" and must rely upon the eye to read syntagmatically for a determining context to discern the differences. But it is just that context that Addison's text disrupts (or we might say that disruption is Addison's context). "Two" follows "one" so naturally in this poem that the listeners will think for a moment that they have heard "two" one more time in the phrase "to times." The poem, by violating that series of phonetic and generic expectations, raises all those questions of representation that Silliman and Oren find at the nexus of political and poetic avant-gardes. Addison's odd sort of love poem does, in fact, by conjoining its prepositions in such unusual ways, formally replicate the emotional collapse of representation that is its subject matter: "you should be / slightly half of me / in part and place of you." It is the lover's refusal to be half of the poet, to be partially replaced by being partially placed in the poet, that lover's putting by, or down, of the poet's proffered rebirth, that leads to the writing of a poem that stands in the place of "the I put on."

Everywhere in his work Addison employs this technique of exploding commonsense usage, of interrogating parts of speech and formal arrangement. The poems have as one of their many points of origin speech, but it is in Addison's hands a "speech parabolic" (11), a speech whose arc has to be graphed along its constituent axes. In "Umbra" Addison records a particularly domestic and surreal arc of speech-writing:

spoke
       said muffled mute hot gerund to be is being is
               the night pitch
               the feeling pie
                         (*Aura* 9)

In that same poem he again links an evangelical Protestant tradition of oral representations of visionary states to a specifically written mode. The visionary oral tradition grows directly out of readings, often readings aloud in performance, from the New Testament book of Revelation (whose author Son House called "John the Revelator"). Addison's revelatory script is a form of such spirit writing that eyes its own form as a source of further revelations: "let / prone veins of fire repent of presumption / the climbing to comma" (12). Here, too, there is a racial mark-

ing of lyric surface. Addison both portrays the human body's
movements as a writing across racialized space and portrays writing as a racialized space for the embodiment of thought:

> She moves penumbral limbs long-lettering the garrulous day
> and drawn across the night thigh pencilled unsharp ends
>   erase
>   white darkness letters written in overwrought space
>   naked outfaces the eyes of letters
>
> (13)

Form as metaphor for form is the motivating force for Addison's
long lines here. The long lines mime the length of the woman's
"penumbral limbs," stretching past pentameter in long-lettered
syllables that sound nothing like Whitman. The lithely moving
legs both pencil and erase lines of thought and feeling as they
move back and forth in space. Writing itself is a "white darkness"
as the figure and background of the written page trade places.

The poem "By line abdomen cradle aura womb" carries this
aesthetic a step farther as Addison first jams statements hard up
against one another, as though to fuse them, then punctuates
syllables as if to render them phrases in their own right: "dark
space.in place aura thigh is par.a.phrase. ink / as distinct deep
intuits a black kink axis in.field.in to / figure out black out in
pink.ink acts" (15). This poem follows "Umbra" in Addison's
chapbook and in many ways glosses the procedures of "Umbra."
The constituent words found inside the word "par.a.phrase" enact an authorizing gesture for our readings of the figures of
speech written here. The expression "field.in to / figure out"
paraphrases the figure–background shifts in the "white darkness"
of "Umbra" 's writing and in the ur-text of the woman's bodily
figurations. Once the reader has fallen into the reading habits
scripted by Addison with his interruptive punctuation, it then
becomes habitual to engage in redoubled readings of each
phrase set of the poem. Thus the "ink acts" of the last line quoted
can be read, to begin, as an instruction to "figure out black" or
as a description in which "figure" and "black" are both "out."
This poem, whose dates of composition are given as 1959–65,
then moves to a consideration of the problematics of presence
and absence in writing and a meditation upon the field of writing (reminiscent of Pollack's field painting and Olson's and
Duncan's projective-field composition strategies), all scripted as

a bridge passage to get from one place to another in the poem:

close-in / / closing field
presence fits / / absence out.closed.out
break fords break bridge. fast   up.ends knit

(15)

The inserted marks of caesurae serve both as last bastion against the closing in of the field in the first two lines (the marked absence that staves off closure) and as the breaking ford of enjambment, a logistics of crossing over from one signification to another. The caesurae in Addison's lines are a sort of suspension bridge fitting absence to presence.

In his poem "After MLK: the marksman marked leftover kill," Addison applies this methodology to an overtly political lament. The title itself puns upon the line that commonly precedes a poem written "after" another poet, in the sense of a written imitation of that poet, usually in another language. Readers may take the preposition "after" in those instances as a sign that the poem they are to read is not meant as an "accurate" translation but as a new poem in a new language written in the manner of or under the inspiration of the absent original. (Translations labeled "after" are usually not published with an accompanying original in a bilingual, facing-page edition.) Addison's poem is written more literally "after" Martin Luther King, as the subtitle sadly indicates, and it is an "imitation" of King in the sense in which William Carlos Williams liked to use that term. This form of mimesis is not an attempt to copy the things of the world but to imitate the creative processes of nature in a forum of mimesis, the poem as scene for the creation of new forms and things, the poem as new form. Addison's "After MLK" is a poem that does not simply offer to represent for readers the life or spirit of Martin Luther King; it is a post-King poem whose language forms, in the aftermath of assassination, as a re-creative, prophetic act. In thinking of the death wound with which "the marksman marked" King, Addison puns upon past legal fictions of civil equality and writes a proleptic figure of a future politics: "watch the little black hole / in the new world order undeliver-rated life-space" (23). The neologism "undeliver-rated" appears as a pun upon the "deliberate speed" with which the nation was ordered to dismantle its apparatus of segregated education in 1954, an order whose deliberate ambiguities might now be viewed as having encouraged the "undelivery" of the promised integration. The poem encodes as well another tragic sense of undeliverance, the failure of the Promised Land as life-space to embody itself for black souls. "Undeliver-rated" includes, too, a sense of the underrated, and for readers in the post-Reagan–Bush era of American politics, Addison's encryption of the "new world order" as site of undelivered and now unpromised promise is attended by ironies unforeseen by the poet. Throughout the poem Addison makes use of this same writerly technology of multiplying reinscription to create ever denser areas of overdetermination. Concocting a portmanteau word (both a blend and a counterword), Addison describes a world in which "civilly engineered rights" are "obversely proportional to wishfountainpen power," a construction that portrays as wishing well both the act of the poet himself and the formal ceremonies surrounding the president's signing of his name to Civil Rights legislation, ceremonies during which the signature is affixed with many pens, and following which those and even more ceremonial "wishfountainpens" representing by metonymy the power of the Executive are passed out to Martin Luther King and others in pledge of federal power to guarantee the rights of black Americans. But, following a parodic formula of counterposed powers, Addison knows that the civilly engineered rights will be opposed, because "anti-rights-bodies equal ten/time square / by the co-efficient light minus the magnetic exponential . . ." (23).

As he so often does, Addison includes ironic commentary on his own poetic procedures as a constituent part of his thinking about the post-King "indefinite period." Looking to the "Armageddon Eve" signaled by King's assassination, the poet imagines "run on sentence–structured fellowship.mad theme antics . . ." He links together the histories, prophecies, and poetries of the Old Testament traditions with the chronicles and apocalyptic visions of the New, looking for vindication: "whether in Kings or Psalms or Ecclesiasties, / never blink, in Acts or Revelation: / by goods the goodbye contract of the little black hole" (23). As he approaches the end of his meditations, an end that eludes description by sailing out in ambiguous ellipses, Addison calls together a science of persuasion and a science of explanation. He writes, "So now rhetoric unpacked good physics call forth overcoming" (24). The killing of King was the unpacking, in one deadly sense at least, of the rhetoric of triumphal liberal progress, and the event calls for a further unpacking of rhetoric in acts of political and moral explication. The poet calls for a rhetoric that will assist in the final overcoming of racism, but he is also calling for the simplest kind of physics (every action has its equal and opposite reaction) to enact the promissory rhetoric of liberatory song. It will not be sufficient for a platitudinous white president to assure his television viewers that "we *shall* overcome." A reaction equal to the "anti-hymn" of the assassination must inevitably be called forth:

> in Copernican accounting for a new toned iron sting in
> graft itches
> before the picture of muzzle simultaneously develops
> to mass spree-the-corpuscle of dropout entropic delight,
> to wRap tRap white nightrider wind in Brown paperbags for
> sailing . . .
>
> (24)

Addison's Copernican accounting presents mass social movements and the spontaneous upheavals of revolt following King's murder as a corrective physics following the inexorable laws of the universe. (We might in passing note that Addison's references to black holes and entropy place him also in the lineage of postmodernity that includes such writers as Thomas Pynchon and Don DeLillo.) In the last, elliptical line of his poem, Lloyd Addison encodes a nation's responses to *Brown v. Board of Education* and also militant black response to the violence of the white hegemony. The figure of H. Rap Brown rises from among the written characters of the poem to sail in the post–Martin Luther King wake. It is the "nightrider wind" of oppressive American racisms that provides the wind in Brown's sails. (Is it possible that this line also alludes to the infamous "brown bag" test of color consciousness?) In Addison's "Copernican accounting," violence is, as Rap Brown used to say before he was himself trapped by it, as American as apple pie.

Lloyd Addison was acutely aware of his marginal status in the official world of American letters. In a letter to Rosey Pool, who included his work in her anthologies of African-American verse, he wrote that, like him, "Many men . . . stand and have stood between two worlds, marginal men. Only we do not all face the same direction. And that is the difference in orientation, in outlook, and in success. I think that I have always faced the wrong direction" (Pool Papers 4). Addison had entered, without success, the competition for the Yale Series of Younger Poets in 1960, but he understood clearly that, as one facing the wrong direction, he was unlikely to receive accolades from the dominant literary institutions of his time, and he set about creating new and more open institutions, such as his magazine *Beau-Cocoa* and the Umbra workshops. His formal innovations were an obstacle to wider publication. He wrote to Pool in 1960,

> I do not feel obliged to fit so neatly the printer's habit – though printing costs are high – nor the grammarian's stylistic monotony, though monotony may be the more concise and impressive. My format is an essential part of my presentation, and I had never written so well until I evolved this of my own.

Commercial and academic audiences, though, were perhaps after another form of essentialism from black poets. Addison refused to write what he called "Negro sayings" (Pool Papers 4), but he believed that the jazz rhythms and black voices that were an inherent component of the world he wrote about would "accost" any reader open to their presence. Further, he linked his formal experiment to his understanding of black history:

> And so 400 hundred years of slavery in America may be a large or a small matter to consider, according to one's point of view, but surely for many it is a woeful reality and the first order of business to compile its shameful statistics until one and all can write its obituary. It is unfortunate, but only a personal misfortune, that I, as the great grandson of a slave (in chains) cannot put a comma and/or period in the right place in this chronicle, or epic. (Pool Papers 4)

The poems that Addison sent to Rosey Pool were, he told her, "perhaps of the future," and he advised her that magazines rejecting his works had accused him of "ultra-romanticism, of being too cosmological, poetical, etc," but a reading of his few published poems indicates that his marginality truly was a result of his facing the wrong direction – that is, facing in a direction that editors and readers did not generally expect a black poet to take in 1960. Addison did not expect his poems to interest all readers. He told Pool, "I think that if one can break out of the mold, any mold, it should be interesting to witness. But, of course, it need not be interesting to all" (Pool Papers 4). In the Umbra workshop Addison encountered a group of innovative writers and readers who were very much interested, who answered when Addison asked for a witness, and in Addison the Umbra writers found confirmation of their own opposition to "stylistic monotony."

At the end of his 1958 prose poem "Tango," which appeared in the second issue of *Yugen,* Oliver Pitcher wrote that "Nothing is ever where we left it" (17). Lloyd Addison has, for the most part, been left out and left behind by literary criticism examining the progression of African-American writing from the immediate post–World War II period to the advent of the manifestoes of the Black Aesthetic, despite the testimony to his influence from contemporary participants in that progress such as Lorenzo Thomas. When we return to our readings of Addison, we will find that neither he nor his poems are in exactly the place where we left them. Just as we now cannot help reading an eerie and ironic foretelling of George Bush's continued opposition to all Civil Rights legislation in the "new world order" Addison saw in the aftermath of Martin Luther King's death, so must we now read back into Addison's record the poetics of writers who came after him, such as Nathaniel Mackey, Erica Hunt, and Will Alexander. Alexander's prose poem "Hypotenuse Shadows Shouting Buffalo Lyrics," written more than two decades after Addison wrote most of his poems, follows Addison's lead in using the logics of physics and mathematics as tropes for a racialized politics in America. As the speaker of Alexander's poem escapes "to the Albert Einstein trophy case," he contemplates a calculus of violence contemporaneous with Addison's: "At the recreated murder of a botched up Emmet Till, the bomb explodes in the neck of the [jury] foreman, and tears through the eyes of his family so that the vultures make the best of a char broiled human sandwich" (13). Alexander's work participates in a tradition of formally innovative, politically directed, surreal composition that stretches from the postwar era through Umbra poets such as Addison and Pitcher and into the present. Oliver Pitcher, however, is perhaps even less known to students of recent poetry than Addison. Pitcher was not included in the Paul Bremen series of chapbooks that preserved at least a small portion of the record of innovative black verse that American publishers would not preserve. He did publish a small book of poems, *Dust of*

Silence, as early as 1958, prior even to Baraka's *Preface to a Twenty Volume Suicide Note,* and Pitcher was an active early member of the Society of Umbra. He was subsequently included in Arnold Adoff's encyclopedic anthology *The Poetry of Black America,* but he was left out of most other contemporary collections, including, oddly enough, Bremen's *You Better Believe It,* which included so many of the other Umbra writers. (Oren notes that Bremen and Pool had been introduced to Pitcher, along with Addison, Hernton, and Patterson, as early as 1962 [180].) Pitcher's absence from most poetry anthologies, then and now, may be in part the result of his having devoted much of his career to painting and writing plays. But his brief association with Umbra (he is listed as a member in both of the first two issues of the magazine) offered, as Oren indicates, "various models for the younger poets" (180), and those of his works that found their way into print over the years are a tantalizing lead still awaiting the critical readings of literary history.

One of the first things that leaps out at anyone reading Pitcher's poems within the context of Umbra's history is his imbrication in the metaphorical shadow world of color and meaning, in the logics that shadow the logics of race in America. The title piece of his book *Dust of Silence* (1958) alludes to the black Protestant traditions of redemptive sacrifice and to the black intellectual traditions of doubled consciousness. The subjectivity that is "not your father's double-consciousness" is a volatile postmodern positioning that comes after Eliot's handful of dust had been scattered and metanarratives of salvation had been silenced by "our neighbor's dearly-beloved rope" (9). The prose poem opens in the hour of the dusk of dawn, that transitional moment at the edge of night. It is a time when "Smithereens of sound is [sic] now dust of silence," a time when the comforting myths of historical narrative will no longer suffice but the stranger comforts of indeterminacy have been embraced. "There is no cause for alarm since no one knows what day is being celebrated, and there is safety in silence" (10). At the still, vanishing point between day and night, life and death, sacrifice and resurrection, Pitcher gazes at the horizon: "Distant spots of light, puffs of lightning or vague suggestions of incendiaries? only the penumbras could be seen far off on the thin black strip of horizon of Calvary Hill" (10). The text, too, is a "thin black strip of horizon," and it is common for us to think of fine "shadings" of meaning, of areas of signification fading into one another. Richard Harland, in *Beyond Superstructuralism: The Syntagmatic Side of Language* (1993), suggests that "We may think of a word's meaning as a combination of umbra and penumbra: an area of total shadow fading off into a surround of partial shadow" (26). But just as the subtitle of Harland's book betrays its own figure of speech (How *would* one look from "the syntagmatic side of language" to the "other" side?), so the suggestion that we think of something *as*, that we consider meaning *as* umbra and penumbra, suggests that all really is, metaphorically, penumbra. There is in language no "total" shadow of meaning (just as it is ultimately impossible to be beyond a shadow of doubt), and there is hence no falling off into a partial surround. The taxonomy of race in American consciousness, our fathers' as well as our own, operates within a similar totalizing and contradictory logic. Racial definition in this country has attempted, at least since the early days of slavery in the English-speaking areas, to banish the very possibility of penumbra under a totalizing rubric of blackness. What DuBois and so many other African-American writers discerned so clearly is that white society's attempts to delineate a clear and distinct line of demarcation between itself and blackness will not hold. Those writing inside the horizon line of color could see that these cultural boundaries were a penumbral area of cultural indeterminacy, that horizons are always advancing and retreating across the mutual landscape. As Pitcher wrote, "only the penumbras could be seen."

The name "Umbra" was a positive assertion of cultural blackness, but it was never totalizing. The Umbra group included some white writers, like Art Berger. In the signifying realm of Pitcher's poem, black sacrifice did not lead inevitably to some great getting-up morning when all souls would be washed white. In contrast, his vision revealed to him "a clay pox from dust unrisen on drizzling Easter" (10), a trope whose language portends Addison's later writing of the "undeliver-rated." The white robes that Pitcher could see were not those of an angelic train; they were owned by those same neighbors who wed themselves to the politics of terror with their "dearly-beloved rope." In "The Twittering Machine" of his poem, Pitcher warned, adopting biblical diction, "to avoid the ushers in white robes at the / end of the line, I say unto you, get off / at the stop BEFORE the next" (18). Pitcher's irony may be measured in this last instruction,

which resembles so strongly the impossibilities of white expectations of blackness. White Southerners wanted black people to be
invisible, but nearby. White Northerners, some at least, wanted
black people to be free, but to be free somewhere else. (*Uncle
Tom's Cabin* is perhaps the paradigm here.) Southern newspapers
were likely to accuse lynched black people of having committed
suicide and then having burned the evidence. The only salvation
Pitcher's humorous lines can find is to get off at the Zen-like
stop BEFORE the next stop. Pitcher's formal devices are often
used to underscore these ironies. The phrase "end of the line"
does not come at the end of the line of verse but instead, with
heavy enjambment suspending our reading between the lines
separating the definite article from its object, it comes at the
beginning of the next line. Another enjambment causes the
reader to think, however briefly, that Pitcher's colloquial advice
is simply to "get off," perhaps by any means necessary.

Many such devices recall the ironies of the blues, and "Dust
of Silence" pays tribute to that source by means of citation,
enjambment, and substitution. When we read the line "some of
us have moved to the outskirts of" (18), it appears that we have
joined a company of blues migrants following Louis Jordan's
lead in his recording of "I'm Gonna Move to the Outskirts of
Town." Pitcher's is a more cosmological move, though no less
rooted in the realities of black lives. The "some of us" in his
poem "have moved to the outskirts of / time when nobody was
looking" (18). (Could the "nobody" who is looking be related to
both Emily Dickinson's and Bert Williams's "Nobodies"? Is such
an intertextual, historical miscegenation unreadable by current
criticism?) Another poem, "Harlem Sidewalk Icons," pays tribute
to the inventiveness of vernacular storytelling, to the traditions
of the blues, and to Hughes, who regularly wrote lines like the
conclusion to this stanza:

> Man, in some lan
> I hear tell, tears wep
> in orange baloons will
> bus wide open with
> laughter.
> > Aw, cry them blues Man!

(22)

This poem is in the same mode as Sterling Brown's "Slim in Atlanta," a poem that tells with raucous humor what happened when Atlanta passed a law requiring black folk to do their laughing in a telephone booth. It is possible that Pitcher had not seen this poem (though surely he found it after his move to Atlanta), since Brown's book *Southern Road* was experiencing one of its repeated periods of unavailability during that time. What we can track here is more important than matters of direct influence (or even anxieties of influence), however. In Pitcher, as in Addison, we see a new generation that had not yet thought of itself as postmodern (Baraka entitled his anthology of postmodern fiction writers *The Moderns*) moving the ironies and formal features of the blues into a newer poetics inspired by, but departing from, the colloquial texts of predecessor poets such as Hughes, Brown, and Tolson. Pitcher is possessed of the blues singer's love of wordplay. In "Finger Exercises for Majoriska" Pitcher tells of a poet who "came to a just end. One day / at high noon while writing about / the moon, he was sunstruck" (14).

As a painter, Pitcher had a characteristic appreciation for the materiality and pliability of his materials. Like those modernist painters who did not want the painterly textures of their surfaces to give way to their models as a transparent medium providing unmediated access to a transcendent subject, Pitcher showed himself unwilling to regard the chirography of his texts as a transparent medium giving itself up to speech. Pitcher's "Sidewalk Icons" were taken from street speech, but they were not street speech. The icon was characterized in part by the very artificiality of its representation. Pitcher's "Harlem" is musicked speech written down, speech relined and re-presented as visual text. For Pitcher there never has been an opposition between orality and the literary. There had been an oppressive devaluing of black speech by the American critical establishment (usually, in fact, a devaluing of a constructed representation of black speech), but Pitcher's revolution against that racist devaluation was not a simple revaluation by reversal. He wanted an orality reformed in art script. In an introduction that he wrote, many years after his own book of poems appeared, for an anthology of writings by members of the Atlanta University community, he remarked of the book's contents that "Most of the writers who use the idiom of street talk, have hammered it, mastered it, into a fine arts graffiti" (4). Pitcher's fine arts graffiti is a sort of street-corner calligraphy.

He performed this visual textualization of the spoken in his poems as early as 1958. In "The Icononclast's Closet," Pitcher proffers an inventory of "old-found" toys. Among the odds, ends, and debris, he enumerates "bits of paper; credos, documents, agreements, treaties" (*Dust* 20), each of which is labeled with the same ironically altered slogan. In his book, Pitcher reproduces the revised slogan in a graffitilike scrawl, all in capital letters, spread across the space of the page as if spread across the side of a building. It looks as though the slogan was originally written, "FOR THE BETTERMENT OF ME," but, editing this statement of motivation, the poet has scratched an *X* across the still visible word "ME." (It would be some years yet before Derrida would use the same graphic device to illustrate the concept of writing under erasure, and poets of the New York school were just beginning the practice of printing such "canceled" lines.) Pitcher has then added the substitute word "MANKIND." These notes, credos, and self-important agreements, the poem tells us, were "scratched out, rescribbled, tucked away in a vest pocket" (21). Jerry Ward spoke of N. J. Loftis's *Black Anima* as "black speech rerapped" (207), and Pitcher's writing of the rescribbled graffiti of his own text is yet another naming of the reformation and deformations of mastery I have been calling, after Ed Roberson, the calligraphy of black chant. Like that of Addison and Spellman, Pitcher's aesthetics again leads to a concretizing of the abstract, a reification of the impalpable in imagery that is musical, visual, and, as the fact that it is written makes obvious, scriptable. In parodying the reactionary mind as a paragon of emptiness, for example, Pitcher's poem "The Iconoclast's Closet" adopts the abstractions of geometry. For him, conservative thought is a line linking two naughts, and if we recall from our geometry classes that a point has no length, width, or depth and that a line is points in a series, having neither width nor depth, we can then read in Pitcher's lines the utter pointlessness of the reactionary ethos. "His mind," as Pitcher scathingly describes it, "is a curved line starting at void ending at vacuum tripping over raspy negatives all the way" (20).

Pitcher's was, as we have seen, a politically committed art that linked radical social analysis to the radical artifice of innovative poetics. Another mark of his postmodernity was that he viewed contemporary black arts as the repetition, with a racial as well as temporal difference, of the acts of revolution that were modernism. Nothing is ever repeated per se, and so to repeat formal modernist ruptures of signifying practices in another time and place, in another dimension of race and class specificity, is to repeat afterward and otherwise, and hence Pitcher's is an African-American "post-" to the revolutionary modernisms of the past. In introducing his Atlanta University writers, he proclaimed, "What James Joyce did for (or to?) British English, urban blacks and regional dialects are [doing,] creating still another dimension in American English. Actually, these writers are carrying an ancient banner and fulfilling unwritten promises to . . . Rimbaud" (4). Such radically "other" dimensions of revolutionary modernity are most readily discerned in a book like Baraka's *System of Dante's Hell,* in which the canonical locus of Dante's *Inferno* becomes the site for Baraka's harrowing of the forms of modernity and for the reclamation of a black postmodernity. But already in 1958, Pitcher's *Dust of Silence* provided models for the structures and the ethos Baraka was moving toward independently. Pitcher's "Washington Square: August Afternoon" reads very much like the dissociative early circles of Baraka's urban inferno:

> the poet who gave up the middle class, upper and lower, as hopeless (sprawled on the fertilized French poodle grass scorched brown; he, not the class, for security insults, melody embarrasses.) Too early risen, weighed down by the Rosey Eclipse, he hears the sound within his head of the Nail hammered into hardwood and knows, allez oop, the day beckons. He throws back his head, the head of a stunted rooster (no, not at all like an alley cat) he trumpets and challenges the day with a deliberate cough, ppplllttt! and "Hopeless! Hopeless!" He's found his song; he saunters off to someone's sparrow roost called home, so small it holds nothing but pocket editions. (19)

The coughing poet greeting the "Rosey Eclipse" of the day is as much a response to Aimé Césaire, whose *Return to My Native Land* was written "at the end of the small hours" (37), as it is the fulfillment of an unwritten promise to Rimbaud. And that promise is itself overironized, addressed as it is to a poet who, having written *A Season in Hell,* then entered a period of unwriting when he joined the colonial enterprise in Africa. Pitcher's poems are a double-bladed response to Rimbaud, remastering the weapons of the surrealist prose poem, deforming mastery as had Césaire, and posting them by return mail in the postcolonial enterprise of revolutionary black writing.

Depending upon whose account we attend to, Norman Henry Pritchard, Pitcher's colleague in the Umbra group, either was kidnapped or participated in a feigned kidnapping by his colleagues in the swirl of events that marked the end of Umbra as a functioning workshop group in New York. (The magazine continued briefly on the West Coast under David Henderson's direction.) The uncertainty surrounding these events is ironically reflected in Pritchard's subsequent abduction, by force or benign neglect, from literary histories and from the anthologized record of African-American writing. This poet, whose face was once so prominently featured on the cover of *Liberator* magazine and who published as recently as 1970 with such a well-regarded publishing house as Doubleday might as well have been a featureless, unpublished bohemian, considering his nearly total disappearance from critical view. When Kevin Young was writing his article "Signs of Repression: N. H. Pritchard's *The Matrix*" (1992), he found that Pritchard's reputation was so thoroughly repressed that the poet could not even be located. Young writes, "Pritchard – whose present whereabouts are unknown to members of his former circles – seems to have fallen not so much out of favor as out of the picture altogether" (38). When what was then seen as the more "nationalist" wing of the Umbra group "kidnapped" Pritchard, with or without his cooperation, all they apparently wanted was the Umbra bankbook that he held for the group and kept at his parents' house, where he was living. (The Umbra account held either twenty-five or two hundred dollars, depending on whether Tom Dent's or Joe Johnson's memory is more accurate on this count.) In the intervening years, Pritchard himself has been withdrawn from the cultural capital of American literature.

Oren, in his interviews with the purported Umbra kidnappers, seems to have gotten no closer to a definitive narrative. Askia Muhammed Touré told Oren;

> We seized Norman and refused to let him leave because we
> felt that if we could not be heard democratically then dog-

gone it the journal would not come out. We were certainly firebrands . . . We held Norman as hostage, drove with him to Brooklyn to his parents' home and secured the bankbook and sat on it in order to prevent *Umbra* from coming out. (199)

This is a fascinating scenario, but probably exaggerated. It would seem highly unlikely that a man taken by force (Oren has been told alternately that a gun or a knife was involved) would enter his parents' home while the "abductors" waited and then turn over the bankbook. Ishmael Reed, who was reputed to be one of the abductors, has told Oren, "I can't imagine anyone kidnapping Norman Pritchard. He's a large fellow, capable of taking care of himself" (199). By whatever means were necessary, though, the bankbook was gotten out of Pritchard's possession, and if Dent's memory is accurate Reed must have been involved in some way, since it was Reed and "Charmy" Patterson who returned the passbook to Dent after a short period (Oren 199). No one thought to record Pritchard's own account at that time. Some years later his two major collections were published, *The Matrix: Poems, 1960–1970* in 1970 and *EECCHHOOEESS* a year later, he appeared in a remarkable number of anthologies for a poet of his age, including Richard Kostelanetz's collection of concrete and sound texts, *Text–Sound Texts* (1980), and then he slipped out of sight. It was as if he were not only writing in such a way as to "decompose the reader," to use the critical terminology of W. Francis Lucas, but to decompose himself as a public persona as well.

According to the biographical notes supplied by Doubleday when they published *The Matrix*, Norman H. Pritchard was born on October 22 (a birthday I share with him) in 1939 in New York City. While pursuing his B.A. degree at New York University he was president of his campus Fine Arts Society (without being kidnapped by his colleagues) and was an active contributor to the university's literary magazine. He did some graduate work at Columbia, gave readings at venues including Sarah Lawrence College, Barnard, and a meeting of the Poetry Society of America, and taught briefly at the New School for Social Research. During his years in Umbra and afterward, he published his works in *Athanor, Liberator, Season, Negro Digest, Sail, Poetry Northwest*, the *East Village Other, Gathering*, and many additional magazines and journals. Besides the numerous anthologies of African-American writing that included his work, he contributed to thematic collections such as Walter Lowenfels's *In a Time of Revolution*. The contributor's note accompanying Pritchard's poems in one anthology indicates that he was then working on a novel, but no novel has yet appeared in print.

Pritchard was quite capable of turning out the most perfectly regular of metered couplets when he chose to, as in the poem "Parcy Jutridge," which appeared in the anthology *Dices or Black Bones:* "in thin where utters coast the light / few trace their mirrors on a fuel" (69). And yet, for some still to be explained reason, Pritchard has never been taken up by more recent champions of metered verse such as the New Formalists. "Parcy Jutridge" bears an unmistakable affinity to the experimental poems in standard verse forms of more celebrated poets such as John Ashbery, but the extreme unconventionality of Pritchard's language forms was unusual even at the time of composition. On a casual reading one might almost assume that Pritchard was following aleatory procedures like those used by John Cage or Jackson MacLow. But there is a nagging sense that these lines do make sense, akin to the feeling we get, while reading the invented words of Lewis Carroll's "Jabberwocky," that we can recognize the creatures being described, despite the fact that the description occurs in an unknown idiom. If one can "trip the light fantastic," then certainly one can "coast the light," and that would seem an apt description for what our utterances do, particularly those that we, not reduce to, but raise again in writing. "Utters" may be creatures of speech, shaped perhaps like otters, or we may be riding along an utter, in the sense of "extreme," coast, where things, like the air, are attenuated "in thin." Similar readings multiply along the thin reflecting surface of the following line. It is almost as though the underlying meters, with their predictable familiarity, ensure that we will in the end make sense in and out of Pritchard's poem.

That surely is one key to the formal universe of Pritchard's works. He has recognized that form in itself (though it is never found in itself apart from that which it is the form of) conveys and guides the making of meanings by readers, and that forms may underscore or counter the significations of the language that shapes them. One reason the dialect of the Jabberwock seems so instantly comprehensible even to the youngest native

speakers of English (perhaps particularly to the youngest) is that
Carroll's "nonsense" phrases are constructed in strictest accord
with standard English syntax, that they occur in a poem that
religiously follows the formal traditions of its genre, and that the
invented words conform to regular rules of word formation in
English. (For example, the "adjectives" of this idiom invariably
are placed in the grammatical positions occupied by English
adjectives and often end with "y" sounds; the plurals are formed
with the final "s," etc.) In Pritchard's verse (and this is really true
of all poetry), the poem's shape and rules of construction may
prove as important to our eventual interpretations as the "content," and in many instances the form is the reader's primary
experience of the poem. This is not to say that Pritchard did not
share the cultural and political imperatives of the other writers in
the Umbra group. His writing was, as he put it in "Metagnomy," a
constant searching among the real "to seek / to find / a lance /
to pierce the possible" (101). Even so straightforward-seeming a
goal as this was subjected to formal disruption by this poet. When
he reprinted the poem in his book *The Matrix* in 1970, just a
year after its appearance in *The New Black Poetry*, Pritchard extended his seeking lance as a dissecting tool turned upon its own
language, searching among the very letters of the words for
further possibilities. In this revised version, the lines just quoted
appear as follows:

```
To     s     ee     k
to  f    in    d
a   l   a    n    c    e
to    pier   c   e        the p o s s i b l e
```
(Matrix 41)

Suddenly our eyes find the "pier" that had always awaited us in
the original line, and just as suddenly we find a new form of
internal rhyme in reading the *d* and the *e* at the end of the
second and third lines against the "the" in the last line. These
discoveries may not seem great revelations, but they certainly
offer us a demonstration of the very "piercing of the possible"
that is their subject matter. Creeley's adage that form is never
more than an extension of content has seldom been so tested by
extension as in Pritchard's texts.

Always Pritchard looked on the underside of usage for what
might have been occluded by familiarity. To Lorenzo Thomas,

Pritchard's investigations were a distinctly African-American practice, an extremity of signifying marking its own routes through the master texts of "good" English, and this was one of the attractions of Pritchard's model for Thomas, who was the younger poet by just five years. In "The Shadow World," Thomas argued that "Pritchard investigated the African underpinnings of 'Black English' before most of us even understood the significance of the term. Pritchard's early experiments, which were to lead to a 'transrealism' that resembles concrete poetry, resulted in poems written in tampered English in which the combination of sounds approximated vocal styles and tones of African languages" (54–5). Thomas adduced as an example the poem "Aswelay," which exists both in the form of a published text and in the form of a performed sound text recorded on the Broadside collection *New Jazz Poets*, a performance that Percy Johnston said was impossible to duplicate "aloud, in silence, or [by] any method" ("Minton's" 46). Thomas's term "transrealism" might be useful as a rubric for the discussion of a poetics that not only employs the surreal imagery of a Césaire but, in addition, radically transcends the logic of common syntax and even of word structures. Such a transreal poetics assaults the internalized *langue* itself, disrupting its normative workings and violating the naturalizing effects by which it is seemingly rendered transparent. The transreal poetics of N. H. Pritchard are a critical interdiction suspended between the very letters in which we inscribe subjectivity.

We also see in Thomas's use of the term "transrealism" to describe the "tampered English" of this African-American form of matching transgressive syntactic and poetic structures to transgressive social positions the continuation of an African-American critical tradition. From Baraka's "changing same" and Russell Atkins's "psychovisualism," through Thomas's tampering "transrealism" and Stephen Henderson's critical deployment of the folk terminology of "worrying the line," to Ed Roberson's "calligraphy of black chant" and Nathaniel Mackey's "discrepant engagement," black poets and critics alike have systematically set about the tasks of theorizing black poetics and developing nomenclature appropriate to the needs of their subject and of their social critique. Black Americans have always engaged and produced philosophy and theory and have always constructed vocabularies of poetic theory. Frequently, as in the case of Henderson, those vocabularies have been drawn directly from black vernacular traditions. Even when the vocabulary itself was new coinage, the phenomena it was designed to describe were often viewed, as in Thomas's commentary on Pritchard, as being rooted in linguistic practices of black Americans traceable to African cultural origins. These theories and vocabularies, however, like the poetry they described, have generally been segregated from predominantly white American national literary genealogies. It has only been in recent years that a significant number of white critics, few of whom give any indication of having ever read Thomas, Pritchard, Elouise Loftin, or even more formally traditional writers such as Gloria C. Oden, have seized upon and employed the terminology of black critique. Now, though, we find that we are in the midst of a curious replication of what once was known as the "one-at-a-time" phenomenon. Whereas the white reading public once seemed incapable of expanding its interests beyond a Richard Wright or a Ralph Ellison or a James Baldwin, some white critics now too often seem prepared to expand their critical vocabularies of black literature no farther than what has been offered by a bell hooks or a Henry Louis Gates. In the same way that Jacques Derrida did not foresee the manifold ways in which his tactical use of the term "deconstruction" would enter the language as the name for an array of sometimes only vaguely related procedures, Gates surely could not have desired, when he published *The Signifying Monkey,* that his adaptation of the vernacular term "signifying" in the critical analysis of black expressive forms would become the end point rather than the beginning stage of some people's readings in black critical traditions. It is now common for white critics whose citations reference no African-American criticism prior to the 1980s, whose readings do not encompass the prior works of W. S. Scarborough, Arthur P. Davis, Saunders Redding, Darwin Turner, Sterling Brown, Eugenia Collier, Stephen Henderson or even Alain Locke (let alone a Percy Johnston or a Larry Neal), to make "signifying" the all-inclusive term of black literary forms in their analyses. (Just as "deconstruction" now appears comically in our daily newspapers as a term for anything at all odd or hip, so "signifying" has begun to appear in the strangest of usages, detached from its vernacular grammars. T. J. Anderson III, in a recent review of Art Lange and Nathaniel Mackey's anthology *Moment's Notice,* makes a point of

remarking that in Baraka's poems we can see the author "signifying the text," as though signifying were some process akin to
preshrinking [79].)

Not only might renewed readings of the avant-garde poetics of
Pitcher, Pritchard, Carrington, and others serve to resituate our
comprehendings of African-American traditions in poetry; they
might also lead to a renewed reading of earlier stages of black
critique. Recent debates about the suitability of structuralist and
poststructuralist theories to the reading of African-American literature might take a significantly different cast if they were recontextualized against the background of Lucas's description of
"decomposition" in the poetry of Pritchard and Atkins's use of
the term "deconstruction" in the setting out of his theories of
psychovisual critique as early as 1956. The bruising debate between Gates, Joyce A. Joyce, and Houston A. Baker featured in
the pages of *New Literary History* in 1987 provides a notorious
example. In the concluding sections of Professor Joyce's second
statement in the discussion, she claimed that "Among the most
modern of the novels written by Black writers . . . only Reed's
relatively early *Mumbo Jumbo* shares a striking 'decentering,' 'playful' affinity with Beckett and Barth. Stated again, poststructuralist
methodology imposes a strategy upon Black literature from the
outside" (382). There is, of course, already a large logical problem here that Joyce chooses not to address. If even one novel by
Reed shares the qualities that Joyce claimed typify works that
lend themselves to poststructuralist methods, then such methods
are not an imposition brought wholly from the outside. Indeed,
Mumbo Jumbo, a book that often asserts African origins for the
most "modern" Euro-American forms, is a strikingly peculiar
book for her to mention here. More importantly though, Joyce's
complaint is yet another example of a critic grossly narrowing
the universe of black writing in the interest of undergirding a
questionable critical hypothesis. Professor Joyce found "only
Reed" (as Allen earlier could find only Baraka) among such
formally adventurous, and sometimes even playful, fiction writers
as Baraka himself (how could she omit *The System of Dante's Hell,*
a novel with clear influences upon Reed?), Leon Forrest, John
Edgar Wideman, William Melvin Kelly, Charlene Carter, Charles
Johnson, and Clarence Major. Further, Joyce's narrowed perspective would have left her hard pressed to explain the appearance,

just shortly after her essay was published, of such astonishing novelists as Xam Wilson Cartiér. This narrowing becomes yet stranger in light of an earlier comment by Joyce. In the first section of her portion of the discussion, entitled "The Black Canon: Reconstructing Black American Literary Criticism," she produced an essential textual resistance of black verse to post-structuralist methodology as a reason that critics using these methods have not yet written significantly about black poetry. "It is no accident," she asserted, "that the Black poststructuralist methodology has so far been applied to fiction, the trickster tale, and the slave narrative. Black poetry – particularly that written during and after the 1960s – defies both linguistically and ideo-logically the 'poststructuralist sensibility' " (342). We know that she had read Baraka, since she cited him elsewhere in her discus-sion, but she appeared completely oblivious to the very existence of Reed's colleagues in the Umbra group, Pitcher, Pritchard, and Addison, and her comments would certainly have encountered resistances of their own if applied to the work of better-known poets of the period, such as Major and Wright. Once again, readers guided by such intemperate essentializing would have had difficulty making sense of these claims in light of the subse-quent work of poets like Harryette Mullen and Erica Hunt. What is needed, in my view, is a restorative process of readings, not to "prove" the ultimate applicability of postmodernity or poststruct-uralism as an apparatus for "processing" black texts but to gain a more complete comprehension of just what it is that black writers have been doing. It is probably not the case that poststructuralist methodologies have not been applied to these poets because the poetry itself somehow repels them. It is far more likely that the critics Joyce has in mind have not, as she appears not to have, read enough of the poetry.

Plainly, Pritchard's "ventilations" of his texts, leaving a lettrist visual text on the page in which readers may probe, playfully or otherwise, among the possibilities, is of a piece with Addison's interdictive punctuation, operating both to slow our reading rush toward the premature assignment of final meaning and to thicken the material resistance of the words as chirography. Sometimes the content of such ventilated texts may seem banal (as many of the poems of e. e. cummings may seem trite once we have reassembled the scattered print), but Pritchard causes us to attend more closely to the nontrivial processes of meaning making in the act of reading. *EECCHHOOEESS,* for example, places the following line on a page of its own:

l   i   keso   mestro   rmwi   thou
         taname   e

(59)

In the same way that, when reading "junt," our eyes may seize upon the one "real" prefix, "anis," so most readers will probably jump to the formal address of "thou," automatically seeking recognizable text codes, before we realize that we have scanned a line that spells out the slightly sentimental, though misspelled, simile, "like some strorm without a name." Is "strorm" the name for a nameless storm? Is this what the thunder said? It remains impossible, when reading a book that contains poems like "junt," to judge when we have stumbled upon a misprint and when we are "meant" to read in the blown-apart "strorm."

Less problematically, a familiar instance of formally "making strange" is a page like the one that occurs earlier in Pritchard's "VIA," which is occupied by the single, centered word "ksud" (41). This is simply mirror writing, and we quickly discern the "dusk" that is the real-word referent of the real-world referent of the poem. This is a signifying upon the text and upon the script; writing backward is also a traditional form of spirit writing (and, we could add, among the earliest cyphers practiced by children). Additionally, and perhaps most importantly, it is another case of the umbral logic we have seen operating in the works of Addison and Pitcher. Though it is "not your father's" *Dusk of Dawn,* Pritchard's "ksud" signals a continuation, albeit as mirror image, of black modernity's tracing of the racial determiners of linguistic meaning. Pritchard's poetry of invented terms and word deformation is a precursor to the work of poets such as P. Inman and David Melnick (most apparent in Melnick's book *Pcoet*), but despite the fact that Pritchard's books achieved much wider circulation than the books of those writers, because he was published by commercial and university presses, he is not so much as mentioned by Paul Hoover in his Norton *Anthology of Postmodern American Poetry.*

More opaque by far than a poem like "junt" is Pritchard's poem entitled ".–.–.–.". This poem passes beyond Addison's use of punctuation to interdict the coming together at the word level of morphemic and orthographic elements in order to construct a visual text entirely from punctuation. This concrete poem is, like so many others, iconic, as if to counter possible charges that such works exist in a nonreferential obliviousness to the social. Nelson Goodman has said, and the judgment is equally applicable to concrete works whose materials include neither alphabetic characters nor punctuation, that "this emphasis upon the nontransparency of a work of art, upon the primacy of the work over what it refers to, far from involving denial or disregard of symbolic functions, derives from certain characteristics of a work as a symbol" (69). As a poem, ".–.–.–." causes us (those of us willing to read it at all) to reflect upon the arbitrariness of even the iconic. The shape on the page of the poem, figured in symbols that call to mind Morse code, alternates the punctuation used to indicate a full stop with the punctuation used to hold together lexical items across a hiatus. (A dash causes a pause in our reading, whereas a hyphen makes the hiatus disappear in pronunciation, just as parentheses cause a pause but a hyphen does not.) There is no linguistic reason that any given combination of dots and dashes signifies a particular letter of the alphabet in Morse code; hence the code is the mode of sign seen to be wholly conventional. But the fact that most people will see the shape spelled out by Pritchard's periods and dashes as the representation of a human figure is also dependent upon a conventional procedure of interpretation. The shape is sufficiently abstract that it could represent a number of things, or no thing at all. (The "head," for example, has no indicated connector to the "body.") Yet the figure looks enough like other icons of the human body we are accustomed to reading, like the generic figure representing "man" on a restroom door, or the humanoid figures on a pedestrian crossing sign, that it would be difficult not to see the shape of the human being coded here. Pritchard questions mimesis by giving us an icon, which I suppose makes him a sort of iconoclast. Kevin Young argues that "Pritchard questions the mimetic assumptions of both historical material poetry, such as George Herbert's 'Altar,' and the Black Arts movement, ironically by relying on each movement's oxymoronic insistence on physicality and (Black) reality, respectively" (40). The insistence in the case of the Black Arts movement was oxymoronic, sometimes deliberately so, because it was expressed metaphorically, and thus the questions raised by Pritchard about the movement's mimetic assumptions had already been raised in such movement poems as Baraka's "Black Art," though it was some time before the leading theoreticians of the Black Aesthetic began to account for this root contradiction. Baraka's poem calling for a return to the bedrock of black material reality, his poem calling for poems with material effects in the real world of the social, relies at its outset upon a metaphor: "Poems are bullshit, unless they are / teeth or trees or lemons piled / on a step" (116). This either means that all poems *are* bullshit, a possibility many would be willing to admit, or it requires a certain amount of hermeneutic work on the part of its readers. Such work may in fact lead to and accompany political action, and Pritchard did not write in objection to such action. What the ironic materiality of Pritchard's poems does call for, as Young indicates, is an openness to theorizing about the usually unacknowledged reliance upon these mimetic fictions, a willingness to consider possible consequences of this assumption that language can present an immediate, unmediated experience of black, nonverbal, realities. Pritchard's poems, then, do at least decompose a too quickly accomplished move to claims for the transparency of art. The same is true of such chanted sound texts among Pritchard's works as "Gyre's Galax," which subjects the phrases "Sound variegated through beneath lit," "twinly ample of amongst," "In lit black viewly," and "In dark to stark" to a series of swirling permutations powerfully reminiscent of such early electronic music texts as Steve Reich's "Come Out," which, it must be remembered, was composed for a benefit performance to aid the defense committee of several black youths arrested during the Harlem riots of 1964. (The voice heard speaking in that work is that of one of the defendants, Daniel Hamm.) "Gyre's Galax" is an example of the performative poetics that Baraka was increasingly to adopt during this period, and the poem's version of "worrying the line," Stephen Henderson's verbal analogue for such voicelike instrumental techniques as the blues guitarist's bent notes, bears the same sort of formal relationship to the blues repetitions of Hughes's lyrics that the overblowing chordal squalls of Pharoah Sanders's tenor saxophone bear to the earlier techniques of Coleman Hawkins.

There is also about Pritchard's works a bluesman's ironic regard for the commodity aesthetics that ensnare him. A poem entitled "WE NEED PEOPLE" opens with the language of advertising, that impersonal form of mass address which strains to sound as if it speaks to you alone. It is the language of the circular found in your mailbox: "WE NEED – please read this and see if you qualify, if you do not care to take advantage of this please pass it on to a friend" (*EECCHHOOEESS* 29). Just how, a reader must then ask, do we take the measure of our qualifications for this ever repeating, once-in-a-lifetime offer? The poem has asked to be passed on, though. Anyone who does not care to take advantage of the poem should pass it on to a friend:

> beside twisted ready before
> without those mostly or an under
> plundered nearly through feasted
> delighted so as to be carried
>
> (29)

The influence of Stein is obvious; she might have appreciated Pritchard's preposition sandwiches in the first two lines of the quatrain. More distinctly Pritchard's own stamp, a trait that carries through the satiric jab at commercial appropriations of public language that begins with the poem's opening announcement, is the use of enjambment to redouble the meanings clustered around the phrase "under / plundered."

Pritchard always had his eye on the altering artifacts of our culture in this way. Much as Baraka recalls, with a great deal of nostalgia, the advent of the paperback book in his *Autobiography* (and he seems, as a young artist in the Village, to have equipped himself with an appropriately hip paperback for his forays among his friends in much the same fashion as he had earlier carried a trumpet player's "gig bag" when he went out among his school friends), and as Pitcher closes one part of his prose poem to "Washington Square" with the description of a house "so small it holds nothing but pocket editions," Pritchard begins "From Where the Blues,"

> Stacks of paperbacks
> against whiteless walls
> foliate the landscape
> of the incubal inclosure.
>
> (51)

The sound quality of the phrase "stacks of paperbacks" is the same mode of construction at work in the line "beside twisted

ready before" in "WE NEED PEOPLE," but the semantic functioning of the two lines is quite different. "Stacks of paperbacks,"
in addition to its delights as organized sound, offers readers a
straightforward description of a typically intellectual bohemian
abode, to which "foliate the landscape" is a metaphorical addition of the type normally found in popular lyric verse. In *Beyond
Superstructuralism,* Harland wants readers to know, "The fact is
that sentences make *points,* not pictures" (41). Pritchard's poems
require a somewhat broader move beyond mimesis than even
Harland's. Harland might argue that "From Where the Blues"
does not make for a portrait of the artist as a young fan of
Billie Holliday; rather, it says something about that young fan's
experience of Holliday and her music. Pritchard's stance is not a
complete rejection of aboutness. Referentiality happens, even to
the most nonrepresentational of art forms. What Pritchard may
hope to chart is the signifying glossolalia of black language as
intervention in the world, not just as a recording and recoding
of the oral.

In "Metempsychosis," Pritchard uses short lines and enjambment to highlight already heavy internal rhyming and to cause a
reader to pause more frequently between words than might be
common with most lyrics. The poem looks forward to Bob Mar-
ley's song "Chant down Babylon," and it takes as its beginning
point the very "there" that Gertrude Stein could not find in
Oakland:

>once two trees
>stood
>in a where
>there echoing
>a prayer chant
>chanted hammer
>in words
>from an unknown
>tongue
>lifted
>the silence
>moans
>
>   (*Matrix* 58)

Pritchard's "chanted hammer / in words" is the tool he uses to
decompose the master's house; it is the tampered English of his

reforming work. Heidegger held that language is the "house of Being" and that man dwells poetically in the world. Eloise Loftin, no public advocate of the Heideggerian phenomonological approach to literary criticism, wrote in her "Pome: for Jamima," that "poetry is the only house / worth living in" (35). Gerald Jackson, another Umbra poet, offered a tragicomic reflection on that theme in an untitled poem that puns upon both the old adages about throwing stones and upon newer terminologies referring to drug and alcohol highs: "My house – my rock – stoned" (43). (There would also seem to be an intertextual relationship to the parable of the man who built his house upon a rock. Jackson is able to do a great deal with just five words and two dashes.) The image proves finally too domestic for Pritchard's language. According to Lucas, in Pritchard's poetry "Being is debarnacled and set adrift" (12). In the appropriately titled "Magma," Pritchard's writing is a line tracing that drift of Being. Sounding very much like his contemporaries Cecil Taylor and Clark Coolidge, Pritchard forms paratactic streams of molten language, strings in which individual word forms attach themselves to one another in phrases, then drift apart to rejoin in alternate construals:

> hollow or filimentary or silled
> in which of these can hold a grasses rock
> stock and fallow stretching broad
> the chord stung she could run
> scotch hipped to her never left alone
> wants herselves for the ever was come
> to these sprawling among the dialed
> pent up upon where no one
> will have ever noticed
> these daisys pending the sun for it's fall
>
> (12)

In contrast to Addison's overpunctuated, start-and-stop form of parataxis, this poem is almost totally lacking in punctuation. In the further absence of capital letters, one can begin and end sentences or phrases nearly at will. This is not to say that any interpretation may be supported by the text, despite the fact that the number of potential interpretations is probably infinite. To posit that the set of possible meanings is an open set is not to say that the set can contain anything. The words Pritchard has placed on the page impose some constraints upon hermeneutic action. But the indeterminacy of phrase construction parallels and propels the indeterminacy of meaning in the poem. It is often not possible to determine finally if certain lines are en-jambed or end-stopped. In those instances the lines must be read both ways. The briefest accounting of a few of the meaning effects available to us in this text gives a good sense of Pritchard's direction in the 1960s. (The poem appeared in the June 1967 issue of *Liberator.*) When we pause at the end of the second line, we may imagine a rock lodged in grass, or the proverbial grass that grows on rock (unless the rock is rolling), but when we go on to the next line and complete a phrase that reads "rock / stock and fallow" it is impossible not to hear in the intertextual distances the vernacular phrase "lock, stock, and barrel." This technique is one we also see in Jackson's "My house – my rock – stoned." But many of the shifting meaning constructions in "Magma" result from those indeterminacies that are produced by differences between orality and scripture. If we simply listened to the poem, we would be unable to distinguish by means of con-text between "the cord stung," a phrase that would seem amply motivated by the phrase that follows ("she could run"), and what is actually printed in the poem, "the chord stung." Note too that Pritchard has used a musical referent, a chord, to manifest a silent difference, the difference between the morphemes repre-sented by "cord" and "chord." Such written supplementarity of significance is what Henry Dumas called for in *Play Ebony Play Ivory* when he asked for an art that would "make chords that speak" (4). (In fact, Dumas used exactly this example in the poem "Jackhammer," where he wrote: "I see the long historical chord pumping the man / this jackjack in the city groin / pumping the man" [18].) Likewise, listening to the final words of "Magma," we might well not sense the presence of the silent apostrophe, the poem's sole piece of punctuation. Since we have just heard that something is "pending the sun," it would be quite natural to hear the "its" as possessive and to produce a reading in which daisies await the fall of the sun. When we can see the punctuation, we can read the meaning that daisies pend because the season is fall. It is not the case that one reading eliminates the other, like the coming into contact of matter and antimatter. We cannot keep ourselves from hearing the one significance even as our eyes read the other. They both exist in unstable proximity as we go on reading. So much remains pent up upon Pritchard's lines. So much depends upon the very indecisiveness of his syntax. It is always in the space between our readings that Pritchard's lines decompose and multiply. His poems exemplify the spirit of the concluding lines of Redmond's history of Afro-American poetry: "Between the *lines* are the rattle of choruses, the whine (hum) of guitars, and the shriek of tambourines, framed by rivers that will not run away" (422). It is between the lines that we must, at least until he is publicly recomposed, read Norman H. Pritchard.

In his 1978 interview with Charles Rowell, Lorenzo Thomas remembered the prophecy spoken to him by a writer friend when Thomas decided to make Houston his home: "Well, you know, if you stay down here you're not going to be a Southern poet; you're going to be a forgotten poet" (Rowell, "Between" 31). Though he has been more recently published than Pritchard and certainly more widely published than Pitcher and Addison, Thomas is another important poet missing from too many major anthologies and from nearly all critical histories. In Thomas's case this situation is doubly ironic, for his own essays as a critic and scholar have been invaluable to historians studying developments in American poetry in the latter half of the twentieth century. Those few historians who have directed their attention to the Society of Umbra and its influence upon the Black Arts movement have invariably found themselves going to Thomas's published accounts for a firsthand witness.

But if we can get a witness, we cannot always get a hearing. Thomas, too, has been missed by even the sharp eyes of editors such as Michael Harper and Anthony Walton, in their anthology *Every Shut Eye Ain't Asleep,* and by Paul Lauter in the *Heath Anthology of American Literature.* Paul Hoover, on the other hand, does include a selection from Thomas in the *Norton Anthology of Postmodern American Poetry,* and Douglas Messerli's *From the Other Side of the Century* reprints more Thomas poems. Characteristically, however, for the period 1976–93, we are most likely to encounter Thomas's works in an anthology of alternative poetries like Michael Lally's now dated *None of the Above.* Though a useful essay on Thomas's career to date, written by his Umbra associate Tom Dent, appears in the *Dictionary of Literary Biography*'s volume on post-1955 African-American poets, Thomas infrequently appears in discussions of contemporary black poetics. He was included in

Lally's anthology and was often published by such avant-garde
publishers as Telephone Press, Kulchur Press, Blue Wind Press,
and by Angel Hair Books, but the name of Lorenzo Thomas
nearly never appears in critical studies of American postmodernism. Thomas was one of the most prodigious of the young talents
gathered under the Umbra umbrella, and his work has been
read attentively and enthusiastically by such champions of the
avant-garde as Charles Bernstein, but most of his past work has
been allowed to pass out of print, and the last major gathering
of his poems, *The Bathers,* was published in 1981, under Ishmael
Reed's imprint. Thomas has continued to write and publish, and
his activities as a critic, editor, teacher, and arts activist have had
a profound influence on younger writers, including Harryette
Mullen.

It was as a remarkably young arts activist that Thomas entered
the Society of Umbra. He was still a teenager, a student at
Queens College, when he began attending Umbra meetings
(Dent, "Thomas" 41). Even as a high school student he had
cultivated a sense of himself as a "Greenwich Village poet," and
he had joined together with several high school friends to start a
magazine, *Ripple* (Rowell 28). Thomas was also accruing early
experience as a public speaker that would later stand him in
good stead when he joined in Umbra's legendary public readings. A member of the National Conference of Christians and
Jews, the teen-aged Thomas "went around to schools, synagogues
and churches giving . . . little speeches about brotherhood and
equality" (Rowell 28). Like so many other African-American cultural activists, Thomas had a Caribbean background. His mother's parents were Jamaicans, she was born in Costa Rica, and his
father was from Saint Vincent. Thomas himself was born in Pan-
ama and first came to New York when his parents immigrated to
the United States in 1948 (Dent, "Thomas" 316). His first language was Spanish, and his entry into English proved as memorable as his geographical relocation; he had the sense already at
the Havana airport, as he recalled those days for Rowell, that he
was entering "into an entirely different world from that [he] had
been living in [for] the first five years" (19). Perhaps because of
his youth, Thomas forgot Spanish as he learned English, but this
act of resituating himself upon the territory of another tongue
forever after oriented him in a highly politicized and counterhe-
gemonic attitude toward the language in which he would later

write poetry. Feeling the need to "repress" Spanish in order to fit into the English-speaking society of the other children in his new homeland, Thomas also embarked upon a massive and continuing project of reterritorializing English. "I was redefining the language I was forced into," he explained to Rowell (19). As he grew to comprehend the many ways in which American English is racially marked, his desire to wield English more effectively than the native speakers around him redoubled. "There was also, of course, the whole business of being Black and coming from a whole family of race conscious people, and the idea that if you are Black you had to be more qualified than necessary" (20). As he began to write, his desire to enter into English, and not just to qualify as a native speaker but to exceed the qualifications of the writing and speaking subjects surrounding him, led to his positioning himself as someone writing simultaneously inside and outside traditions of English in order to rewrite and reposition those traditions.

Throughout his published works, Thomas can be seen subjecting the literary heritage of English poetics to a transfiguring interrogation. In his memoir of the Umbra period and its aftermath, he describes the modes of reappropriation of traditions practiced by the Black Arts movement: "Under Baraka's direction, somehow informed by Ezra Pound's aesthetics, the Harlem organization was determined to MAKE IT NEW" ("Shadow" 68). Pound's aesthetics itself was one of the things to be remade anew. Thomas's 1970 serial poem "Fit Music" models his own positioning with regard to Pound and to traditions that both Pound and Thomas were to make use of:

> Yet Confucius went on plucking the *k'in* and
> Singing the Odes.
>
> Ezra Pound, certified madman
> Is melancholy. In his book
> On the shelf. Overdue. What
> A mean life.
>
> (*Bathers* 75)

The Confucian Odes, like other things, are changed when they are played upon the blues guitar, and Pound, whose comments about black writers (such as William Stanley Braithwaite) were almost invariably brutally biased, probably could not have foreseen the manner of "making new" that the poetics of imagism and vorticism would lead to in the hands of Baraka and Thomas. Thomas's borrowings from Pound draw an overdue notice, perhaps an usurious fine. Such meanness matches the meanness of Pound's own suburban prejudices (as well as the mean circumstance of his life in Saint Elizabeth's), and by registering them together with Pound's madness Thomas signals his intention to take what fits his own music from Pound while leaving the dross behind. The notes that Thomas provides to his poem give a fit answer to the exclusivity of the company contemplated in T. S. Eliot's "Tradition and the Individual Talent." Thomas's quotation from Pound's translations of Confucius ("Without character you will / be unable to play on that instrument" [70]) suggests that the lack of moral character historically evidenced by many of America's literary greats may have unfitted them for their instruments. Eliot, who, Pound predicted, would not approve his inclusion of "blackmen in a bukk about kulchur" (*Letters* 288), would not have been receptive to Thomas's insistence that among those poets we must acknowledge "for their timeliness and aptness of thought" (66) are Brian Wilson (composer of "Little Honda") and James Brown ("Godfather" and "Soul Brother Number One"). What Thomas makes of the tradition offered by the more traditionally acceptable politics of Robert Frost, who, despite his very occasional befriending of individual African Americans such as Melvin Tolson, was every bit as bigotted as Pound, is exactly the kind of deterritorializing ethnic irony practiced by Tolson.

Thomas's "Inauguration" opens sounding just like Frost at the Kennedy inauguration. On that brilliantly sunny, cold, and windy January day in 1961, Frost had difficulty reading from his typed text and appended a recitation of "The Gift Outright," a poem whose celebration of manifest destiny, whatever its other merits, is, at the least, problematic. To those whose ancestors had been the objects of America's many wars of territorial expansion, Frost's lines must be considerably less celebratory than that day's audience appeared to find them: "Such as we were, we gave ourselves outright / (The deed of gift was many deeds of war) / To the land vaguely realizing westward" (348). Thomas places his reader in turn upon that same historic promontory occupied by Frost's poem: "The land was there before us" (*Chances* 15). This opening seems as unproblematic as could be imagined. The readily available pun instructs readers in the land's priority (as if this were to be an environmentalist's lyric) as it describes the land laid out before us. It is as we read through the heavy enjambment that becomes evident upon our arrival at the second line that the first of Thomas's multiple ironies comes into view: "The land was there before us / Was the land." The recombinant grammar of English would allow us to hear the poem as stammering repetition: The land was there before us . . . before us was the land. But in the absence of mediating punctuation we must read and hear a literal dialectic at work in which one dialect contests another in an intertextual play for power. One ironizing gesture of the poem is to transcribe, in the traditionally represented dialect of one black English, Frost's famous poem. Listening to Frost's inaugural recitation, marking an occasion of great ambiguity for black spectators in particular, whose hopes had to have been leavened with a certain skepticism, a writer such as lyricist Oscar Brown, Jr., might well have wanted to ask the white poet, "What you mean 'we,' white man?" Thomas's response is to take both the first-person plural of Frost's poem and the dialect grammar sometimes associated with blackness into his hands in a massively revisionist act. Frost's "The Gift Outright" is problematic in part because the seemingly inclusive "we" of the poem registers a series of exclusions, beginning with the poem's assumption that "we" are all figurative, if not literal, descendants of the English. These exclusions were recorded in the Constitution's counting of slaves as three-fifths of a person and its repetition of the phrase "except Indians," and by such later inscriptions as the Chinese Exclusion Act and the *Plessy v. Ferguson* decision. At one level Thomas's poem intrudes upon the excluding circles drawn by whites who say "we" in poems like "The Gift Outright." As white celebrants circle the wagons of their self-sustaining identifications, Thomas's first-person plural abruptly crashes the party, leaping into the circle to remind readers that "us was" here before the Mayflower landed Protestant Pilgrims at Plymouth Rock. Such an interdiction of "white" pronouncements interrogates, too, the racial markings of "our" language. English was not the native tongue of most Africans taken into slavery. It became the native tongue of American-born blacks. Africans acquired English under the enforced tutelage of white masters. As Europeans, in the process of becoming white people, and Africans, in the process of becoming black people, spoke to one another, they were dialectically implicated in one another's mastery of what was becoming American English.

Thomas's "Inauguration" makes it impossible for American poetry to conduct itself as wholly white mythology. In the colored colloquy of American discourse, white and black are never alone, never nations with separated language traditions, no matter how much anyone might wish it were so. People came, or were brought to North America, and, according to Thomas, "Then things / Began happening fast" (15).

Thomas's inaugural disruption is no simple reversal of signifying power, however. If the land has come to belong to and be the black American as well as the white, then all will have to own the legacy of our acts and histories. Further into the poem it becomes clear that "us" functions as an acronym for the United States, advancing Frost's and Thomas's first persons together. Thomas parodies Frost's insistence that "The deed of gift was many deeds of war." The bitter irony of Thomas's lines is reminiscent of Bob Dylan's 1960s anthem "With God on Our Side," but the first-person plural of Thomas's poem has plural significations: "God must be one of us. Because / Us has saved the world. Us gave it / A particular set of regulations" (15). In "Heavenly Bodies" Thomas presses these inaugural ironies back to the time of the Great Emancipator himself, Abraham Lincoln, whose actions and attitudes toward African Americans, slave and free, were as ambiguous as John F. Kennedy's were later to prove. Signifying upon one of Lincoln's most famed aphorisms, reappropriating and remaking it, Thomas again lays claim to the body of the nation as both curse and bitter blessing: "God sure loved the negro / To give him America" (*Bathers* 92).

This kind of contestatory, intertextual interrogation of English literary traditions is the closing note of Thomas's most recently published selection of his works, *The Bathers* (1981). Ending that volume is a piece entitled "Another Poem in English," which takes as its point of departure what is perhaps John Donne's best-known line of verse. From that antisolipsistic vantage point, Thomas moves into a percussive deformation of stanzaic form, mapping an archipelago of nouns and verbs upon the surface of his page:

John Donne would think of an island
After all this noon is written
All afternoon I think of several
Words

	change	ribbet	foment	format
Plan	plane	solder	alchemy	Army

(158)

This passage echoes the earlier passage in *Drive suite* when Carrington and/or Bremser wrote in rapid fire a drumming sequence of "big" words, though it is doubtful that Thomas had seen that earlier poem before the composition of "Another Poem in English" in the early 1970s. Thomas's constellation of word forms uses shorter words than *Drive suite*, but to much the same end. The sounds of the words alone are sufficient to draw them together into metonymic figures, and readers will naturally begin a process of drawing semantic as well as phonic relationships among them. "Plan" and "plane" are on the same page of most dictionaries (and occupy the same plane of the poem), and both may serve as locus for an army's movements. "Ribbet" is the sound a frog makes in American English, which will bring us back to the *f*'s from frogs back to "foment." Alchemy, like armies, foments change. Alchemy, like rivets, which rhymes with "ribbet," solders things together. Solder holds parts of a plane together, and planes transport soldiers, and so on ad inifinitum. Each reader will enter this array from a different point and will configure its semantic materials differently, but the sheer impossibility of just leaving the words alone, of *only* allowing oneself to hear them as sounds, is a final demonstration of the truth that no man is an island. As Thomas sits thinking of words, when noon is written, he is inextricably imbricated in the fabric of the social intertext. Although some of his poems carry no overt references to race, there is always an additional racial reading asserting itself, since he is, after all, like "any other sad man here / american" (Baraka, *Dead* 47). Despite America's continued omission of black Americans from public declarations of what America is, America would not be America without African Americans. America has wanted to have black people here, working, rather than in Africa, self-employed. America has wanted black people to communicate with the rest of the population in English, all the while insisting that black Americans were constitutionally lacking in the requisite skills of mastery. In other words, as Thomas writes in "Other Worlds," America has said to the black people in its melting pot,

We would rather have you here than absent
Though you fall vomiting into the soup.
We would rather have you here, in English
Than train you in less grand acts of decline

(*Bathers* 56)

Thomas closes this 1968 poem with a simple instruction: "This is very important, read it over again."

If we are to reread it, it must have already been written. Thomas, along with so many other poets who came after the modernist revolt, has viewed the printing of the poem as a performance piece. It is simply not the case, in his view, that the poem exists only as spoken performance (the print being reduced to a set of instructions for the performance), nor that there is a strict separation between the written poem and an oral realization. Like so many of his colleagues in the Umbra group and elsewhere, Thomas turned to jazz for an analogy to explain his conception of the poem as practice. His explanation to Rowell was that he thought "of poetry as performance, and one studies one's craft for the purpose of being able to perform well. The individual poem is not that important – and that's the interesting thing about poetry, too. It's like music in that the practice and the artifact are the same thing" (24). During the period of the Black Aesthetic movement, frequent complaints were lodged against what was seen as a European tradition of isolating the work of art as artifact from its social circumstance. Interestingly, this charge, which certainly seems apt as a complaint against some of the more extreme New Critical versions of what it means to read the poem "itself," arrived on the heels of the reemphasis upon process, performance, and seriality that the New American Poetry derived from William Carlos Williams and others as a way of contesting that same artifactual regard for the poetic text. Poets like Baraka and the Umbra group are the connectors here by which a postmodern rebellion against the idea of the poem as icon was joined to an ideology of the social functioning of the poet posited as African-derived tradition and brought into the Black Arts movement.

Thomas, like Baraka, Spellman, Johnston, and Neal, was able to identify ample black precedents for this conjoining of ideologies. He pointed to the Afro-Caribbean poet and political leader Aimé Césaire as one of his stronger early influences (Dent,

"Thomas" 318), and Césaire's surrealism was as powerful a model for the poets of the Black Arts movement as was the ideology of Negritude that he theorized along with Léopold Senghor. But like Johnston, Baraka, and Kaufman, Thomas also found a fertile "folk" precedent for the politicized ironies in his version of the surreal. Chicago's *Living Blues* magazine recognized the power of this connection, one seldom articulated by students of American verse, by publishing a special supplementary issue in 1976 dedicated to surrealism and the blues. In his interview with Dent, Thomas cited as his influences, along with Césaire, such lyricists and performers as Robert Johnson, Lightnin' Hopkins, Clifton Chenier, and Juke Boy Bonner (Dent, "Thomas" 324). The blues are clearly constituted within an oral tradition, but even prior to their recording they have participated in the reiterative logics of the graphic mark. Baraka's concept of the "changing same" is the marking of an ideology of reiteration within subtly altering forms with a signal difference. The call and response of the blues-based form reiterates that logic and signals that difference. The written does not oppose the sung. "The practice and the artifact are the same thing."

Thomas by no means ignored the false hierarchies by which oral expression, particularly by African Americans, has often been demeaned in American literary discourse, but neither did he reify those hierarchies by merely repeating them in inverted form. He never denied the strange liminality of the advent of writing, but he does exhibit the bluesman's commonsense approach to such things. In "Embarkation for Cythera" he wrote,

> The idea of a written language
> > when before,
> the words in our
> > mouths were enough.
> > Not that it takes anything away
> from the people we are,
> > > "Education"
> You don't write "corn" if you
> > mean okra.
>
> > > > (*Bathers* 23)

Well before English-language readers had ready access to Derrida's critique of the supplemental logic of grammatology (the poem is dated 1964), Thomas demonstrated his understanding of how that which had seemed self-sufficient in language comes to appear grounded necessarily in that "extra," the supplemental markings of writing. Thomas's humor here, like Leroy McLucas's in his poem "Negotiation," poses an invigorating counter to any who might argue that an inherent elitism adheres to the "educated" or to the written.

Additionally, Thomas followed Baraka in his insistence upon reasserting an ancient African tradition of inscription and spirit writing. Although Thomas's assessment of the Black Arts movement's conceptions of "right sound" and of the functionalism of black poetry was that they produced a fair number of "misshapen" and "bad takes" (Rowell 25), he still saw those attempts as following in a lineage traceable to early Egyptian civilization. "As I read Gerald Massey in *The Book of the Beginnings* and *Egypt the Light of the World*," he told Rowell in the course of their interview, "I discover that in ancient Egypt there was a scribal concept" (24). That scribal concept, which parallels both later sub-Saharan African scribal practices and African-American spirit writing, was a writing of the mysteries, a writing of signs that, when pronounced, would bring God into evidence. That scribal concept acknowledges writing as both marker of absence and means of bringing the ineffable into our thoughts. In the title poem of *The Bathers,* Thomas transcribed Egyptian glyphs within the context of present political struggle, writing the present as predicated upon the past of writing. In the act of bringing an ancient African text to bear upon the contemporary and local texts of American racial politics, Thomas reenacted Martin Delany's audacious acts of signifying in his book *The Origin of Races and Color,* when that nineteenth-century writer copied the texts of ancient Africa into his text as a means of contesting the textual power of racist Americans. Delany's text might almost be taken as a sort of Rosetta Stone permitting us to read the unpronounceable hieroglyphs of Thomas's poem within a polyglot context of black writings.

In "The Bathers," the figures formed by the shapes of Civil Rights protesters within the high-pressure stream of water aimed to drive them from the stage of history become living glyphs, transformative signs. This 1970 poem in tribute to the transfiguring moment in American history that occurred during the Civil Rights campaigns in Birmingham, Alabama, is, like the campaign itself, an interactive and multimedia text, a hypertext in a literal sense. It is a scribal glossolalia and a writing that remarks the inability of its own English to encompass the language of the glyphs (*Bathers* 59):

Lotus. Mover on the face of the waters . . .

Sleepless Horus, watch me as I lie
Curtained with stars when ye arise
And part the skies. And mount the Royal
Bark

They said the ancient words in shameful English
Their hearts rose up like feathers

Many have pointed to that moment when the images of heroic Civil Rights marchers under attack by police dogs and powerful streams of water from fire hoses appeared on the television screens and newspaper front pages of the entire world as one of the great ruptures in hegemonic discourse in our time. Ruling narratives of triumphalist Western progress quickly found ways to recuperate this moment (and today even archconservatives proclaim themselves to be acting in the tradition of the Civil Rights movement), but for an instant the brute consequences of dominant patterns of racial thought were impressed upon the consciousness of America and the world in a fashion that shocked even some of the upholders of those dominant patterns. Thomas portrayed this as a possibly redemptive rebirth of a nation. It is not that he was under the illusion that white America changed its mind in some substantive way about race and rights when it saw its ugliest reflection in the yet more distorting mirror of television. But Thomas found here a defining historical text when an African spirit was reborn among his lost North American children, when Orisha could be dimly made out "amid the waters with hatchets," and when even klansmen and Southern "law enforcement" officers might be viewed as bringing God into evidence:

Where Allah's useful white men
Came there bearing the water
And made our street Jordan
And we stepped into our new land

(62)

Thomas's is a transumptive revealing of the figures of this history that replicates the transfiguring rereading that took place on that day in Birmingham, a day when the figures of racist power and authority were rewritten and recontextualized as ineffectual and dangerous fools attempting to turn back the stream of historical progress. The humiliating acts of segregationist authority, intended to impress upon the marchers the futility of their rebellion, were instead reread as the dying gasp of a vicious anachronism. That day, according to Thomas, "The figures on the truck inspired no one" (62).

Such proverbial reversals of signifying motion form the poem's opening tropes. In Birmingham, the Fire Department was brought onto the scene to extinguish the fire in the minds of men and women. Instead it spread the flames:

We turned to fire when the water hit
Us. Something
Berserk regained
An outmoded regard for sanity
While in the fire station
No one thought of flame
Fame or fortune did them

We did them a fortune. We did
Them a favor just being
Ourselves inside of them

(59)

Thomas's tracing of the reversed powers of signification also marked a deconstruction of the terms of American racial identifications. The most massively unremarked irony of American race is the fact that whites have depended irremediably upon the existence of blacks as their defining other. The vaunted white culture that segregationists sought to keep pure by keeping it symbolically separate from blackness required that blackness for its very existence. In Thomas's opening stanza, the blacks Birmingham would expel from its central public spaces are the very favor of its defining animus. And in the transformed nation brought about in the baptismal waters of Birmingham, a transformed future becomes visible. In the ethnic ambiguities of the indefinite second person, Thomas described a future born from the being of "ourselves inside of them." "In the nation coming your children will learn all about that" (59). As Thomas copied the ancient glyphs into his poem, placing his work in the scribal traditions of ancient Africa, so he now drew African and Judeo-Christian prophetic traditions together in a defining jeremiad:

>   . . . ancient hands raised
> This water
>
> As the street preachers
> Have a good understanding hear them
>
>   O israel this O israel that
>
> Down here in this place
> Crying for common privilege
> In a comfortable land
>
> Their anger is drawing the water
>
>   (61)

Here, again, Thomas joined the free verse forms of postimagist American poetics to the legacy of a particular metered modernity. "The Bathers" repeats once more the ironizing tropes of Gospel song. "God's gonna trouble the waters" is the prophecy brought to us on the wings of song, but the appropriate response is not truly fatalistic. The troubled waters are both destroying and saving, hence the powerful symbolism of Baptist adherence to total immersion. Hence also the unexpected (by Sheriff Bull Connor and his associates) response to Birmingham's form of pragmatism. The song does not instruct us to run for higher ground; neither does it contemplate death by water: rather, we are to "wade in the water, children." What might have seemed to the white city fathers a simple and effective means of dispersing the gathering forces of the Civil Rights movement instead put Birmingham on the world map as synonymous with bigotry and inhumanity and as the site where the tide turned. When Birmingham's civil authorities sent the waters crashing against the massed demonstrators, they could not have imagined the symbolic power that they were transferring to the objects of their hatred: "Some threw the water / On their heads. / They was Baptists" (62). "The Bathers" rise from the waters of anonymity as forever after recognizable figures in the stream of historical narrative.

In an earlier poem, "Twelve Gates," Thomas had, like Olson and Baraka before him, and like Césaire in *Return to My Native Land,* laid bare those mechanisms produced in the wake of the Enlightenment whose humanism provided a rationale supporting the institution of property *in* persons. Césaire asks after

> those who invented neither gunpowder nor compass
> those who tamed neither steam nor electricity
> those who explored neither sea nor sky
> but without whom the earth would not be the earth
>
> (74)

Thomas's "Twelve Gates" inquires after the same histories:

> The invention of reason.
> And those who own nothing what of those walking around
> Without land, without cash value, properties. Without
>
> Nothing in their name. Whose destinies
> Are not marked or marked down. What of
> The ones who are meant to rise in the world
> By their names. Whose names are not known.
>
> (*Bathers* 54)

Césaire's surrealism is an explicit counter to the history produced by the Enlightenment dream of historical progress towards a God-given, Eurocentric telos. Césaire's language, the site of colonial instruction and strategic rebellion, is his locus for contesting Western reason. The Adamic moment in which Césaire reclaims the naming powers of New World language, recovers the power of great speech, is followed by a moment in which Césaire's French serves as the marker of his departure from Francophone appropriations of the power to determine that which is or is not evidence of reason:

> Words?
> Ah yes, words!
> Reason, I appoint you wind of the evening.
> Mouth of authority, be the whip's corolla.
> Beauty, I name you petition of stone.

But ah! my hoarse contraband laughter
Ah! my saltpetre treasure!
Because we hate you, you and
your reason, we claim kinship with
dementia praecox.

(*Return* 55)

The mouth of authority in Birmingham opens to emit a stream of violent erasure, a stream meant to obliterate the mass movement of those "walking around / without land," all in the name of civil order and reason (with all deliberate speed). But in Thomas's view the anonymous bathers become signifying figures of history. The baptizing waters transform the young into lions, into "vau the syllable of love" (59), into the animated characters of a narrative linking the ancient writings of Africa to the prophetic languages of the present. As Césaire desired, the bathers say "storm," say "river," say "tornado" and "tree"; that is, the writing in which they exist says these things. Their symbolic speech marks a rupture in American history, one that is remarked by Lorenzo Thomas in a poem that is the record of its occasion.

Following the dissolution of the Society of Umbra as a functioning workshop, some of the members joined Baraka as he moved uptown to Harlem and formed the Black Arts Repertory group; some eventually resettled in other parts of the country (Dent and Pitcher in the South, Thomas in the Southwest, Reed and David Henderson in California); some remained in New York, working independently; and a few drifted out of the literary scene entirely. In the brief years of its activity as a public group, however, Umbra had provided a forum for many of the new directions in poetics that had been evolving among black writers in different parts of the country. The Society of Umbra forms a link between the experiments of the 1950s and early 1960s and the poetry of the Black Arts movement, which attempted to build a black aesthetic around the formal structures developed by black experimental artists adapting modernist techniques to their own ends. In the years immediately following Umbra's last meetings, a number of new black magazines appeared, including the *Journal of Black Poetry*, and older magazines such as *Negro Digest* (rechristened *Black World*) significantly increased the number of their pages devoted to poetry and criticism. Those anthologies that appeared to map the contours of African-American verse during the Black Arts period invariably included a strong representation of Umbra poets. But as clearly as the linkage between the earlier black avant-garde and the poetics of the Black Arts movement was made at the time by writers such as Baraka, Major, Neal, Stephen Henderson, Jordan, and Randall, and as clearly as the links have been made in subsequent critical evaluations by Dent, Thomas, Oren, and others, it is a link that has been infrequently examined in more recent studies of black verse, and that is almost entirely absent from the curricula of American and African-American Studies. From roughly the mid-1970s through the late 1980s there was a general attenuating of critical attention to the fuller spectrum of black poetry, and later publishers evinced little interest in replacing (let alone reprinting) the wealth of eclectic anthologies of black verse that had once, briefly, been at the center of studies of black literary culture. Given the large number of Umbra artists still living and writing, it may be that this group could again serve as a bridge between periods of literary experiment, could again help critics to attain a broader sense of the directions taken by black writing in the years since the end of World War II.

One crucial task awaiting such a comprehensive history is the location and study of additional texts of experimental poetics by black women. A number of interesting individual poems by women appeared in *Dasein* and *Umbra,* as well as in anthologies such as *We Speak as Liberators* and *The New Black Poetry.* Many of these women writers, however, have never had books published or, as in the case of Julia Fields, wrote the majority of their poems in "mainstream" poetic forms (though the content was often considerably more radical). There were, always, promising signs of the impending increase in publications by black women and in critical attention to their works. There were also those who, like Toni Morrison, were early advocates of more adventurous new poets even when they restricted their own published work to prose. Audre Lorde's first chapbook appeared in the same Poets Press series that published Spellman and David Henderson. Another poet, then signing her work as June Meyer, appeared on the scene with startling new works like "All the World Moved":

All the world moved next to me strange
I grew upon my knees

in hats and taffeta trusting
the holy water to run
like grief from a brownstone
cradling.

(Jordan, *Some Changes* 24)

Still, the book in which this poem was eventually collected, the author's last name having changed to Jordan in the interim, did not appear until 1971.

It is likely that the reason so few formally avant-garde poems by black women were in print in the 1950s and early 1960s is the same reason so few poems by women were to be found in the magazines and anthologies published by Beat and Black Mountain groups. The coteries of avant-garde poetry in America were largely operated as male enclaves, even when, as in the case of *Yugen,* one of the coeditors was a woman. Clearly the male avant-garde poets did encourage and assist some women poets (indeed, each "school" seems to have had its requisite token woman). Baraka, for example, published the collection *Four Young Lady Poets,* though the ladies there gathered were all white. (Baraka's later anthology *Confirmation,* coedited with Amina Baraka, gathers together a significantly diverse set of writings by African-American women.) But black women were for the most part offered little incentive to pursue poetic experimentation in America. Even the Society of Umbra, which had women members and published women's verse in its magazine, seemed sometimes to adopt a smothering attitude toward some women artists' imperatives. Women poets often read at Umbra gatherings. Fields read to Umbra members in April of 1965 and reported to Rosey Pool that the Umbra group had greeted her reading enthusiastically (Pool Papers 52). Tom Feelings brought Rashidah Ismaili-Abu-Bakr to her first Umbra meeting and helped her to get her first poem published in the magazine *Liberator,* which had also published Pritchard. Ismaili, whose later book of poems *Missing in Action and Presumed Dead* bears laudatory comments by former Umbra colleague Calvin Hernton, recalls that even in Umbra things were sometimes unequal. Speaking of the Friday night workshop meetings at Dent's apartment, she recalls that "After a few hours of discussion of the latest poems and the contents of so-and-so's novel, the girlfriends would start to arrive. I had to leave early because of my son, and I remember having the feeling of being left out" (586). Things did not improve markedly with the advent of the Black Arts movement, as Ismaili tells it. Despite the prominence of women poets like Sonia Sanchez and Carolyn Rodgers, women often felt they were being restricted to conventionally "feminine" functions: "We were to dress 'African,' assume the persona of 'the Motherland,' and raise little revolutionaries," according to Ismaili (586).

Nonetheless, works of real originality increasingly appeared from women poets, like the writer Jayne Cortez, who moved to New York from California and whose works show a decidedly different approach to jazz-based poetry from that adopted earlier by Baraka and Spellman. Cortez, herself a musician, had long-time personal affiliations with avant-garde communities of musicians and artists dating back to her early years in Los Angeles. After she moved to New York, her work in poetry began to be published with some frequency, and it became rapidly apparent that she had developed a poetics parallel to but generally independent of the work of the Beats and the Black Mountain and New York school poets. Cortez shared with male poets like Johnston, Spellman, and Thomas the powerful connecting of surrealist methodology to a blues sensibility rooted in a reclaimed (or sometimes constructed) African scribal tradition, but she also brought to the mix a woman's realm of reference. In her poem "I Am New York City" the personification of the metropolis is specifically feminine:

> approach me through my widows peak
> through my split ends my
> asthmatic laugh   approach me
> through my wash rag
> half ankle   half elbow
> massage me with your camphor tears
>   salute the patina and concrete
> of my rat tail wig
>
> (*Scarifications* 8)

To remark this black feminine constellation of referents is not to posit an essentialist argument about Cortez's poems. In fact, these lines from "I Am New York City" should be read intertextually, as a contrapuntal rereading of traditions within blues lyrics. The history of African-American lyrics includes both the literal and the figurative use of call and response. In the same way that the blues singer or jazz musician responds to the call of his or her own lines, and in the same way that the audience at a live performance enters into a call-and-response relationship with the artists, joining them together in a community of innovation and meaning making, the recording history of blues and its popular music descendants is marked by the constant appearance of "answer" records, as when "Work with Me Annie" drew the response lyric by Etta James, "Roll with Me, Henry," a song that was retitled "Wallflower" to get past the censorship of the radio programmers. Cortez's lines about "split ends" and "rat tail wigs" are a woman's answer to, among many other things, a lineage of male-authored blues songs about short-haired women and their wigs. (Lightnin' Hopkins's "I don't want no woman if her hair ain't no longer than mine" is one ready example.)

Poets like Cortez and the members of the Umbra group also established a public space into which younger women, many of whom had come of age as artists reading the works of Baraka, Major, and others of that generation, could enter and find some support for experiments of their own. Elouise Loftin, for instance, belonged to an age group whose members, although they could not take for granted a wider public acceptance of the newer poetries, could at least benefit from the models set before them by that generation of African-American poets that first broke with the formal patterns of their modernist predecessors. It was still a matter of the "changing same," a matter of repetition with a signal difference. Poets such as Baraka and Thomas did not leave entirely behind them the example of such artists as Hughes, Brooks, and Tolson, but neither were they satisfied to continue inhabiting the stanzaic forms and political habitats of those then still living earlier poets. Likewise, the members of the generation born after World War II could learn enormously from Baraka's and Spellman's generation, but they were not content merely to mimic the pioneers of the Black Arts. What would reappear as the changing same in the work of poets like Loftin, who was born in July of 1950, was that ever fertile mixture of blues surrealism that joined a writerly concern with material form with a poetics that drew heavily upon the oral heritage. Loftin's poem "scabible," from a book of verse whose title, *Barefoot Necklace,* foregrounds that blues–surrealism continuum, combines the tightly compressed syntactic disruptions of poets like Carrington and Addison with the childhood pop culture frames of reference of early LeRoi Jones:

rows of piggy bank fed coins
headless yo-yos in apple pie
fingers desecrates piano
calves cool out with a spoon
hit-man issued to barb-wire moon

hey diddle diddle
watch your fiddle

(28)

It is difficult to imagine a poem like "scabible" appearing in
Phylon or *Negro Digest* prior to the revolution in poetics registered
in such postwar small-press magazines as *Free Lance, Dasein, Yugen,*
and *Umbra.* Unfortunately, it appears that it is once again difficult
for poems like Loftin's to gain access to a reading public today.
She was, while still a student at New York University, the poetry
editor of *Black Creation* magazine, and her work appeared in such
large-circulation publications as *Essence* and *Présence Africaine.*
She was anthologized at an early age, and her work appeared in
the encyclopedic *Poetry of Black America* when she was only twenty-
three years old. Loftin enjoyed the strong support of some Umbra writers. Reed, for one, wrote a highly favorable review of her
poetry in the *Washington Post.* In excerpts from that review that
were reprinted on the back cover of *Barefoot Necklace,* Reed supplied the highest praise:

> Elouise Loftin writes Abby Lincoln – visceral – screaming
> poems . . . and she can glide tenderly like Sarah Vaughn's
> voice, as in "For a Spirit." And when she gets "street" [it's]
> not the strained condescending "rap" of some rhetorical
> descendants of Ingersoll, but Bed-Stuy "street" . . . She has a
> song and she can sing it.

Even with the well-placed praise song of such a well-published
writer, Loftin's poems have passed into the same critical invisibility that veils most of the work of Reed's Umbra colleagues. Rarely
do any critics setting forth to describe the poetics of black
women cite any text by Loftin, and I have so far been unable to
locate any critical study of postwar American poetry in general
that makes reference to her poems. In the title poem of *Barefoot
Necklace* Loftin writes of

a history and desire of what
in the world you will show as yourself
myself alone is who i am

(15)

Even at a time when American literary criticism has finally made a modicum of space on its agenda for the writings of African-American women, it has still too frequently left poets like Loftin alone. At a time when the politics of identity have often guided critical readings of American verse, the possible range of written subjectivities has too often been narrowed in critical accounts by the elimination from consideration of many poems that might stand in the world and show themselves as alternative histories of (and) desires.

My concern at this early stage of a study of the poets of black experiment has been to demonstrate the existence of discrete communities supporting avant-garde work in African-American poetics in the years following the World War II and to give some indication of the potential significance of these communities to possible histories of African-American verse. There are other communities deserving of further inquiry, such as the grouping of artists around Chicago's Association for the Advancement of Creative Musicians, and there may be other groups yet to be identified for critical study. Further, there are several extremely important individual writers during this period, some of whom I hope to include in later stages of this ongoing work, who, although not overtly associated with a particular, geographically located "school" or workshop, were constituents in a national, and eventually international community of avant-garde artists communicating with one another directly and through the available networks of little magazines and small-press publishers. In San Francisco, and briefly in New York, Bob Kaufman was an important figure in Beat circles, one whose books of poetry from City Lights Books and New Directions carried his influence far beyond the loyal friends of his immediate circles. Neeli Cherkovski has said of Kaufman that "Both in his poetry and because of his presence in the community of poets, he has left a legacy unequalled by others. That is a big claim, but I think an honest and accurate one" (8). Like Baraka in New York, Kaufman was an activist in San Francisco's avant-garde ranks, fending off police raids at the Co-Existence Bagel shop in 1956 and, in a plan hatched with Allen Ginsberg and others one night in 1959 at Cassandra's Coffee House, establishing the mimeographed magazine *Beatitude*, whose legendary issues rank with *Floating Bear* as an outlet for the new poetries in this period (Bryan 3). Clarence Major, who, as we have noted, attended a few meetings of the Umbra group and contributed work to their magazine, seems always to have been in motion during the early years of his career. His letters submitting works to various magazines were posted from Chicago and Omaha as well as from New York and, as had so many other young black innovators, he saw the need to create new media of publication. Major's *Coercion Review* ran from 1958 through 1961, and Coercion was also the imprint of his early poetry chapbooks, *Love Poems of a Black Man* and *Human Juices*. Major, like many of his contemporaries, corresponded with Baraka and submitted manuscripts to his many publishing projects. Later Major was to guest-edit an issue of the *Journal of Black Poetry*, and his International Publishers anthology, *The New Black Poetry*, is an invaluable resource for students of the African-American poetries of the 1950s and 1960s. In Boston, Stephen Jonas was an integral member of the circle of innovative poets that included Jack Spicer and Robin Blaser. A poster from that period advertising a Boston reading by Blaser, Jonas, Spicer, and John Wieners displays the characteristic mixture of black music and irreverent revision of modernist poetics that inspired so many of these poets. At the top of the poster we read, "EZRA POUND EATS WORMS"; at the bottom, we read, "Nothing has been so good since Bird died." Poems by both Blaser and Spicer were included in Allen's *New American Poetry*, but none by their intimate associate Jonas were selected. Jonas, too, was in frequent contact with Baraka, and for a time the two young poets planned a book by Jonas to appear in Baraka's Totem/Corinth series.

Two poets whose books did appear from Corinth were Jay Wright and Tom Weatherly. Wright, like Cortez, was from the Southwest, having spent his childhood in New Mexico and his final years of high school in California. His Corinth book, *The Homecoming Singer*, was the first of his major collections. He has published a series of equally impressive volumes since and has been the subject of a special issue of the literary journal *Callaloo*. Tom Weatherly is considerably less known to literary scholars, despite his inclusion in the *Dictionary of Literary Biography*, no doubt in part because of his sparser record of publication. Weatherly's remarkable first book, *Maumau American Cantos*, published by Corinth, still awaits adequate critical analysis. It was followed by a small collection from the determinedly avant-garde Telegraph Books, entitled *Thumbprint*, and another collection, entitled *Climate*, that appeared as part of a two-author booklet from Middle Earth Books. Though Weatherly is mentioned in a prose poem by Ashbery, few of that much examined poet's critics have evinced any interest in following up on this tantalizing lead. In the 1970s Weatherly taught at Rutgers University, Bishop College, Grand Valley State College, and Morgan State College, and he has worked in Poets in the Schools programs as well as in a program at the Department of Corrections on Rikers Island. Weatherly's own Natural Process Writers' Workshop and his work with the Saint Mark's Poetry Project extended his influence over subsequent poets even farther than did his limited-edition books of the period. He shares with poets like Addison, Pritchard, and Carrington the distinction of having gone unnoticed by nearly all histories of American postmodernity. If we compare his career (always a dangerous basis for conclusions about reputation) with that of other poets, such as Lorna Dee Cervantes, it would seem that Weatherly may have been ignored as much for what he writes and how he writes as because of the quantity of his publications. Cervantes, having published only one book with a university press, has been included in nearly every anthology of contemporary American literature, including the Norton and the Heath collections, whereas Weatherly has never appeared in any of the anthologies likely to find their way into a university classroom. Similarly, Norman Loftis, whose poetry has attracted the praise of Ashbery and Auden, and whose poetry collection *Black Anima* was brought out by Liveright, a publisher capable in its day of placing books of verse in leading bookstores, has never had another major book of his poetry published, and his work is omitted from most currently available anthologies. Loftis has gone on to award-winning work as a film producer and director and has published additional writings. Alpha/Omega Books published his novel *Life Force*, and in 1993 he arranged for the publication of his unusual work of arguments in philosophy and theology, *Condition Zero*, by Peter Lang publishers.

These writers paved the way for the next generation of innovative black poets, which included Nathaniel Mackey, Erica Hunt,

Ed Roberson, Will Alexander, Harryette Mullen, and others. The generational linkage is often direct. Michael Harper selected Mackey's *Eroding Witness* for publication in the National Poetry Series, and Mullen's first collection, *Tree Tall Woman,* published by Energy Earth Communications, appeared accompanied by an approving blurb from Thomas. Even so, black poets committed to nonconventional or experimental modes of composition can expect at best an uncertain response. Many of the most interesting poets of recent decades have endured the greatest difficulty in attempting to publish. Anthologies of the early 1970s introduced readers to some of the most exciting work of the time in individual poems by DeLeon Harrison, Glen Stokes, William Anderson, and Lawrence S. Cumberbatch, most of whom have never had books readily available to a potential reading public. Cumberbatch's poem "I Swear To You, That Ship Never Sunk in Middle-Passage!" is not overtly about the fate of black poets, but it serves as a blues poet's commentary on the invisibility blues:

> Tugging at the containment
>   all yields for the sake of bursting feet
>   scuffling in the furrowed yesterdays
> Inn beyond "one man's" whirl,
>   funky dark as the hovel,
>
> us children never sink
> dancing on the water of futility

(28)

Will Alexander was not to have a full book of poems published until the late 1980s, when his collection of surreal prose poems accompanied by his own illustrations was brought out by Jazz Press. More than a decade was to pass between the appearance of Harryette Mullen's first book and her second, a collection of prose poems entitled *Trimmings* and published by a lively new press, Tender Buttons. Erica Hunt, though she was included in Ron Silliman's landmark anthology of L=A=N=G=U=A=G=E poetries, *In The American Tree,* did not get a full book of poems published until Roof Books printed her *Local History* in 1993. If Major is right when he says that to be a black poet is to be unpopular, then poets whose works interrogate what literary society conceives to be blackness, what languages and what forms are critically associated with constructions of cultural blackness, might expect that their works may meet with something less than immediate approbation. But writers whose poems are inscribed as a history "of what / in the world you will show as yourself," who do not confuse the poem with the self but who write the poem as a graphic record of the self in the world, might at the least insist on resisting their own erasure. African-American poets pursuing forms of discrepant engagement, decomposition, psychovisualism, transrealism, the calligraphy of black chant, and a host of other modes of "worrying the line" might at the least hope they can get a witness. In *Lucid Interval* Ed Roberson wrote,

> a black man ought to have such
> signs on his cross-
> roads taken pictured too   landmark status:
> a small writing desk   in a quiet corner
>
> worn deep in the mass of no less subject
> than white tree worshippers of paper
> their cannibalist sacrifices
> flipping through them   offered that order
> be maintained white   where his ink dark-
>   ened those sheets
>
>   (62)

PART TWO

SLIPPING INTO DARKNESS

I am so black that
I am black
In theory
And in fact.
/ . . . /
I am so black
That I was black
When blackness was profitable
For white people only.

Julia Fields, "How Black"

4

"OUT THERE A MINUTE"
The Omniverse of Jazz and Text

how sound comes into a word, coloured
by who pays what for speaking

Audre Lorde, "Coal"

Proper evaluation of words and letters
In their phonetic and associated sense
Can bring peoples of earth
Into the clear light of pure Cosmic Wisdom

Sun Ra, "To the Peoples"

The word shall descend
          upon us
    before we learn to speak
          and it shall
stop us before we break

Henry Dumas, "Saba"

you'd never understand what i'm not sayin

Elouise Loftin, "Popcorn"

With the heat death of the Beat movement and the collapse of a fashionable poetry and jazz moment, literary criticism largely lost interest in reading the contemporary intertexts of black music and verse. With the present Beat revivals, marked most ostentatiously by the extensive media attention to anniversary conferences and festschriften in New York and at the Naropa Institute, breathing new life into a movement whose corpse had never been entirely removed from the stage, we are also witnessing a powerfully popular revival of public poetry performance, includ-

ing well-attended poetry "slams," heavyweight poetry champion-
ships that are covered by television news; "stand-up" poetry movements; a "spoken-word" tent accompanying the most recent
"Lollapalooza Tour"; and the appearance of spoken-word videos
on the Music Television channel. These phenomena are notable,
among many other things, for the negligible representation of
jazz performers and the ridiculously small number of black poets
included in the productions. This revival has extended even to
the commodification of the Beat generation. Allen Ginsberg now
appears in print ads for Gap clothing ("Allen Ginsberg wore
khakis," the ads tell us), but Ted Joans, who mounted the half-
parodic "Rent a Beatnik" program in Greenwich Village has yet
to be asked for his endorsement. Novelist William Burroughs,
whose recordings have become steady sellers in the spoken-word
category, has recently been featured in television advertisements
for Nike shoes, implying that being a former heroin addict and
shooting one's wife may be less of a roadblock to media market-
ability for writers than a black skin. Given the nearly universal
testimony of the original Beat figures to the fundamental importance of jazz in their own works, it is odd indeed that jazz is now
so often reduced to an electronic sample when it is permitted
entrance at all to the new bohemia. Younger performers, like
their older Beat models, often adopt what they take to be the
trappings of jazz in their dress and speech, but it frequently
seems that their aesthetic follows a paraphrase of a Jayne Cortez
poem: "We want the stylings, but we don't want the people."

One might have expected that the proliferation of cultural
studies and the rapidly expanding bibliography of critical studies
of Rap and Hip Hop might have had the residual effect of
modestly increasing critical attention to jazz and poetry, but
that has not yet happened. If anything, the current academic
fetishization of Rap has served to obscure further the continuing
experimentation with text by jazz composers. Reviewers and critics have commented at length on the turn to jazz sources of Rap
groups such as Diggable Planets and Us3, and an increasing
number of Rap artists have recently included live jazz performance in their stage presentation, but few writers have placed
this work in the larger context of earlier or more recent jazz
compositions embedding poetic texts. The surge of interest in
Rap has led to the resurgence of the careers of such groups as
the Last Poets, but although the music press now routinely cred-

its that group and Gil Scott-Heron as progenitors of the later socially conscious Rap of Grandmaster Flash and those who followed after, neither the popular nor the academic presses have given much space to the still earlier recordings of poetry by Amiri Baraka, Archie Shepp, or even Charles Mingus. We have benefited from a recent spurt of widely available and well-edited anthologies of literary texts related to jazz. In just the past few years, Yusef Komunyakaa and Sascha Feinstein have published their volume *The Jazz Poetry Anthology;* David Meltzer has brought out his collection, *Reading Jazz;* and Nathaniel Mackey and Art Lange have coedited what may be the best anthology of this type so far, *Moment's Notice: Jazz in Poetry and Prose.* There has been a strange twist to all this activity, though. Most important jazz has been created by African Americans; most of the works published in commercially available anthologies of jazz writing are by non-black writers. *Moment's Notice,* which presents the most accurate record of the multiracial involvement of poets with jazz, includes a poem by Kofi Natambu that might profitably have been read to the gathered critics and celebrants at the recent Beat conferences:

> Jazz poetry was not discovered by
> Allen Ginsberg or Jack Kerouac
> let alone Kenny Rexroth
> Nor was it a literary invention of the
> Beat(up) school, the New York School or
> any other official institution of 20th
> century AVANT-learning
>> It started if you really wanna know
>> (and you damn well should) in a white
>> whorehouse in East St. Louis, Illinois
>> in August 1928 where a bunch of drunken
>> unemployed Negro poets were sitting around
>> trying to sound like Louis Armstrong as a
>> rickety Victrola ground out 1900 choruses
> of "Tight like That" in the early morning
>
> (342)

If literary critics (even those who might privilege the oral) have been for the most part uninterested in studying such innovative poets' recordings as the Broadside collection *New Jazz Poets,* which includes poems by Percy Johnston and a good sampling of

Umbra poets, or the Essence album *Destinations,* with its selections by Norman H. Pritchard, Calvin Hernton, and the now much better-known Paul Blackburn, or the recording *Four Cleveland Poets,* with its recitations by Russell Atkins, we have, with a few notable exceptions, seemed woefully ignorant of the extensive body of recordings of avant-garde jazz works incorporating poetry by black writers. Though critics have devoted entire volumes to the examination of Rap and its cultural contexts, frequently producing valuable insights, we have yet to see an entire critical book devoted to the study of black jazz texts, and a sort of Gresham's Law of literary discourse and verse commodity has taken hold, proving prophetic Kalamu Ya Salaam's complaint made a quarter of a century ago: "Unfortunately, because these albums sell we can look forward in the near future to many more albums of 'Black rapping' and less of 'Black poetry' " (32).

It seemed for a time in the 1950s that recordings of jazz with poetry were appearing everywhere, and it has been all too easy to forget that Charles Mingus had been composing such works twenty years earlier, or that Duke Ellington's *A Drum Is a Woman,* incorporating poetry, was already being recorded when Kenneth Rexroth, Lawrence Ferlinghetti, Jack Kerouac, and Kenneth Patchen headed into the studios. Jazz poetry had long been an interracial as well as an intertextual phenomenon. Barry Wallenstein reports that Charlie Parker "was known to carry around copies of Patchen's poems and to recite them from memory" (617n), and reading the correspondence between Charles Olson and Robert Creeley impresses one with just how strong a common influence Parker's music was on the development of projective verse. Sometimes the widespread public attention given to white poets' performances with jazz accompaniment gave added impetus to black poets who had always worked with jazz materials to release their own "product." In October of 1958, Arna Bontemps wrote to Langston Hughes,

> I was interested last night in the TV readings by Carl Sandburg on the Milton Berle show. Poetry with Jazz. Even he has gone for it. He gave 1919 as the date of his first jazz poem: "Jazz Fantasia." He also talked of the first [New Orleans] and Memphis jazzmen to hit Chicago, at a time when he was a young newspaperman and very alert to such arrivals. Point: something of this sort for you would seem to

be a natural. It would be a terrific way to boom your *Selected Poems*. (376–7)

Hughes had anticipated his old friend's suggestion this time, for by March of 1958 he was already in the studios of Verve Records recording his poems to the music of Leonard Feather and Charles Mingus and their groups. This was only one year after Rexroth and Ferlinghetti's *Poetry Readings in the Cellar* was released on Fantasy Records, and it was the same year in which Kerouac recorded *Poetry for the Beat Generation* and *Blues and Haikus*. Aside from Hughes, however, few black poets were in a position to secure such recording opportunities, and it was not until the mid-1960s that a large number of recordings of African-American poets performing their poetry in jazz contexts began to appear (though there were always recordings of solo recitals by black poets).

The results of the poetry and jazz "movement" of the 1950s were not always as aesthetically successful as Hughes's work with Mingus and Feather on *Weary Blues*. Looking back at that period in *Reading Jazz*, Meltzer remembers,

> During the brief rise and fall of the Beat Generation, poets (myself included) read poetry in nightclubs accompanied by jazz musicians. Some – Rexroth, Lawrence Ferlinghetti, Kenneth Patchen, and Jack Kerouac – recorded their efforts. To my ear, the first three failed to either swing or sing. They recited or declaimed verse while a jazz combo vamped behind them. A jazz ensemble played arranged compositions for Patchen to enter into in a manner akin to Schoenberg's use of *sprachstimme*. While there was a formal musical setting for Patchen's work, Ferlinghetti and Rexroth seemed separate from the music, the jazz only background to the poem, not interactive with it. I thought Kerouac was the most successful, grasping the jazz "spirit," both on record and in his writing. (178)

Meltzer goes at once to the crux of the issue, the interrelationship between the music and the poetry. Too frequently, enamored of the ideal of improvisation, poets simply took to the stage or to the studio to declaim their creations, trusting to the spirit of the moment and the musicians' ability to anticipate the text's direction, often sorely trying the sympathy of their audience. Jazz is an improvisatory music, but jazz musicians' improvise within preset paradigms (such as a standard "head" chart or a sketch of a theme), or they improvise together in rehearsal until they are able to create sound forms that they find productive for the group as a whole. There were two reasons for the high quality of Hughes's *Weary Blues* sessions. First, Mingus (who was not credited on the original album because of conflicting contractual obligations) and Feather had sketched the music in advance with specific Hughes texts in mind. Secondly, the Hughes poems on this recording, even the free verse poems, are so deeply rooted in traditional blues forms that his recitation sounds as if he is simply reading, rather than singing, song lyrics. The next generation of black poets would take a freer approach to forming their lines, just as the next generation of musicians after Mingus would build upon his work in the creation of Free Jazz, but poets like Baraka would often return to Hughes's example for sustenance.

The Beat poets' relationship to the music was, like Rexroth's, usually more contingent. Rexroth and Kerouac certainly knew a lot about musicians and listened with a keen ear to jazz, but they evidenced little clear understanding of how the music was put together, and thus their approach to locating their own lines within the music was generally intuitive. The music was, as Meltzer says, more frequently background (or even distraction) than equal partner in a new genre. Rexroth was assuredly more attentive to these issues than Kerouac, and Rexroth carefully rehearsed certain tunes to go with certain poems. Still, Rexroth's recitations are seldom more than his usual reading style placed against an old standard.

Kerouac's relationship to the music with which he surrounded his poems was still more contingent. For example, the fact that Steve Allen ended up providing piano accompaniment for his poetry reading at the Village Vanguard in New York and on the subsequent album *Poetry for the Beat Generation* was almost pure accident. As David Perry reconstructs the events, Kerouac's first Vanguard set, unaccompanied, was a disaster (5). Allen suggested that a jazz piano accompaniment might help and was then drafted for duty in the second show. Kerouac's second album, *Blues and Haikus,* was more of a planned event, though the session itself was played spontaneously. Bob Thiele, the producer, suggested a second set of sessions to follow the work with Allen, and Kerouac suggested hiring saxophonists Al Cohn and

Zoot Sims as his session men. The session men handled the date much as they would have handled any pickup session. They dutifully improvised around Kerouac's readings (which they had not heard before), collected their paychecks, and left (Perry 5). The generally high quality of the music on these recordings is a testament to the ability of seasoned side men to sound good in a rehearsal setting. The generally interesting quality of the writing is a testament to Kerouac's own long years of woodshedding. Responses to the mixture of the music of Cohn and Sims with the words of Kerouac have varied tremendously. For Ginsberg, Kerouac's "*Blues and Haikus* remain . . . the classic of all Beat era jazz poetry recordings, yet to be matched for delightful recitation – verve of pronunciation, deep color of vowels & consonantal bite, exquisite intelligent consciousness in crossing T's & tonguing D's against the teeth with open lips" (8). It is more than a little interesting that Ginsberg says absolutely nothing here about the jazz on this "classic of all Beat era jazz poetry recordings." Meltzer, certainly more of a musician than Ginsberg, thinks that these sessions "are wonderful examples of dialogue absent in the other records" (178), but for Wallenstein, one of the very few critics to have written substantively about this genre of collaborative work, "the integration of music and voice is awkward, . . . as if the horns were playing the poem just recited" (611). In fact, there is truly little discernible difference between Kerouac's mode of reading with music and without music, which is not an entirely bad thing. The influence of jazz, Be Bop in particular, is there already, on the page and in his voicings of his own texts. Had Kerouac been possessed of greater technical knowledge and facility, he might have created yet more interesting improvisational spaces between his poems and the music of his collaborators. In the end, though, Gerald Nicosia may be right that *Readings by Jack Kerouac on the Beat Generation,* "Kerouac's only album without actual musical accompaniment," is "perhaps the best demonstration of the musicality of Kerouac's art" (9).

If the public and the professors quickly lost interest in the Beats' jazz-poetry phenomenon, young writers did not. New York's bohemian scene was already attracting new groups of poets and musicians who proceeded to do something new with the idea of jazz texts. Though jazz musicians and poets had always intermingled, perhaps no black poets and musicians since the days of the Harlem Renaissance had so actively involved themselves in one another's works. Again, the poetry of Hughes and the Be Bop of Parker, Dizzy Gillespie, Thelonious Monk and Bud Powell were the spaces of intersection. Amiri Baraka, as a student at Howard University, had been one of those young people who huddled around Sterling Brown's record player studying blues and jazz with the author of *Southern Road*. In a "Note" in a 1961 issue of *Floating Bear*, Baraka outlined two means by which the newer jazz musicians of his generation made use of their predecessors' breakthroughs: "What 'Trane' has done is simply make some resolution of all the fragments that were so in evidence in the early 50's. Ornette, &c. went *back* to Bebop. Trane had simply added whole integers" (56). Writing over his pseudonym "Johannes Koenig," Baraka traced two forms of a postmodernity in *music* that he thought paralleled his own relationships to modernity in poetics. One mode gathered up the loose ends and unfinished projects of the modern; the other returned to the modern and located within it new beginnings. The result is a set of aesthetic motions that are at once in the tradition and counter to its direction. As Ronald Radano later said of Anthony Braxton, the black artists who created an African-American postmodernism were bringing into being a "voice [that] would develop from its black roots" as a critique not only of the "categories of official culture but of jazz and 'black music' as well" (120).

Baraka's "Note" in *Floating Bear* was written prior to John Coltrane's *Ascension* recording sessions, sessions that saw the bringing together in one critical moment of the two modes of postmodernism Baraka had discerned in the new music of Coltrane and Coleman. In the interim, Coltrane had digested the breakthroughs of Coleman's *Free Jazz* experiment of 1960 and had melded Coleman's concept for guiding free ensemble playing with his own ideas about deconstructing the opposition between solo improvisation and ensemble "background." Significantly, the *Ascension* sessions included a number of the younger musicians with whom Baraka was working and with whom he discussed his aesthetic ideas, among them his neighbor Archie Shepp, himself a poet, actor, and playwright. Shepp was in many ways characteristic of that generation of innovators who followed immediately in the wake of Coltrane and Coleman. Almost as soon as he had arrived in New York, Shepp had begun to move within the circles of new black artists such as Baraka and Cecil

Taylor, and among the early public appearances that brought Shepp before a large audience was his lengthy engagement in the cast of Jack Gelber's play *The Connection,* a cast that also included Taylor. (Jackie McLean appeared in another version of the cast.) One of Shepp's own early plays, *A Cellwalk to Celestine,* derived its title from a musical composition of Taylor's, with whose band Shepp played for some time. Shepp typically viewed aesthetic issues in terms of a continuum between music and literature, often, as did Baraka, employing an analogy from one art form to elucidate his approach to another. In the liner notes to his *Live in San Francisco* recordings of 1966, he looked to an Irish modernist author to explain something of the black postmodernist direction he was working out, an increasingly nationalist postmodernity in those years: "The whole Western esthetic since the Renaissance seems to be based on the fact that white men introduced the art of notation to music. James Joyce tried to forget that. Not musically. As a writer, he tried to forget it." Shepp, originally from Fort Lauderdale, had an even more extensive reading background in literature than many of his colleagues in the new jazz, a group of notoriously wide readers. He had studied drama and literature at Goddard College, receiving his B.A. degree in 1959. Within six years of completing college, Shepp was releasing recordings of his original compositions on albums that received international distribution, and from the very beginning of his recording career he experimented with jazz settings of poetry. He also continued to associate with avant-garde writers, speaking at public forums with Baraka and attending meetings with the Umbra group. The cover photograph for Shepp's album *On This Night* was, as it happens, made by LeRoy McLucas, whose poems "Graph" and "Negotiation" were included in the first issue of *Umbra.*

The literary magazines of the late 1950s and early 1960s, most notably *Yugen* and *Floating Bear,* often published statements on the emerging new wave of jazz forms, along with poems inspired by the music. Many poets followed Baraka's lead in contributing reviews of records and performances to both jazz and poetry magazines (and Baraka was often the middleman, getting review assignments for his friends). In later years, Baraka and poets Larry Neal and A. B. Spellman collaborated for a time in publishing *Cricket,* a black music magazine intended to counter the white-dominated world of magazines like *Down Beat.* Clearly, the new generation of innovators in African-American poetry saw the new jazz not just as a source of inspiration or a parallel to their own projects but as virtually identical with their projects, and many of the older musicians like Sun Ra encouraged this merging of aesthetic revolutions.

One public sign of the arrival of a new musical aesthetic (born of Bop, and thus a revolution within a tradition of revolution) was the October 1964 festival in New York billed as "The October Revolution in Jazz," which ranks with the Armory Show earlier in the century as a clear signal of cultural shift in the history of American arts. The October festival, organized by Bill Dixon and held at the Cellar Café, featured more than twenty performing groups and included such musicians as Sun Ra, Milford Graves, Dewey Johnson, Paul Bley (a white pianist who had worked early on with Coleman), and Jimmy Giuffre. Baraka, then still known as LeRoi Jones, organized a series of jazz concerts in Greenwich Village, and Milford Graves remembers him reading his poetry at some of those performances (Such 26). In March of 1965, Baraka was instrumental in the production of another festival of "New Black Music," which included performances by Shepp, Betty Carter, Albert Ayler, Sun Ra, Coltrane (who was to record *Ascension* only three months later), and Charles Tolliver. The Impulse label of ABC Records released a selection of live performances from the festival under the title *The New Wave of Jazz,* reducing organizer Baraka's proposed title, *New Black Music,* to a subtitle. The original concert was held as a benefit for Baraka's Black Arts Repertory Theater/School and marked the public joining of the new movements in black music, poetry, and politics. Baraka described the recording as "the touchstone of the new world" (*Music* 175), appropriating Matthew Arnold's critical terminology for a radically black-nationalist aesthetic. The characteristics that Baraka attributed to the new musicians are clearly those of the new poetics he was advancing from the late 1950s into the 1960s, and his African-American adaptations of projective verse theories are prominently evidenced. Baraka described as central modes of the New Black Music:

> *Projection over sustained periods* (more time given, and time proposes a history for expression, hence it becomes reflective projection.
> *Arbitrariness of form* (variety in nature).
> *Intention of performance as a learning experience.* (*Music* 175)

The New Wave of Jazz was followed quickly by the ABC Impulse album *New Thing at Newport*, featuring Coltrane and Shepp, with Shepp including an original poem as part of his concert at the generally more traditional Newport Festival. (Not even Coleman had appeared in the official Newport program as of that time.) For some years thereafter the Impulse label was practically synonymous with the "New Wave" of jazz, even advertising itself as a commercial locus for this seemingly anticommercial music, and many of the Impulse recordings made use of poets' texts.

Some of the Impulse sessions were among the most successful efforts to bring the post-Bop revolution in music together with the post–projective verse and post–Langston Hughes revolution in black poetics in such a way that the commonality of aesthetics would be illuminated rather than obscured. The difficulty of this endeavour was the same difficulty that Wallenstein identified in his criticism of Kerouac's *Blues and Haikus*. Listening to the recorded works of the later, Free Jazz musicians, Ekkehard Jost argued, in his book *Free Jazz* (1981), "When spoken poetry and music are combined, the message of the words is obviously much more prominent than when a text is sung. There is a real danger that the music will be reduced to a mere sound backdrop, or – as is the case in many rigged-up 'jazz and poetry' experiments involving words and music not written for each other – that the two will run as it were on separate tracks" (105).

One of the most egregious examples of a rigged-up conjoining of music and text is to be found on the Miles Davis album *Live-Evil*. Here the text and the music are quite literally on different tracks, but with none of the interesting effects so often found when modernist and postmodernist artists juxtapose seemingly unrelated materials. The fourth side of the album is taken up by a piece entitled "Inamorata," which includes a spoken text by Conrad Roberts. The music for this selection sounds much like that on the rest of the album (Davis's standard touring repertoire at the time), until the moment arrives for the beginning of Roberts's recitation. It sounds as if the mixing of the instrumental tracks had been accomplished before someone had the afterthought to include a text. Instead of the text being mixed *into* the instruments in such a way as to produce an illusion of simultaneity, the engineers simply decreased the volume of the music and overlaid the recorded recitation. The results are mixed. Roberts sounds as if he is in the room with the listener, whereas the band seems to be playing in another time zone altogether. The music is not just reduced to a background; the text, an indifferent creation at best (though beautifully read by Roberts), virtually colonizes the territory of the recording, oppressing the music.

Though Miles Davis had a number of literary friendships over the decades (with Quincy Troupe, for example, who coauthored his autobiography), he seems to have given little thought to his relatively few experiments with texts in his music. Perhaps his best work of this kind is on the *Sun City* recordings produced by Little Steven Van Zandt for Artists against Apartheid. This was essentially volunteer studio work for Davis. He came into the studio and laid down trumpet lines for already recorded songs. But Van Zandt's mixing, particularly on "Let Me See Your I.D.," where Davis's improvisations join Gil Scott-Heron's reading of his own free verse, is far superior to similar ventures on Davis's own recordings. The most extensive work Davis undertook with spoken verse was his posthumously completed collection *doo-bop*. These sessions, which grew out of his conversations with Def Jam Records' Russell Simmons, represent the trumpet player's attempt to create a jazz–Hip-Hop fusion to parallel the jazz–rock–soul music fusion he had given birth to with albums like *Bitches Brew*. It would be grossly unfair to judge *doo-bop* too harshly, since it was finished without Davis's participation and therefore cannot represent his full intentions. (For example, Troupe has told me that he himself was supposed to record one of his poems for a selection on the album but in the end did not). Davis's playing on *doo-bop* is assured, and he adapts to the rhythm tracks produced with rapper Easy Mo Bee effortlessly, but the Raps on the collection trivialize the project. Easy Mo Bee's "Blow" opens as follows:

> Here I am Easy Mo Bee, kickin' it live
> With the legendary Miles Davis
> Just my favorite
> And his trumpet can't be played with,
> Tampered with
> Or picked up and thrown to the pavement

The tracks are an entertaining mix, beginning with a phone message from Miles and seguing into an invigorating Davis trumpet line. But the almost mandatory James Brown sample this time only serves to remind listeners of how tame Easy Mo Bee's work really is. When the rapper tells us, "Me and the Chief will just blow," the temptation is strong to repeat back to the producer the lyric to the Brown tune he's sampled, "Give it up or turn it loose."

Getting the mix just right proved to be a problem even for musicians who collaborated with poets whose own work might match their innovative force. When Ornette Coleman sought a poet with whom to record one of his "harmolodic" compositions, he chose one of the most active of the Umbra group, David Henderson. The title piece of the collection *Science Fiction* might have served as a demonstration of the extension of Coleman's emerging theory of "harmolodic" composition. In Coleman's view, harmolodics, like Russell Atkins's psychovisualism and deconstruction, is an interdisciplinary approach whose methodology is applicable across a range of media. Harmolodics, he has written, "can be used in almost any kind of expression. You can think harmolodically, you can write fiction and poetry in harmolodic. Harmolodics allows a person to use a multiplicity of elements to express more than one direction" (qtd. in Litweiler 148). The first print reference to Coleman's theory appeared in the liner notes to his symphony *Skies of America,* recorded with the London Symphony Orchestra a year after *Science Fiction,* where he refers to a forthcoming theoretical book on the subject. Although the book was never completed, Coleman's harmolodic practices have been transmitted in the music world through musicians who worked with him, such as James Blood Ulmer, Ronald Shannon Jackson, Don Cherry, and Charlie Haden. Cherry has explained that "In the harmolodic concept, you're reaching to the point to make every note sound like a tonic," and bassist Haden has described the approach as "a constant modulation in the improvising that was taken from the direction of composition, and from the direction inside the musician, and from listening to each other" (qtd. in Litweiler 148). These explanations remain a bit mystical (though, as Coleman's biographer John Litweiler has pointed out, the composer has on occasion provided a more practical set of notes and chords to help puzzled interviewers), and the application to poetry must be largely along metaphorical lines. All the same, we can gather some sense of the harmolodic conception of group creation from what was attempted in *Science Fiction.*

It is important to our understanding of the nature of postmodern jazz-text creations that we know that the poem had been written down prior to the performance (as was true of most of the poems I discuss in this chapter). However great the influence of oral and musical traditions upon the poet (and they were powerful, in the case of Henderson), the fact remains that the poem was not wholly improvised in the moment of the performance. Like all chant, and like the music on this recording itself, the performed poem was the realization of a repeated textual form. The text was the occasion of the performance of the poet, and the musicians and poet (and recording engineers) together created a new form. Similarly, once recorded, the text and its music became graphically stable (though subject to physical alteration), but the listening and signifying experiences are not stable. The context of reception is different with each listening, and past listenings form the context for repeated listenings. The audience for a recording such as *Science Fiction* are improvising agents themselves, constructing new object-forms from the jazz text recorded by the artist.

One key to listening to a jazz text of the sort found in "Science Fiction" is understanding that Coleman's approach to ensemble work differed radically from the traditional relationship of solo to accompaniment in Swing and Bop. As Coleman explained in the liner notes, "The kind of music we play, no one player has the lead." This meant, too, that there was no trading eights between soloists (though there was constant interchange of material), but it also meant that the relationship between the poet's voice and the instruments was not what most listeners would probably have expected. Henderson's recitation of the poem is not in any sense "accompanied" by the players; his voice is just one element in the ensemble. Contrary to Jost's observations with regard to most jazz-poetry performances, the spoken word here does not make the "message" more prominent, because it is never the "lead" voice. Even so, the recorded version of this work is less satisfactory than most Coleman compositions, and again this is largely the fault of the production techniques. Henderson adopted a reading style on this session quite unlike his usual mode of live performance, spacing each word, allowing the words to hang isolated in aural space surrounded by the music before they join up syntactically with other words. That effect is heightened by the heavy application to his voice of an electronic echo. The words thus "resonate against one another," as Robert Palmer says in his album notes, while they also resonate with the ambient tones of the musicians. Added to this mix is another recorded voice, that of a crying baby. Though in one sense this may be seen as an overliteralizing of the subject matter of Henderson's poem (which begins with a meditation on birth), it could also be read as emphasizing the nonverbal signifying potential of the human voice. Henderson's poem is rhetorically effective. "How   many   enemies   make   a soul?", we are asked out of the swirling vastness of the instrumental improvisations. At the poem's close the poet declares, "My   mind belongs   to   civilization," just before a tape speedup seemingly lifts the music into outer space. The production, though, limits these effects through a poorly planned mix. As on Davis's "Inamorata," the music and the poem were obviously recorded at different times, and the musicians seem to be playing without any cognizance of the poem. The voice does not overwhelm the music, as it does on "Inamorata," but neither does it sound as though it were truly part of the same improvisation. With subsequent developments in recording technology it is now possible to record tracks years apart and still create the illusion that they are responsive to one another (indeed, it now really is possible for the singer to phone in his or her performance), but, in the opinion of Litweiler, "Science Fiction" is "a long, static performance" (141) of considerably less interest than other compositions from the same sessions, such as "What Reason Could I Give" or "Civilization Day." The work with Henderson forms a thematic link with the rest of the album and is an intriguing attempt, but it needed to be recorded more carefully if it was to display the possibilities of the harmolodic approach to jazz texts.

Of the musicians who had already established themselves on the jazz scene before Coleman arrived in New York in the late 1950s with his Free Jazz, Charles Mingus, whose movement from Bop into freer structures bridged the generations, experimented more frequently with the incorporation of recitations into his performances than most, and he generally found effective solutions to the problem of balancing instrumental and verbal texts in the same piece, as he had with his portions of Langston Hughes's *Weary Blues*. Mingus's own poetry, however, tended to be premodernist in form, and his music is often of far greater interest than the verse. On the compilation album *Let My Chil-*

dren Hear Music, this is most evident in "The Chill of Death." The Mingus poem of that title was first composed, along with the music, in the late 1930s, and both poem and music are marred by large doses of sentiment. To a background of lush orchestration Mingus recites, "The chill of death as she clutched my hand / I knew she was coming, so I stood, like a man." There is little here to indicate that this same man would go on to write such masterpieces as "Fables of Faubus" or "Epitaph." An interesting development occurs once the recitation is completed, though. An alto saxophone solo takes off from the end of the poem (inspired and suggested by Charlie Parker, according to the liner notes), and suddenly the sentimentalism vanishes, even though the orchestration remains somewhat lush. The resulting effect is an odd suturing of the premodernist to the modernist, as if Mingus were engaging in a Parker-like destruction and reinvention of his own earlier compositions. One of Parker's most repeated strategies was to destroy the melody of a sentimental favorite like "Moonlight in Vermont" and reinvent it as a modernist Bop masterpiece, all the while preserving the harmonic ghost of the original. Mingus's "Chill of Death" seems to respond to its own sentiment with a kindred form of deformation and remastery without ever completely abandoning its romantic origins.

Far more like his work with Hughes, and like the majority of his text-based performances, is Mingus's composition "Freedom," which he recorded as part of his brilliant but ragged concert at Town Hall in New York in November of 1962. The musicians gathered on the stage that evening included Clark Terry, Pepper Adams, Danny Richmond, Eric Dolphy, and others of similar stature. Copyists were reportedly still busy reproducing the score for the arriving musicians that night, music that included the now well-known and much acclaimed "Epitaph." The recording has the feel of history in the making, and it was still very much in the process of being made as the artists found their way through a set of complex compositions. "Freedom" is a Civil Rights anthem that begins with a couplet that could have been written by Hughes himself and then complicates itself with a more latinate vocabulary. As the piece begins, what sounds like tympani keep time while the assembled instrumentalists chant a wordless melody in unison, clapping their hands and striking a tambourine on the heavy downbeat. Mingus recites, sounding like the irreverent trickster that he was, "This mule ain't from Moscow; This mule ain't from the South. / This mule's had some learning, mostly mouth to mouth." As Mingus concludes his anti–Cold War and antiessentialist recitation with the advice to "stand fast," part of the band begins to play while Mingus and the rest of the ensemble sing a chorus, "Freedom for your brothers and sisters, but no freedom for me." At the close of that chorus, during which the horns build an almost agonizing tension, the drums shift the rhythm to a double-time, syncopated dance mode, strongly reminiscent of 1930s Swing, but the soloing horns take liberties with the chords that no Swing band would likely have permitted. After the round of improvisations is concluded, the drums return to their dirgelike rhythm, and Mingus repeats his recitation. "Freedom" is a deeply moving and ironic political and musical statement. It is a modernist collage built on black vernacular traditions, and it remains one of Charles Mingus's great achievements.

It remained for musicians and poets younger than Mingus, younger even than Coleman and Coltrane, to bring the musical revolutions of Mingus, Monk, Coltrane, and Coleman together with the emerging new African-American writings in an effective way. It is not until the mid-1960s that we begin to see a significant number of recordings in which the new wave of black jazz and the postwar experiments in black poetics come together as a new genre of post-Beat, black avant-garde statement. Those mid-1960s recordings would open the door for the rush of record albums by black poets and would-be poets that clogged the sound track of social turmoil in the late 1960s and early 1970s. (Who could ever forget Nikki Giovanni's album of poems read to Gospel choir accompaniment, seemingly with no sense of irony, or the mind-numbing contribution of the Last Poets to the Hollywood blaxploitation film *Right On?*) In the opinion of Kalamu Ya Salaam, there was a notable decline in quality from Baraka's recording *Black and Beautiful, Soul and Madness* to the Last Poets' eponymous release, to the Black Voices' *On the Streets in Watts,* a decline directly related to the sudden interest on the part of commercial record producers in the money-making potential of decontextualized black rage (a reawakened interest in the wake of Rap, as the Last Poets, but not Baraka, have once again been featured in movies like *Poetic Justice*). If Gil Scott-Heron could get appearances on television on the strength of his record *The*

Revolution Will Not Be Televised, the thinking seemed to go, then perhaps there was a market there to be exploited.

For all his virtues as an eloquent, and even elegant communicator, however, Scott-Heron was not a proponent of revolutionary formal experimentation in verse, and although Hollywood brought its briefly profitable flirtation with black poetry to a screeching halt (to be renewed with the advent of Gangster Rap), successive waves of jazz-poetry innovators carried on their work in the penumbra of capitalist modes of communication. Baraka, who has also recorded poetry to Rhythm and Blues accompaniment, took the lead in this jazz-poetry work too. His most intriguing jazz collaboration was produced for ESP Records, a label that had released ground-breaking early works by Sun Ra, the Fugs, William Burroughs, Pharaoh Sanders, and the Revolutionary Ensemble and that demonstrated its penchant for the esoteric by occasionally printing album liner notes written in Esperanto. In 1965 Baraka recorded a recitation of his poem "Black Dada Nihilismus" with the New York Art Quartet on their eponymous ESP disk. The quartet was formed by musicians with whom Baraka was already familiar, and about whom he wrote frequently in his capacity as a jazz critic. In his "Apple Cores" column in *Down Beat,* while discussing the first releases from Bernard Stollman's ESP Records, Baraka had mentioned the musicians of the quartet and indicated that they were artists "who must be heard at once" (*Black Music* 121). The drummer, Milford Graves, had studied tabla drumming with a musician from India, and Baraka thought this one reason that Graves's snare drum work seemed "completely different from the usual drum and bugle corps ratatat most drummers get" (121). Saxophonist John Tchicai was an Afro-Danish artist who had performed with Shepp and Cherry in Europe and had been enlisted by Coltrane for the *Ascension* project. Of Tchicai's approach to his instrument Baraka wrote, in 1963, "He plays the alto like he wanted to sound like Coleman Hawkins playing like Ornette Coleman. But he sounds mostly like nothing you've heard before" (*Black Music* 97). The bassist for the recording, called *New York Art Quartet,* was Lewis Worrell, who had also played with Sonny Murray and Albert Ayler. The trombonist was the young Roswell Rudd, one of a small group of white artists, including Paul Bley and Charlie Haden, who made original and lasting contributions to the new music. Rudd was a frequent associate of

Shepp's and would later work with the Jazz Composers' Orchestra. It is a Rudd musical composition "Sweet V" that encompasses Baraka's recitation of his poem from his book *The Dead Lecturer* on the album.

Critics who read Wallenstein's description of this recording in his essay "Poetry and Jazz: A Twentieth-Century Wedding" before listening to the recording itself may be surprised at the difference between his characterization of the recording and what is actually in evidence on the record. Many would no doubt agree with Wallenstein that the poem is a brutal and apocalyptic work (612), but it is difficult to see anything "didactic" about it. Nor is it an easy matter to accept his description of this piece as a "rant" (612). It may be the case that he is simply reading back into the past attitudes he has adopted toward later Baraka works, many of which could well be termed didactic. Baraka's poem calls for "Black scream / and chant" (*Dead* 63), but there is no screaming from the poet on this recording. It would be some time yet before Baraka would make recordings in which he practiced his more dramatic approach to recitation, in which he attempted to bring some of the instrumental techniques of the new jazz into the performance of the spoken word. Baraka's work with the New York Art Quartet builds its terrifying tensions out of the dissonance between the apocalyptic words of the poem and the almost overly calm fashion in which Baraka reads it. In fact, Baraka's rendition of the poem with the New York Art Quartet is nearly identical to his cool and suspense-filled performance, without music, recorded at an August 1964 Asilomar conference taped by Pacifica Radio. Wallenstein feels that "Baraka's book *The Dead Lecturer,* and the recording of this poem from it, more than any other single effort, seem to give license to rage" (612). Despite the escape hatch represented by the word "seem," it does seem that Wallenstein puts more weight upon the reception of this recording (which did not, after all, receive significant air play) than the evidence will bear. One might argue that any license to rage derived from the history of oppression the poem is built around, not from the poem's tone. And although Baraka's developing mode of delivery was widely copied by other poets, black and white, surely few could have taken any license to rant or rage from the coolly delivered horrors of this reading of "Black Dada Nihilismus." That is a point whose importance goes far beyond a local disagreement over the reading of a single poem. There has been a tendency among some critics to dismiss Baraka's later works as mere sloganeering, but this dismissal is built upon a failure to read the full variety of his poetry after *The Dead Lecturer*. The demonstrable fact is that Baraka has always exhibited a wide range of tone, both in his writing and in his readings. Just as his later work juxtaposes such didactic efforts as "Against Bourgeois Art" with more meditative poetry, such as the several lyrical sections of "Whys/Wise," the loud riffing of his declamatory mode has always been interrupted by moments of quiet, almost whispering insistence. What is dramatically disconcerting, as in the case of "Black Dada Nihilismus," is that Baraka's quietest delivery sometimes is used for his most apocalyptic visionary verse.

This touches upon one aspect of Baraka's aesthetics that has remained constant throughout the evolution of his several stages of political thought. Since adopting Marxism in the 1970s, Baraka has often quoted at readings and talks Mao Tse Tung's famous quip to the effect that "All art is propaganda." But, as I have heard him do on several occasions, he also repeats the less well-remembered rejoinder Mao offered to his own observation: "Not all propaganda is art." In the mid-1960s he set forth his ideas about the relationship between art and instruction, and these ideas still appear to guide his work thirty years later. In his 1965 essay "New Black Music," Baraka argued that "Expression does not set out to instruct, but it does anyway . . . if the objects of this mind-energy are so placed that they do receive. Reflection intends to change, is a formal learning situation. But getting hit on the head with a stick can do you as much good as meditating" (175). These functional descriptions of expression and reflection (incorporating an ancient Zen joke) would seem to mark the boundaries between which much of Baraka's subsequent poetry has been ranged.

Rudd's musical composition "Sweet V" opens with meditative percussion sounds, as Milford Graves moves from cymbal to snare, slowly adding a bass drum note. Baraka and Lewis Worrell begin together, the bass player providing plucked notes under the poet's reading of his text. Baraka reads his title, "Black Dada Nihilismus," and moves directly into the poem. What cannot be heard here is the fact that the printed version of the poem begins with a period. But the blank space in the poem's first line finished off by the initial period in Baraka's text is, in a way,

performed by the percussion solo that leads into the poet's
reading:

> .Against what light
> is false what breath
> sucked, for deadness.
> Murder, the cleansed
> purpose, frail, against
> God . . .
>
> (*Dead* 61)

As the snare and the plucked bass runs proceed, they seem to
underscore the frail starting-and-stopping rhythms of the poem.
But it is a frailty that has an accumulating power, a misleading
quiet, a barely audible purposiveness that will not be swayed from
its direction. It is, as the poem puts it, "Hermes, the / / blacker
art" (62). That crackling frailty follows into the second canto of
the poem, again seeming to exemplify the truth of the poet's
words, "Plastique, we / / do not have, only thin heroic blades"
(63). The metallic sounding of the high-hat cymbals here adds a
literally thin and heroic tone. When Baraka speaks (not screams)
of a "dull, un / earthly / hollering," it is this quietly clattering
rhythm section that imparts such an unearthly tone to the performance. The closing high-hat and the thick bass are in contrast
to the sharper sounding of the open cymbals or the saxophone,
and their dull hollering presages the retributive murders spoken
of in the poem. The drum patterns build to a busy crescendo as
Baraka softly chants the litany of names that occurs near the end
of the poem:

> For tambo, willie best, dubois, patrice, mantan, the
> bronze buckaroos.
>
>> For Jack Johnson, asbestos, tonto, buckwheat,
>> billie holliday
>
>>> For tom russ, l'overture, vesey, beau jack
>
> (64)

If this poem does license rage, then surely this peaceful invocation of the departed is a source of that license. The names in this
rhythmic list belong to people who were persecuted or thwarted,
or who had their art perverted by white desire. Here the assassination of Patrice Lumumba is memorialized alongside the names

of entertainers such as Mantan Moreland, who were driven into the portrayal of minstrel figures and closed out of opportunities to create their own art by their own lights. Here Baraka's own grandfather Russ is placed within a lineage of black revolutionaries that includes Denmark Vesey and Toussaint L'Ouverture. Here hapless Buckwheat is memorialized as the requisite "other" buddy to white ambition, like Tonto, and this more than a decade before the figure of Buckwheat was again made a commodity on *Saturday Night Live* and in a new generation of *Little Rascals* film. Baraka's praise song for the forgotten and abused predecessors concludes in a prayer to the "lost" West African god Damballah to "rest or save us / against the murders we intend / against his lost white children" (64). As Baraka reads quietly the last line of his poem, echoing its title, "black dada nihilismus," Tchicai's saxophone enters in response, in keeping with the fragile but slicing tone of the earlier sections. Baraka once likened Tchicai's alto tone to "a metal poem" (*Black Music* 154), and the musician's tone as he first states the theme of "Sweet V" is exactly that sharp lyric Baraka describes. It is an imploring but somewhat dangerous sound that Tchicai produces as he leads into the theme, joined by the trombone of Rudd, the song's composer. The two horns take turns soloing against the thematic materials. Graves moves the group into a faster time signature as Tchicai improvises. The chorus actually sounds a great deal like some of Coleman's duets with Cherry in their early music.

What is of particular interest in the improvisations is that Tchicai and Rudd appear to be improvising from Baraka's materials as well as from the choral theme. Not all of the instrumental responses to Baraka are as literalizing of his statements as the rhythm section's opening accompaniment appears to be, but the crucial point to be made is that there is a doubleness in the musical response that greets Baraka's call. The solos in "Sweet V" improvise from Baraka's semantics as well as from his tone and rhythms. Musical notes are not as denotative as spoken words, but they can, through the construction of and deviation from conventions, come to carry significant connotative weight. According to David G. Such, in his study *Avant-Garde Jazz Musicians Performing "Out There"* (1993), "Most Western scholars and listeners tend to agree that all types of music have at least some degree of referential value" (113). This is certainly a proposition that would not seem foreign to West African musicologists (one has only to think of the "talking drums") or to students of the blues (in which harmonicas and slide guitars constantly emulate the speaking voice and in which a guitar player might well be heard addressing his own instrument, "Talk to me!"). The primary musical theme of "Sweet V" might indeed sound "sweeter" than we would expect, given the poem, but it stays very close to the opening rhythms of Baraka's poem. The individual solos, on the other hand, sound in many places as if they were construing answers to the poem's prayers. As the poem itself rejects one form of the modern, "the protestant love, wide windows, / color blocked to Mondrian . . ." (61), the intertwining lines of the saxophone and trombone sketch a postmodernist riposte to the harmonic obligations of Be Bop's modernism.

Unlike most of the Beats' experiments in reading to jazz, the musicians on the *New York Art Quartet* recording of 1965 sound as if they have not only listened to Baraka's poem but have taken positions inside its stanzas from which to elaborate their contribution to the new ensemble structure built upon the poem. This is true of most of the recordings Baraka has made since that time, both the jazz texts and the recordings with a Rhythm and Blues band. Just two years after his work with the New York Art Quartet, Baraka was able to record his anthematic statement of the Black Aesthetic, the poem "Black Art," on an album of material by Sonny Murray released on Baraka's own Jihad Productions label. Like Sun Ra, who released a stream of recordings of his band's works in progress on his own Saturn label, Baraka had understood that a black-owned and directed company might be required if the new music and the new poetry were to be made available to black audiences without censoring of the type that reduced the proposed title *New Black Music* to a subtitle at ABC Records. The 1967 recording entitled *Sonny's Time Now* reunited Baraka with bassist Lewis Worrell and also included Albert Ayler on tenor sax, Don Cherry on trumpet, and Henry Grimes as a second bass player. Perhaps Baraka's most extensive project in this genre, though, was the 1981 recording *New Music–New Poetry*, with David Murray on tenor saxophone and Steve McCall on drums. This project found Baraka working with an artist, Murray, who represented a generation that had come of age listening to the revolutionary music of Coltrane, Coleman, and Eric Dolphy while reading the revolutionary texts of Baraka. Murray was too much an original talent to be satisfied with merely imitating Coltrane, but neither was he interested in enlisting in anybody's campaign to return jazz to some presumably pristine condition prior to the Free Jazz movement's disruptions. McCall's extensive work with the trio Air helped him to develop the skills needed to work simultaneously as timekeeper and equal voice in the improvistory trio format.

There is much that is didactic in this recording, such as the possibly unintentionally funny line, "Long live the death of bourgeois clowns!" The interactions among the musicians and with the live audience very nearly overcome those more heavy-handed passages. In its best moments the recording shows us what can happen when musicians and artists attend carefully to one another's registrations of meaning. In the poem "Dope," for example, Murray and McCall build their improvisations on the melody of the hymn "Leaning on the Everlasting Arms," while Baraka shouts his exorcism of devilish evangelical prevarications that have been rendered as the truth of the moment by the media hegemony. In their performance of "Against Bourgeois Art" the musicians play decidedly non–"Top 40" lines as the poet denounces commodity art, art in which there is "not one image, except of checks / passing, Pollockdollarsigns Dekooning fortunes, Larry Rivers pots at the / end of the rain bow." This does not represent a wholesale rejection of the moment of abstract expressionism or its aftermath. Baraka's own revolutionary poetics had been partly formed in the crucible of that moment (and Rivers had produced the sets for a Baraka play in those Village days). It does represent a rejection of the reformulation of transgressive art as decoration, expensive decoration at that. A part of Baraka's mode of postmodernity is his violent reaction against the co-optation and commodification of aesthetic modernity represented by the transformation of the conflictual elements of modernism into the official culture of high modernism. Baraka's effort involves a return to the more politically radical side of modernists such as Langston Hughes, the side that was repressed as Hughes's texts were slowly (and sometimes reluctantly) canonized. As Baraka turned against cultural nationalism and adopted a Third World Marxism, he began to speak more frequently of a form of "socialist realism" than he had earlier in his career. It is important to remember, though, that his idea of socialist realism was closer to Brecht's than to that of Lukács. Even more important is the recognition that through the course of his very public transformations one thing that has remained constant in Baraka's poetics has been a commitment to the social realism of the blues, an aesthetics that roots itself in the daily lives of black Americans and that derives its forms from the vernacular inventiveness that produces unusual syntax and imagery. Thus the first lines in Baraka's trio performance of his poem "In the Tradition," which takes its title from Arthur Blythe's recordings of masterfully restaged masterpieces of jazz composition, sound very much like the early Baraka of *The Dead Lecturer* and like the late Baraka of poems such as "A Meditation on Bob Kaufman." As Murray and McCall set the tone, Baraka reaches back through the oldest of African-American signifying traditions: "Blues walk weeps ragtime / Painting slavery."

Just as musicians of David Murray's generation came of age with both Coltrane and Baraka in their ears, younger generations of poets were deeply read in the scripts of the first postmodernist African-American poets and composers. It was a natural move for poets who reached maturity reading writers like Baraka and Olson, who thought of the page as a field of operations and as a score for a performative (even when silent) reading, to take a more performative approach to their own writing than had the generation of Robert Hayden or even a poet as steeped in the oral traditions of storytelling as Sterling Brown. Following after the Beat experiments with jazz and poetry, and having been part of the record-buying public when the first black jazz-poetry records became widely available, they also naturally turned to their own experimentation with jazz forms.

Elouise Loftin, born in June of 1950, was fifteen years old when Baraka's recordings with the New York Art Quartet were released. She was only seventeen when Coltrane died. When she was twenty-five she recorded her poem "Sunni" as part of drummer Andrew Cyrille's composition "Haitian Heritage." The connection between Loftin and the first generation of the Free Jazz, or New Black Music, innovators was more than usually direct on this recording. Cyrille, the session leader for the date, had spent many years as the drummer in successive Cecil Taylor Units, and the recordings were made at Ali's Alley, whose proprietor (who also assisted Cyrille in editing and mixing the tapes) was Rashied Ali, drummer in Coltrane's later groups. The sessions additionally included David S. Ware, a tenor saxophonist, also with experience in Taylor's groups, who was subsequently to experiment with recitation on his own *Great Bliss* recordings, and vocalist Jeanne Lee, who frequently improvised unusual scat lines in a trio with Cyrille and saxophonist Jimmy Lyons. Cyrille's attitude toward ensemble work was in keeping with the Free Jazz practices of Coleman's *Free Jazz* sessions and Coltrane's *Ascension*. Cyrille has provided an overarching shape (perhaps a "metashape") for the music, but he expected his musical collaborators to be "player-composers," not simply studio musicians. His method included the poet as one of the player-composers. Elouise Loftin is listed and pictured on the album cover along with the other members of the band Maono, and where each musician's instrument is specified next to his or her name on the roster, Loftin is credited simply as "poet." Cyrille wrote in his liner notes that "many musical suggestions and ingredients used, the stylistic musical attitudes adopted, and the manifest continued interest of the improvised passages, were provided me by the players and poet assembled here." In Cyrille's eyes, then, Loftin was not just a poet brought into the studio for the purpose of reciting to a backdrop of free jamming; she was a cocomposer, and her preexisting text, the poem "Sunni," was the thematic material around which Cyrille constructed the first section of his "Haitian Heritage," which was entitled "Voices of the Lineage."

The composition commences with Jeanne Lee's wordless unaccompanied singing, as if an originary signifying voice, chanting its way into language, were calling the rest of the music into being. The drums then begin, slowly at first, sounding much like the communal drumming of West Africa and Haiti, like the Yoruba-inspired drumming of Voudoun. Lee's voice returns, in a deep register, to form a duet with the percussion. When Loftin's voice arrives, forming a triad with the percussion and with Lee's vocal soundings, we hear the first words of a recognizable language in the piece:

> She haunts the hidden stores
> for old blues tunes
> that she learns but knows well
> and sings long and loud

The two women's voices, one speaking at midrange while the other sings wordlessly in and out of the lines of verse in a lower tone, set up a commentary on one another and perform the "Voices of the Lineage" that name the song. What Cyrille is after is a linkage joining diasporic voices, joining West Africa to the Caribbean and to North America. The triad of text-reading voice, song, and percussion thus shapes itself to a sort of Triangle Trade of historic signifying. The seeds for this approach are to be found in Loftin's text, which links the blues and gri-gri of North American and Caribbean diasporic blacks to the cultural practices of an African past:

> Protected by her gri-gri
> from a truth bearing poet
> She knows no limits
> has been known to smile and has friends
> that she guards from our enemies
> Searching African soil beneath her feet
>
> (Loftin, *Barefoot Necklace* 38)

Lee's voice forms a sort of illustrative glossolalia around Loftin's voice. Lee's vocal sounds are not the traditional scatting of Be Bop. Adding sighs, grunts, growls, and angular glides to an array of techniques that also includes quite well-formed traditional tones, Lee takes lines of melody apart and uses the fragments to frame Loftin's words. When the poem comes to an end, it is with a prophetic image:

> Her mother's womb had a window
> so she knew exactly what she
> was coming into

What we come into here is an extended drum solo built over the Haitian drumming of Alphonse Cimber. While Cimber plays, Cyrille surrounds the hand drums' patterns with intricate figures on his trap drum set. Following Cyrille's section, the poem is repeated, but this time Lee stops singing and recites the poem behind Loftin, producing the effect of a kind of round or fugue. As the two women's voices wind around one another, one lower than the other, we seem again to be hearing an aural analogue of the linguistic lineage that weaves its way through the communities of the African diaspora. The two recitations rejoin each other on the affirmation "yes," a word that forms a line by itself in the printed text included in Loftin's book *Barefoot Necklace*, and the women complete the second reading of the poem, not in exact unison but just seconds apart, each imparting her own inflection to the lines. After the second reading of the text, Lee improvises another set of nonverbal melodies above a second drum solo by Cyrille, this one played primarily on the toms. Finally, Cyrille subsides, and the "Voices of the Lineage" concludes the first cycle of "Haitian Heritage" with Lee's vocals and Cimber's Haitian drum. The effect of the twelve minutes of drumming and chanting is overpowering. It is as though the initial invocation by Cimber and Lee called into the space of the music all the generations stretching from the African origins to the blues of contemporary New York. The concluding minutes of this segment are entitled "Agowé, Hūntō," or "Spirit in the Drum," and their calling leads to the second section of "Haitian Heritage," almost exactly balancing the twelve minutes of "Voices of the Lineage" and hence framing "Spirit in the Drum" between lineage and, as the second part is entitled, "Levitation."

There is another characteristic of Cyrille's use of poetry in "Haitian Heritage" that represents a pattern followed by many jazz-poetry collaborations of the past thirty years. "Sunni" is one of Loftin's most normative poems, as far as formal considerations and syntax are concerned. (In *Barefoot Necklace* this poem is part of a scattered series that includes "Sunni's Unveiling" and "What Sunni Say.") The companion poem "What Sunni Say" makes use of such syntactically disruptive lines as "shoot me for / the moon through / the burning spreading head" (31), whose enjambed prepositions rush a reader into the intriguingly rhymed "spreading head." Clearly the poem "Sunni" was selected for the recording in part because its content addresses the diasporic movement that forms the major theme of Cyrille's composition, but it would also seem that poets and jazz artists have generally tended to choose texts that seem most "accessible" to a listening audience, perhaps out of a concern that a more "difficult" poem might be lost in the music. Whether that has in fact been a motivation of the artists or not, recordings in which the poetry is as formally radical as the music, as in Baraka's work with the New York Art Quartet, are relatively rare. The most notable exceptions to this pattern occur in the works of artists such as Joseph Jarman and Cecil Taylor, artists whose own writing is as transgressive of mainstream lyrical modes as their musical compositions have been transgressive of more popularly accepted approaches to rhythm and harmony. In only one instance among the many recordings I have surveyed for this essay, a set of recordings by drummer Ronald Shannon Jackson, have I located

a nonpoet jazz artist sufficiently audacious to produce performances that deform and deconstruct poems originally written in
more accessible modes, poems by Shakespeare, Poe, and Sterling
Brown.

Although his own poetry is not nearly so technically adventurous as Baraka's, Archie Shepp was much influenced by his early
contact with Baraka, and he has devoted more of his attention as
a composer, and with greater success, to the incorporation of
spoken text within jazz performance than nearly any other jazz
artist of his era. Shepp has been far from alone as a jazz musician
who also writes verse: Sun Ra and Oliver Lake are just two of the
many musicians who have published collections of their poetry.
But Shepp has been far more prolific in composing and recording musical settings for his own texts and the texts of other
writers, and he has been more willing than any composer since
Mingus to take the risk of public recitation in the context of a
jazz concert, including a performance early in his career at the
Newport Festival.

Perhaps his earliest recording of one of his jazz texts was on
his landmark *Fire Music* sessions of 1965. Shepp recorded his
moving lament "Malcolm, Malcolm – Semper Malcolm" on
March 9, 1965, just four months before he was to produce an
unusual jazz reading as part of his concert at the Newport Jazz
Festival. According to Nat Hentoff's notes to *Fire Music*, Shepp's
first widely circulated jazz poem was originally a work dedicated
to the late Civil Rights leader Medgar Evers and formed part of a
longer work scored for alto saxophone entitled "The Funeral."
(Coincidentally, alto saxophonist Marion Brown, also a frequent
composer of jazz poems, joined Shepp in the studio for the *Fire
Music* sessions.) Following the assassination of Malcolm X, who
had, by the time of his death, rechristened himself once more
and established his new Organization for Afro-American Unity,
Shepp reshaped and retitled both his poem and the music. As
Hentoff describes it, the piece in its final form "is meant to
symbolize the various elements in Malcolm's life and spirit, and
in the life and spirit of this country's black people. Including
Charlie Parker." Hentoff quotes Shepp on the subject of this
composition as saying that Malcolm "knew the pride of black,
that négritude which was bigger than Malcolm himself. There'll
be other Malcolms."

In his 1966 essay entitled "The Changing Same," Baraka's

comments show that he had listened closely to Shepp's early recordings as part of his effort to work through the meanings of the modern and its aftermath in relationship to African-American vernacular traditions. Shepp, for Baraka, in both his public addresses and his music, articulated his writings from a point of juncture between the traditional, the modern, and the postmodern. Shepp's writing rearticulated vernacular traditions at the heart of modernity as a way of moving past the deep freeze of high modernism. Baraka wrote,

> Archie's is a secular music, that remains, demands secularity, as its insistence. He probably even has theories explaining why there is no God. But he makes obeisances to the spirits of ancient, "traditional," colored people ("Hambone," "The Mac Man," "The Picaninny") and what has happened to them from ancient times, traditionally, here (*Rufus, Swung, his face at last to the wind. Then his neck snapped* or *Malcolm* or *picked clean.*)
>
> Archie is the secular demanding clarity of itself. A reordering according to the known ("The Age of Cities"). Modern, in this sense. But of "Modern" we must begin to ask, "What does Modern Mean?" and "What is the Future?" or "Where Does One Want to Go?" or "What Does One *Want* to happen?" You hear in Archie's music moans that are pleas for understanding. (*Black Music* 196)

Baraka specifically cites Shepp's "Malcolm" in this context of wondering toward a black postmodernity, and Shepp's *Fire Music* has exercised considerable influence upon subsequent African-American innovators. For one example, Nathaniel Mackey's long-running journal of new arts and writings, *Hambone,* takes its name partly from the very first composition on *Fire Music.*

Though he originally composed the piece for alto saxophone, Shepp plays tenor saxophone on the reformulated "Malcolm, Malcolm – Semper Malcolm," beginning his solo in the upper register, as if in recollection of the earlier version. The realization of this jazz text opens with Shepp reciting to the accompaniment of drummer J. C. Moses and bassist David Izenzon, one of a series of distinctive players of that instrument who worked in the Ornette Coleman group over the years. This trio is a far different line-up from the septet that appears on the rest of the album; "Malcolm" was recorded in a separate session almost a month after the other compositions. Shepp's opening statement seems a description of both jazz and the lives of black Americans: "A song is not what it seems." This opening stanza forms the connection between the life of Charlie ("Bird") Parker and the life of Malcolm X. Izenzon quietly bows his instrument as Shepp's ironic statement enters our ears: "Bird whistled, while even America listened." Izenzon then begins to pluck the strings of his bass while Shepp's poem takes on an increasingly ominous air, yoking together the slow death of the never adequately understood Parker with the sudden murder of Malcolm X: "We are murdered in amphitheaters." Moses plays quick, low tones on the tom-toms with his mallets as Shepp's poem concludes in elliptical lines strongly reminiscent of Baraka and Olson: "Philadelphia . . . 1945 . . . Malcolm . . . My people . . . Dear God . . . Malcolm." Some of the precise allusions may finally elude listeners, but it is probably significant that Shepp's family moved to North Philadelphia around 1945. It could be that the poet's lament includes the loss of the optimism of his own youth, a period when the Be Bop revolution pointed the way toward possible new forms for black expression in America, and when the massive oppressions of racism might not have yet become fully apparent to the young musician. It could also be his way of recalling a period of community that existed among Northern blacks in cities during the war years. As so many white journalists have written of the assassination of President Kennedy as marking a certain loss of innocence for postwar America (though we must always ask Toni Morrison's question, "What is it that Americans are always supposed to be so innocent *of?*"), Shepp's poem marks a nearly final loss of trust in liberal promises of national amelioration. The tearing tone of Shepp's final words, "Dear God . . . Malcolm," melds into the prayerful, high-pitched notes of Shepp's saxophone. The saxophone lines continue the angular and elliptical motions of the poem, forming wordlessly the moans and pleas that Baraka described in Shepp's playing. The melody also provides some sense of an answer to the poem's prayers. The last, insistent chorus, formed of staccato notes linked with a voicelike glide, ends in an upward motion and on an unresolved chord. Instead of the descending "Amen" of most hymns, this piece ends in open ascent, as if the notes indeed pointed in the direction of "other Malcolms" to come.

Tragically, that musical response to the prayers of his own

poem has itself been elided on a subsequent release of "Malcolm, Malcolm – Semper Malcolm." When Harvey Robert Kubernick compiled his compact disk anthology *JazzSpeak* in 1991, a collection inserted in the stream of newly popular spoken-word recordings and attempting to provide some historical context for that stream, he included a violently truncated version of Shepp's composition. The piece leads off Kubernick's anthology, giving some indication of its importance in his view, but just as black poetry has too often been eliminated from Beat histories, Shepp's music has been eliminated from this track. Following the final words of the poem, we hear the first high-pitched moments of Shepp's entrance on saxophone while J. C. Moses lightly touches his cymbals. Then, the track is truncated. In this replication, truly "a song is not what it seems." Kubernick's notes to his collection give unwary consumers no hint of this radical editing, and the audience for *JazzSpeak* will have no way of knowing that the jazz has been jettisoned in favor of the speech. As jazz texts enter the digital age, it appears that artists now are to be murdered on the information superhighways instead of in the amphitheaters.

"Music is not sociology," writes Nat Hentoff in the liner notes to *New Thing at Newport,* the live recording produced from performances of groups led by Coltrane and Shepp at the 1965 festival, "but," he goes on, speaking of Shepp's presentation of his poem "Scag," "when a man can transmute what he has seen in the life of the streets into musical form and substance, the result is art of particularly penetrating and shaking relevance – as in this composition." It may be that Newport audiences did not generally purchase festival tickets in the hope of being penetrated and shaken, but Shepp's unusual performance met with enthusiastic applause. Joe Chambers opens the composition with sets of sharp, double beats on his snare drum, with Bobby Hutcherson joining in unison on the vibraphone. Chambers moves to cymbals as Barre Phillips plays a bowed solo lasting nearly a minute. The rhythm then smooths out as Hutcherson plays glistening runs on the vibes, allowing the chords to shimmer against the stark background. The form of "Scag" reverses the procedure of "Malcolm." On that piece the music seemed to arrive in answer to the poem's pleas. On "Scag," the instruments set up a rhythm that prepares the way for the poem's opening pun. Shepp commences his reading with the line, "Where tracks is, money ain't." Since the poem is entitled "Scag," we know that the surface reference of this line is to the needle tracks in an addict's arm, and to the impossibility of maintaining both a heroin habit and the financial means to support one's life. We also, though, at once begin to revise our reception of the musical passage that has preceded the poem as we now recognize that the drums and the vibes were miming the sounds of a train passing over its tracks, and so the connotation of being on the wrong, unmoneyed side of the tracks arises from the referential possibilities of the music in association with the metaphorical workings of the spoken text. (Further evidence that the two should always be heard together: in light of *JazzSpeak*'s later elimination of Shepp's music, we might now uncover an additional punning possibility in the lines of "Scag." The "tracks" may also refer to commercially recorded music. The tracks may supplant the musician himself, leaving him unremunerated, perhaps even unremembered.) This poem again contains a personal allusion:

Where we were hungriest, we fought,
and some of us died.
Yeah, outright, on buses to Harlem and sometimes
trolleys that led only to 12th and Master
or Germantown.

When Shepp's family moved to Philadelphia, they lived in the Germantown area, which he described to Baraka in an interview for *Black Music* as "mostly a white bourgeois area, but there were these pocket ghettoes like the one we used to live in, right there among the whites. They called the ghetto I lived in 'The Brickyard' " (146). Throughout Shepp's recitation of "Scag" the band repeats its initial, almost trance-inducing rhythm, keeping up the clacking sound of train wheels on the tracks as Shepp links the past history of oppression to a present in which the drug that helped to kill Parker is loosed in a community, inducing lethargy and forgetfulness:

But we never forgot.
We remembered this:
My sister raped,
My fathers bled to death.
And as our various bloods commingled on the ceiling
there, I said,
"Scag ain't dope,
it's death."

Shepp does not produce the past as an excuse for present-day inaction or drug abuse. Rather, he traces an historical lineage in which the sale of heroin is shown to be of a piece with slavery, lynching, rape, and murder, shown to be the extension of a past the nation has refused to face. The poem and its music are an intervention and a call. The poem ends with a sharp drum roll and a crashing cymbal, followed by almost a death rattle on the edge of the snare and a final blow against the bass drum. In an inspired segue, this composition is followed in the recorded version of the concert by the song "Call Me by My Rightful Name," about which Shepp told Hentoff, "At times I like to do something pretty." "Scag" is the record of a moment of improvisation formed within a scored theme and a written text. As if to underscore the very materiality of Shepp's text, as if recording the writerly nature of his work with his ensemble, we can hear the sound of his pages as he turns them before the microphone in the course of the group's improvisations.

During the same year that Shepp recorded these early experiments with his own jazz texts, he was also experimenting with composing musical settings inspired by the writings of others. Perhaps the most ambitious of these is the suitelike title composition of the 1965 recording "On This Night (If That Great Day Would Come)." There are a number of factors that make this composition unusual among Shepp's works. Besides featuring arrangements inspired by the canonical texts of a predecessor, this is Shepp's first recording with a soprano vocalist, Christine Spencer, and it is one of the few releases on which Shepp can be heard playing the piano. Both Rashied Ali and Joe Chambers are heard on drums here, with Chambers playing tympani, and Bobby Hutcherson is again present on vibraphone. Henry Grimes plays the bass. "On This Night" was written in tribute to W. E. B. DuBois, and Shepp explained to Hentoff, again the author of the liner notes, that this piece formed the core of the album. Shepp's piano playing, which provides the first notes of "On This Night," initially shows the strong influence of Cecil Taylor, with whom Shepp had been working and studying in the early 1960s. Shepp's playing follows more traditional harmonic patterns as he shifts into the melody of the composition's first theme, joining Spencer's singing of the unrhymed text. At the close of each sung passage the piano and voice form major chords, but between these passages Shepp reverts to nearly atonal piano passages, and the tympani provide swooping tones as Chambers tightens the drumheads after striking them. In some ways, Shepp has constructed this composition along the lines of the sacred and the secular, recalling Baraka's observations on Shepp's relationship to the modern and what might come afterward. As the text is sung, we hear a kind of postmodern adaptation of the sorrow songs that DuBois wrote about with such intensity in *The Souls of Black Folk*.

The lengthy interlude between the passages of text is given over to a rousing and inventive blues. (This composition is followed on the recording by a tribute to blues harmonica player and singer Sonny Boy Williamson.) During this blues interlude, Shepp moves to his tenor saxophone. He begins by building a lovely chorus in concert with Hutcherson's vibes. On subsequent verses he plays in a style that can only be termed gut-bucket. Drawing on his extensive experience playing Rhythm and Blues as a young man, Shepp ranges his solos across the history of the form, tearing at the boundaries of bar lines and chords, almost spinning out of the confines of the form and into something approaching Coltrane's *Ascension*. All the while, though, Grimes's walking bass and Hutcherson's chords keep calling Shepp's solos back to their blues source. It is a virtuoso passage equal to the work of Coltrane himself. As Shepp's blues resolve themselves in a return to the chords of the chorus, the band turns a corner, and we are back in the opening mode. This time, as Christine Spencer again makes classic lyrics out of the prose of social commentary, Shepp follows her into the melody on saxophone rather than piano. His quavering high notes are an emotional undergirding of the perfectly formed tones of the soprano. The two voices together unite two classic modes of black expression, suggesting that the sacred song of future emancipation, of that "great getting-up morning," finds its telos in the creative capacities of the secular vernacular, art built out of the inventions of daily life.

"The Wedding" is another Archie Shepp jazz text recorded in live performance, this time at the Both/And Club in San Francisco during a 1966 engagement. The San Francisco dates saw Shepp performing with Roswell Rudd and Lewis Worrell, half of the New York Art Quartet, which had recorded Baraka's "Black Dada Nihilismus" just the previous year. Rounding out the group were Beaver Harris on drums and Donald Garrett, a second bass player. "The Wedding" is a narrative poem by Shepp that only hints at the projective techniques of Baraka's early work, but Shepp's composition partakes of the ominous tensions of the jazz version of "Black Dada Nihilismus." The two bass players provide the only accompaniment to Shepp's dramatic reading, one bowing his instrument while the other, more quietly, plucks at his strings. (Patricia Willard's notes to the resulting recording state that the sessions used two bass players on every cut *except* "The Wedding," but she has either failed to listen attentively or is confusing the recording with some live session that did only use one bass, as two bassists are plainly audible on this track.) "The Wedding" is related to "Scag" in that it traces the relationship between the present curse of drugs and the past of social oppression. Shepp intones his text in a tremulous voice, and at the outset it sounds as if he is introducing a fairly conventional narration:

> We sat ten abreast
> On logs that stretched
> The entire length
> Of the room.
>
> (*Live in San Francisco*)

In the end, though, the poem, built around the story of a drug addict's wife giving birth on a church floor, functions more through the accumulation of imagery and discursive statement than through narrative movement. It is as if the motion of the music completed the temporal figurations begun by Shepp's first words. The action of the poem is witnessed by a chorus of older people, the shouting sisters of the church, and "the steely black men whose corned haunches ached from the cold." (Since no printed text is available, I will indicate line breaks in this and other quotations at the point of vocal pauses in the recitations.) In this we see again that obeisance to the spirit of the ancients in the context of a secular modernity that Baraka found so fecund. Houston Baker suggests that "The blending . . . of class and mass – poetic *mastery* discovered as a function of deformative *folk* sound – constitutes the essence of black discursive modernism" (*Modernism* 93). In bringing the sacred and the secular into explosive contact on the floor of the imagined church in his poem, Shepp provides that blending of class and mass. In breaking the already deformative forms of folk traditions in music, in

was certainly the recording *Attica Blues*. In the post–*Sergeant Pepper's* era this type of work was popularly known as a "concept album," but Shepp's predecessors in this form of serial composition were Duke Ellington and Charles Mingus rather than the Beatles. *Attica Blues* is a series of works for large ensemble, each half of the album beginning with a hard-driving blues chorus and concluding with a lighter, upbeat melody. In each half, the opening blues is followed by a short recitation of a text written by William G. Harris. The range of musical compositions links the sacred and secular traditions of black American music and embeds an orchestral jazz history within the context of contemporary music and political statement. Part of Shepp's project in presenting such a broad spectrum of African-American musics in linked series was to foreground the cultural inventions by means of which communities create and sustain themselves. In that same spirit, Shepp recruited "amateurs" to participate in these performances, making the music something in which all could take part, not just an artifact rendered by professionals so that an audience could "appreciate" it. Famed civil rights lawyer William Kuntsler was brought into the studio to read the brief intertexts by Harris, marking a double tribute to Kunstler and to the political activists he has defended over the years. In the same spirit, seven-year-old Waheeda Massey sang the lead vocal for her father, Cal Massey's, "Quiet Dawn," perhaps the most optimistic, and certainly the prettiest, composition on the album, and her presence points to a continuing lineage of improvisation and community making. The longest spoken text on this recording is Bartholomew Gray's "Invocation to Mr. Parker," a tribute to Charlie Parker recited to music composed by Shepp and performed by Jimmy Garrison on bass and Marion Brown on flute and percussion. (Brown had played with Shepp in the saxophone section of Coltrane's *Ascension,* and just as Shepp's first studio recording as a group leader was a tribute entitled *Four for Trane,* Brown continued the tradition by entitling his debut album *Three for Shepp.*) Gray's poem is fairly traditional in form and works within the music much as Hughes worked within Mingus's music on the *Weary Blues.* Gray's poem follows the blues structure of statement, restatement, and resolution, echoing, without exactly repeating, the blues forms that anchor the sessions. The recitation is placed in the midst of Shepp's musical composition "Steam," and, unlike the reading on Miles Davis's "Inamorata," which seems to interrupt the music more than anything else, this textual interlude is mixed and produced in such a way as to sound like a blues counterstatement unfolded from within the soft chords of "Steam."

Three years after *Attica Blues*, Shepp again built a suite juxtaposing varied African diasporic musics and encompassing a poetic text not written by himself. Whereas the blues formed the root strata for *Attica Blues*, Afro-Brazilian music, particularly the samba, formed the motivic structures for *There's a Trumpet in My Soul*. The poem "The Year of the Rabbit" was written and recited by Bill Hasson. In the same way that Gray's "Invocation to Mr. Parker" was made to seem an unfolding of the interior structures of Shepp's "Steam," Hasson's recitation is deftly mixed as an interlude within the serial structures of Charles Majid Greenlee's musical composition "Zaid." While the second part of "Zaid" fades slowly, Shepp's composition rises in the aural stream to accompany Hasson's speaking voice. Brandon Ross's guitar and Shepp's soprano saxophone are the most prominent voices in the rich and slightly echoic music around Hasson, whose tenor voice fits well with the registers of those instruments. As the piece progresses, Greenlee's trombone rises among the guitar and saxophone lines, recalling his "Zaid," which is only in abeyance, not yet completed. Hasson's poem is rather unremarkable in itself, but as it describes its own purpose, "to conjure up love in a veil of despair," the almost veiling mists of the music around the reading voice lend the poem a mystique and a majesty it might not be able to support on its own. Hasson's reading is lyrical, and his contribution has been engineered seamlessly into the mix.

In August of that same year, 1975, Shepp recorded another of his own poems as a jazz text, again situating it within a longer musical composition. Recorded in Milan, Italy, Shepp's *a Sea of Faces* derives its title from the poem that he recites within Semenya McCord's beautiful musical composition "Song for Mozambique." Much as *There's a Trumpet in My Soul* used Hasson's poem as part of a project linking the African diasporic cultures of Brazil and North America, Shepp's poem "A Sea of Faces" is used to join African-American music to its African origins. McCord's "Song for Mozambique" is opened by Shepp's soprano saxophone playing the theme. Bunny Foy then restates the theme, singing a breathy acapella. The song introduces itself, providing a veritable definition of the Swahili word for freedom,

Uhuru. While Foy returns to the melody, humming the verse a second time wordlessly, Shepp recites his poem, a poem that repeats and glosses the word *Uhuru* and that addresses itself. What we might call "auto-apostrophe" was a technique of blues singers long before poststructuralists turned their attention to *mise en abyme.* Inside his poem, Shepp addresses his poem, soliciting its performance of an aesthetic and political ideology:

> Rhyme Pome
> Nigger ain't no more
> He's Black that's sure –
> That stole from Me
> My (w)hole world
> A mystery
> I . . . (k)new

Shepp goes on in a second apostrophe to address the absent/ present spirit of Coltrane, whose trace is audible in Shepp's own saxophone playing. When the text is completed, the opening song is repeated, and then an alternating chant of "Uhuru" and "Freedom" is set up among other voices of the ensemble within the harmonic contours of "Song for Mozambique." One of the male voices, possibly that of Rafi Taha, repeats Shepp's poem a second time, his voice mixed a bit farther back. In a holographic reproduction on the album sleeve, the poem is repeated yet again as calligraphic chant. These overlays of text and song, surrounded by chant and script, text addressing itself as it addresses itself to us, resist any attempt to erect defensible borders between song and sign, speech and writing, music and text. The freedom of the jazz text is the marked freedom of interlingual, transnational concourse:

> Shouting – Uhuru!
> While mute Peruggia
> Stands
> Sunk in a sea of faces
> uplifted
> singing
> today – Uhuru

A city can stand sunk. It can be sunk in a sea of uplifted faces, and it can be uplifted in song. With each reiteration within the recording, and with each replaying of the chant, the signifying motions of the musical text take a different direction. It is always possible to jump the tracks.

Shepp's frequent collaborator in the early days of the New Black Music, Marion Brown, shared his interest in text-based materials. Though Brown generally has worked with verbal texts he has not written himself, his deep and abiding involvement with texts has caused J. B. Figi, writing in the notes to Brown's *Geechee Recollections,* to term him a musician and a poet insepara-bly. "A sense of poetry inhabits his music," according to Figi, "and it's the honing of an immediate art by a reflective one which gives that music its special character: succinct, lyric, delib-erate." Though one might well dispute Figi's separation of art forms along a too neat divide, his comments echo Baraka's locat-ing of New Black Music at the intersection of reflection and expression. In 1966, Baraka said that Brown, "having played with Shepp . . . and shedded with Pharaoh is moving, very quickly" (*Black Music* 134). Brown was among the musicians at the New Black Music concert in 1965, and he later credited Baraka with having introduced him to the work of Jean Toomer, one of the more productive introductions of Baraka's life.

Perhaps Marion Brown's best-known and most significant work is a series of recordings made between 1970 and 1974 and collectively known as the Georgia Trilogy. Jean Toomer's *Cane* is the central impetus for the trilogy and is directly invoked in the second of the works, but the Georgia Trilogy is not, strictly speaking, about Toomer and his work, nor is it limited to an aural tour of Georgia. As Figi puts it, "Just as many *down home* ways originated *back home.* Georgia is Marion's corridor to Africa." For Toomer, the Georgia turnpike that runs as a symbol through the locale of his stories and poems (and reappears as Georgia Avenue in the Washington, D.C., episodes of *Cane*) grows out of a goat path in Africa. For Brown, Toomer's poetic text was a path into his own past and into the cultural past of his race. Following an extended period of work in Europe, Brown and his wife spent a season in Atlanta, and the music of the Georgia Trilogy grew out of Brown's return to the ground of his childhood and his meditations upon Toomer's poems of the Georgia past.

Appropriately enough, the only overt reference to Toomer and *Cane* appears in the centerpiece of the Georgia Trilogy, *Geechee Recollections.* The first record in the trilogy, *Afternoon of a Georgia Faun,* makes no specific allusions to Toomer at all, and yet it is motivated from start to finish by Brown's ongoing conversation with his literary and musical modernist predecessors. The title of this recording (which is also the title of the first of the two compositions that comprise the album) is a virtual demonstration of the polysemous nature of signifying. The obvious allusion is to Vaslav Nijinsky and the Ballets Russes. The period of collaboration between the Ballets Russe and Igor Stravinsky in Paris was one of those transformative moments of rupture pointed to by cultural historians as marking the advent of European modernism. The violent public debates over Nijinsky's choreography and Stravinski's music paralleled American responses to the Armory Show (or later responses to the music of Taylor and Coleman, for that matter). Marion Brown's borrowing of the title resembles Nijinski's own signifying appropriations, for among the Russian choreographer's earliest public works was his 1912 performance of his ballet *L'Aprés-midi d'un faune*, an adaptation of Claude Debussy's 1894 work, *Prélude à l'aprés-midi d'un faune*. Nijinsky, in 1912, performed what was later taken to be a paradigmatically modernist transgression by reformulating Debussy's musical text and restaging the characteristically modernist Grecian forms of movement and mime. Almost half a century later, Brown recontextualized modernity by reappropriating Nijinsky and Stravinski's series of appropriations. Stravinski, of course, achieved some of his modernist effects by way of his appropriations of black American jazz. Brown's act was not mere parody (nor was it really pastiche). He, like so many of his contemporaries, uncovered the Africanity of modernist art (most visually evident in the paintings and stage sets of Picasso and Cocteau) and at the same time reasserted the modernity of black Americans. Again, this recontextualizing of the modern in an "afterward" of cultural history is one mark of an African-American postmodernity.

Like the works of such late nineteenth-century composers as Debussy, Brown's "*Afternoon of a Georgia Faun* is a tone poem," as Brown says in his own description that accompanies the recording: "It depicts nature and the environment in Atlanta. The vocalists sing wordless syllables. The composition begins with a percussion section that suggests rain drops – wooden rain drops. The second section is after the rain. Metallic sounds that suggest light." The wordless text of *Afternoon of a Georgia Faun* turns out to be a prelude to the spoken texts of the trilogy's later works.

Like Debussy's *Prélude* in its relation to Nijinsky's adaptations, the nonverbal sung signs of this first jazz text serve as the condition of possibility for the readings of the later jazz texts. They are the preverbal signing to the postsinging signifying of the subsequent compositions.

Afternoon of a Georgia Faun is a veritable guide to the New Black Music of the post-Bop second generation. The musicians here gathered included Anthony Braxton and Bennie Maupin, who joined Brown on reed instruments; Chick Corea on piano; Andrew Cyrille on drums; and Jeanne Lee as the chief source of those wordless vocables. The band also included Larry Curtis, William Green, Jack Gregg, Billy Malone, and Gayle Palmoré. Everyone played percussion. Brown adopted the ensemble procedures of the large-group compositions of Coltrane and Coleman. As Brown explains it, "the music . . . is a collective experience involving six players, two vocalists, and three assistants. Although I am responsible for initiating the music, I take no credit for the results. Whatever they may be, it goes to the musicians collectively." Brown's introduction of "assistants" is an evolution of the Free Jazz ideology beyond what its progenitors had attempted. The assistants were, as Brown describes their function, "not actually musicians, but people who have a sense of rhythm and melody. My idea here is that it is possible for non-musicians to participate in a musical experience without being technically proficient." Brown also introduced a number of homemade instruments, including his "Top O'Lin," along with traditional African instruments such as the Zomari. These developments were not a naive attempt to rejoin an idealized African community of performance but part of the continuing reinscription of African traditions of music making, in which the community participates directly in the performance and in which innovation takes place within the spaces of repeated forms. When Brown closes his notes on his use of "non-musicians" with the advice, "Try it," he is not addressing himself solely to other jazz composers; he is advising the audience to take an active role in the production of their musical experience. That there is a place for the literary artist in this project is hinted at by the fact that the photograph of Brown and his wife that appears on the album cover was taken by William Melvin Kelley, the author of *Dunfords Travels Everywheres.*

The second record, *Geechee Recollections* (1973), where texts by

Toomer appear within the musical composition, finds Brown becoming more deeply involved with the avant-garde approach to ensemble work championed by Chicago's Association for the Advancement of Creative Musicians (AACM). *Afternoon of a Georgia Faun* included AACM member Anthony Braxton on saxophone. Two more veterans of the Chicago organization, Leo Smith and Steve McCall, joined Brown's group for *Geechee Recollections*. By bringing together such compositions as "Buttermilk Bottom" and "Tokalokaloka," Brown once more drew out the diasporic continuity of international black musics. Further, this recording includes percussion work on traditional instruments of the Akan peoples of Ghana, played by Abraham Kobena Adzenyah. Mirroring its placement at the midpoint of the Georgia Trilogy, Toomer's text "Karintha" appears as the second of three compositions on the first side of *Geechee Recollections,* the first song, "Once upon a Time" (identified as a children's tale), serving as a prelude to Toomer's fantasia about a girl who was rushed too soon into womanhood. Poet Bill Hasson performs the reading of "Karintha," and he is also enlisted as another "assistant" playing percussion instruments. In J. B. Figi's view, "The music is more than incidental to this presentation. It acts as a responsive audience for the storyteller, gathering around Hasson's voice, reinforcing the meaning of the words."

The voice of Hasson reappears on the third recording of the Georgia Trilogy, *Sweet Earth Flying,* but the idea of the music's serving as a reinforcement for the meaning of the words is problematized by the fact that the opening words of "Prince Willie" will be incomprehensible to most listeners. Perhaps, then, the music of this piece will serve to direct the production of meaning *for* the words. Whereas Lee sang wordless syllables on *Afternoon of a Georgia Faun,* Hasson reads a polyglot text that sounds like an existing language to most auditors but remains opaque and ultimately untranslatable. What Hasson has done at the beginning of his text is to fuse "real" words from existing languages with invented words designed to sound Africanesque, recalling Stephen Chambers's 1969 poem "Her" and creating a sort of imaginary Creole text. Acklyn Lynch, author of the program notes for *Sweet Earth Flying,* described Hasson's opening strategy as "attempting to construct a musical language for the speaking voice that reflects linguistic patterns of the African diaspora. He blends words together from West Africa, South America (especially Brazil), the Caribbean and North America . . . and this reminds us that the line between singing and speech in the Black World is very thin." As Lee and Loftin demonstrated on Cyrille's "Haitian Heritage," for black artists it is a thin line between song and speech indeed, and it is a highly permeable line. Likewise, as these jazz texts show over and over again, the line between the written and the oral is so thin as to render any opposition between the two insupportable. Bill Hasson *reads* "Sweet Willie" on this recording. The opening words that he has written he chants in a signifying chain that the listener probably cannot decode but that forms a linguistic link between the language communities of the African diaspora.

Sweet Earth Flying is, like Rudd's "Sweet V," a suite. Hasson's reading occurs in Part IV. Part II has been deleted from the recording. The notes indicate that Part II was recorded at the same session and with the same personnel as the other segments, but it is marked by its absence from the final version, the sequential numbers of the remaining parts pointing to the missing movement. As Part IV begins, AACM organizer Muhal Richard Abrams plays a recurring $\frac{6}{8}$ pattern on the electric piano, while McCall solos on small percussion instruments and Hasson recites his heteroglossic text, in which recognizably Yoruba terms like *Orisha* jostle against vaguely Swahili-sounding syllables. What makes the stream of language fragments and of sounds aspiring to the state of language most effective in this passage, and this was singled out for notice by Brown in his own commentary, is that Hasson has constructed the rhythm of his introductory vocables around the $\frac{6}{8}$ figure that Abrams repeats. With the addition of major chords on top of the rolling piano figure, Hasson moves into English recitation, still interspersed with non-English sounds. No copy of the text is printed with the recording, but what Hasson reads here sounds something like this:

> Boast holes and hanging
> Playing host to nost
> And it's all
> About
> Loving

The opening two lines of the stanza are far more compelling in their mystery and assonance than the all-English stanza that completes Hasson's poem. Brown enters on saxophone at the end of the text, and as he solos Hasson repeats the non-English lines of his poem in the background. As Part IV continues, this technique renders the poet's speaking voice a second soloing instrument, with Brown's horn playing above the piano and drums. What Hasson demonstrates most effectively is that the nonsinging voice, in its rhythms and inflections, can produce as much musical interest as the scat singing of a Betty Carter or an Eddie Jefferson. It is not a purely musical interest, because the listener's mind continually attempts to fit the opaque word sounds inside of some meaning-making structures. Cecil Taylor and Ronald Shannon Jackson were to make yet more radical assaults upon general assumptions about what the human voice should do in music with their own jazz texts. Though Hasson's poem has little to recommend it as a reading text in itself, the rendition of the poem on *Sweet Earth Flying* is one of the more intriguing listening experiences in the genre of spoken-word recordings.

Marion Brown also followed the example of his friend Archie Shepp in taking his jazz texts out of the recording studio and before live audiences in concert. After moving to a teaching post in New England, Brown met the poet and critic Joanne Braxton (probably best known to literary scholars today as the author of *Black Women Writing Autobiography*), and the two of them collaborated on performances. As has been true of the majority of jazz texts here surveyed, the procedure was that Brown would create musical compositions based on preexisting texts by Braxton. The most readily available document of these collaborations is the tape of a National Public Radio (NPR) broadcast of a concert featuring Brown and Braxton at the University of Michigan before an even more than usually enthusiastic Ann Arbor audience. The concert was a presentation of the university's Bright Moments series, named in honor of the late Roland Kirk, and it was broadcast nationally in the *Jazz Alive* program on NPR with A. B. Spellman as host. This concert may have had the largest national audience of any jazz and poetry performance, thanks to the public network's willingness in those days to bring nontraditional programming to a mass audience. The first portion of the concert is a solo presentation by Brown on reed instruments. In the second segment Brown is joined onstage by the poet and two drummers. The first piece performed with this configuration is Braxton's serial poem "Conversion." Braxton does not identify the three sections of the poem as she reads them, but pauses in her voice and shifts in the music signal transitions in the text. Brown plays flute as Braxton begins the first segment:

early   mist
bring back the dawn
i
follow flock

(Braxton 48)

The poem is a narrative, but it is a mystical narrative whose forward motion is registered in imagery that often elides normal syntax. The lines sound a bit like Baraka at the beginning of "In the Tradition." As Braxton reads, Brown's flute darts in and out of her text: "reach blues ancestor." Braxton's is a specifically female meditation, and, unlike Baraka's, it is located in Southern marshlands. She describes a primordial fall, alluding to slavery and loss, as against the music her lyric reads,

to fall from such a height
nobody singing   nobody singing
down the lean black chute
out of night into the heat of the day

(50)

Brown switches to saxophone midway through the poem, as the text shifts its tone to sharper phonetic registers, invoking words like "whips," "cracks," and "mocassins." When Braxton reaches the last line, the music ceases, leaving her voice alone in air as she describes a refuge, "an altar in the wood" (51). With a drumbeat the piece concludes. Also performed at this concert was the Braxton poem "The Palace at Four A.M.," with its description of "a house / where birds fly in and out," read to the clocklike ticking of a drum and a tenor saxophone solo by Brown.

If Brown and Shepp have worked more extensively with texts than most other jazz composers of their generation, perhaps no black poet whose works began to appear in print after World War II has recorded as many jazz texts as has Jayne Cortez. Indeed, Cortez has recorded nearly all of her published poems in jazz arrangements. Beginning in 1974 with *Celebrations and Solitudes*, Cortez has released four collections of these jazz works, including *There It Is, Unsubmissive Blues,* and *Maintain Control.* Some scholarly confusion has already gathered around this neglected body of works. D. H. Melhem's discography that appears with her interviews with Cortez gives a 1975 date for *Celebrations and Solitudes* (211). It is not surprising that she should do so, as later Cortez albums and her *New and Selected Poems* also give this date for her first album. The recording itself, however, a Strata-East release, indicates that it was both recorded and released in 1974. (Wallenstein has the correct date in his short discography.) Nearly all of these recordings were organized and produced by the poet, and as a result she has been able to integrate her writings with the musical compositions far more effectively and with greater variety than most other poets who have recorded with jazz musicians. She has also been more directly involved than usual in the preparation of the music. The notes to *There It Is,* her 1982 release, indicate that all but two of the musical works were "collectively composed." The two that were not were both composed by Cortez's son, Denardo Coleman.

Following in the pattern of such artists as Betty Carter, Mingus, and Baraka, Cortez realized early on that black artists would require full control over the production of their works if they were to escape the censorious mediations of white editing and of capitalist recording industry demands for certain modes of product. Her response was to form the Bola Press, the imprint for all of her recordings after *Celebrations and Solitudes* and for all of her books prior to *Coagulations.* In addition to controlling the production of her jazz texts, she was able to determine the presentation of her printed works, many of which appeared with illustrations by her husband, Melvin Edwards.

Unlike David Henderson on Coleman's "Science Fiction," Cortez's recorded reading to music differs little from her unaccompanied reading style, but then, her works are so deeply rooted in music, and dramatic modes of presentation are so fundamental to her writing, that her texts seem to be written as acapella music. Cortez is one of the more "tonal" readers of poetry among contemporary artists. Continuing the poetics of the Beats and of Olson's projective verse, she writes her lines in breath units, and the measures of these units are usually derived from African-American music. In public readings, Cortez tends usually to read these lines in descending pitch sequences. She reads a first line, organized around one tone and then reads the next descending from a lower starting pitch. Her lines are, in this sense, chantlike, allowing for melodic effects within the chosen tonal range of the individual line. Additionally, Cortez has from her earliest days as a poet taken music as both the subject matter and the aesthetic correlative for her writing.

The works she collected in her first chapbook, *Pissstained Stairs and the Monkey Man's Wares,* published in 1969, had originally been composed for performance by the Watts Repertory Theater Company, a group Cortez had helped to form during her Los Angeles years, for a special production "dealing with Black music through poetry" (qtd. in Melhem 209). As she explained to Melhem in their 1982 interviews, "I started writing poetry about my relationship to Black music, talking about the rhythms or what I liked about it, and of course, talking about the musicians who play the music. It's like praise poetry, the old African praise poetry" (203). Trained in music when young, Cortez naturally gravitated toward the writing of lyric verse, and her extensive friendships with jazz musicians provided her with entrée into a community of potential collaborators. She was married, in the 1950s, to Ornette Coleman, who appeared along with cellist Abdul Wadud (Cortez also played cello at one time) on the 1986 recordings of Cortez's poetry, *Maintain Control.* The son of this marriage, Denardo Coleman, began playing the drums early on. By the time he was ten years old he was already playing on recordings with his father. (The first of these, *The Empty Foxhole,* includes in its liner notes rare samples of Ornette Coleman's poetry.) Since then, Denardo has continued to play in nearly all of his father's bands, and he has played on each of his mother's albums, beginning with *Unsubmissive Blues* in 1980. Both Coleman's biographer, John Litweiler, and Melhem are strangely reticent about this marriage. Melhem does not even name Coleman in her biographical introduction to her interviews with Cortez, stating only that Cortez "was married early, in 1954, to a jazz musician" (182). Whatever problems may have surrounded the marriage and subsequent divorce of these two artists, their early participation in communities of avant-garde black artists as a couple was surely a formative experience for their later works.

In listening to Cortez's series of recordings sequentially, we can see a steady growth in the complexity of musical arrangement, whereas the poet's vocal approach, with small variations, holds fairly constant. This is somewhat analogous to the way that

Miles Davis steadily shifted the forms of music and instrumentation surrounding his own trumpet lines in the last decades of his career. In her first sessions, Cortez was accompanied only by a bass player, Richard Davis. Eight years later, when she recorded *There It Is,* Cortez surrounded her reading voice with no fewer than seven instrumentalists, playing in complex "harmolodic" modes. (That album, I would venture, is the demonstration of the harmolodic approach to jazz text that Coleman's "Science Fiction" could have been.) Cortez has put a great deal of thought and work into achieving the balance that is audible in her production of these albums. As she told Melhem,

> The part that is hard is stretching the human voice. Everybody else in the group has another kind of voice, a musical instrument that's much louder than yours (*laughing*). That's the problem. How not to let the different pitch levels control your work. Most of the musicians who've played with me have all been musicians who play jazz. They are used to inventing off of different rhythm patterns and different sounds. So they relate to what I'm doing in the same way. They interject their own sound and attitudes. I like working with music. It's a collective experiment. A collective composition. (204)

One means by which Cortez directed the pitch and rhythm of these collaborative improvisations was by controlling them in the initial act of composition. Like any singer composing for her own voice, Cortez constructed the melopoeia of her poems to suit her own register and measured them to her own breathing, which sometimes resulted in Whitmanian long lines and other times led to the scoring of subunit lines within the same breath measure, reading like Williams Carlos Williams's late, variable-foot lines. The writing of the lyric text preceded the composition of the instrumental music, but the music resituated the reading, making it a different poem. "The work sounded new and improvised," Cortez says of her performance with a group of musicians in a concert that was part of Joseph Papp's New York Shakespeare Festival Public Theater, "because the approach to the music was new" (Melhem 204). Sometimes, as in the group's performance of "I See Chano Pozo" at that concert, Cortez improvised new lines or interpolated additional words, but her sense of orality and improvisation did not oppose those to the written. For Cortez, each performance of a poem presents an opportunity for signifying improvisation, since each reading is built upon the traces of, and alters, prior readings. Even more importantly, as Cortez insists to Melhem, "of course the work is improvisational before it is written on paper" (204). Even the most determinedly improvising musicians make notes and pass them to one another, and Cortez improvises always with pen in hand.

In her early work Cortez often recorded protests against the commodification and decontextualization of black music. (The ultimate decontextualization is, of course, the white "cover." Back in 1971, Kalamu Ya Salaam warned his readers that "The next step will be an album of Black poetry by a white group" [30]. Now we have such phenomena as Vanilla Ice to contend with.) The second track on *Celebrations and Solitudes*, "How Long Has Trane Been Gone," a poem she had written in 1968, confronts the voyeurism of white audience desire as directly as did Baraka's *Dutchman* just a few years earlier. "All you want to do is pat your foot," she addresses an imagined jazz club audience, "sip a drink and pretend / with your head bobbing up and down." Typically, Cortez inscribes a praise song for John Coltrane that cuts many ways at once. With her poem's title, an allusion to a popular blues lyric ("Tell me how long, how long, has that evening train been gone?"), Cortez places Coltrane directly in the lineage of the blues masters while asking a powerful rhetorical question. Just a short time after Coltrane's death, Cortez is compelled to ask why it is that, in the very moment of canonizing Coltrane, American musical culture was deliberately eviscerating the new musics that Coltrane had helped to bring into being. "There was a time when stations played all black music," Cortez recalls as Richard Davis improvises on his bass, and she means not only that there were all-black stations (there still are some), but that there were stations that played all forms of black music (most no longer will). When WHUR-FM came on the air in Washington, D.C., the station advertised itself as the home to "three-hundred-sixty degrees of black music," and that is the kind of medium Cortez is remembering, a station where one might hear the blues and Coltrane, Rap and black poetry, urban contemporary sounds and the Art Ensemble of Chicago. The experience of listeners in Washington, D.C., is typical. As WHUR's "Quiet Storm" format became increasingly popular, and as it amassed the largest FM audience in its listening region, the range of the music played on the station was narrowed to about five degrees. (Fortunately for the "stateless" citizens of the District of Columbia, Pacifica Radio and the public station operated by the University of the District of Columbia picked up some of the forms of music that were rapidly being dropped by WHUR, but few metropolitan areas enjoy such varied sources for black music.) In 1968, Cortez could still hope to find the music of Coltrane, even the late works, on her radio. In 1994, the NAACP Image Award in Jazz was presented to Kenny G., whose saxophone stylings had largely displaced the legatees of Coltrane from the broadcast media. When Cortez wrote "How Long Has Trane Been Gone," the irony was that Coltrane had not been gone that long, and in those days one might have actually heard a black poet on a radio talk show. Public television, in the early 1970s, broadcast black-oriented arts programs that gave air time to people like Baraka and Ron Carter. By the time Cortez recorded her poem with Richard Davis, she must already have known that the piece was unlikely, in that changing social climate, to receive substantial air play. As Cortez wrote, near the end of her poem, "They divided black music, doubled the money, and left us split again."

The music on Cortez's recordings often serves to redouble the allusiveness of her texts. On *Celebrations and Solitudes,* for example, Richard Davis and Cortez engage in a conversation about the death of Duke Ellington. The poem "Essence of Rose Solitude" is a first-person surrealist vision spoken by a persona who presents herself as an archetypal muse and the subject of Ellington's orchestrations. Discussing her methodology with Melhem, Cortez has remarked, "I try not to get stuck in the mud of art council standards and the spectator's demand for messages. It's called multiplication subdivision, and subtraction" (205–6). Making the same turn that had been taken by such poets as Percy Johnston, Amiri Baraka, Bob Kaufman, and A. B. Spellman, Cortez draws from the compacted imagery of the blues a black American surrealism – what she calls, in part to signal its growing distance from the modernist surrealists of Europe, "supersurrealism" (Melhem 206). As she speaks, placing herself in the subject position of Ellington's own color-coded persona, writing the dreamscape of African-American history that she hears in his rich music, the "essence" she produces becomes increasingly paratactic and abstract:

from turtle skinned shoes
from diamond shaped skulls and canes
made from dead gazelles
wearing a face of wilting potato plants
of grey and black scissors
of bee bee shots and fifty red boils

yes the whole world loved him

(*Mouth* 40)

From what could be a simple initial description of the fashion-able shoes worn by the always stylish Ellington, the lines move through increasingly dreamlike displacements, returning at the end of the stanza to a seemingly straight-forward statement of fact, which has to be read as an overironized observation, coming in the wake of "bee bee shots" and "red boils." The world's love of the man so many called simply "Duke," whose music pro-claimed that he loved us "madly," ends by being as problema-tized, though still a real love, as Ellington's problematic musical tributes to African-American women. Notable here is the palpa-ble nature of this imagery, the insistent physicality of even the most fantastic-seeming imagery. This is a constant note in Cor-tez's writings, and it is everywhere joined to her insistence upon the physicality of writing and the textuality of the word. In "Un-der the Siege of February," for example, also recorded for *Celebra-tions and Solitudes,* she asks, "Who will enter its beautiful calligra-phy of blood?" (*Scarifications* 10). The recording of the jazz texts is a further materializing of the written, and Davis's bass serves to underscore this materiality, to suture the words to the music. At some points we can even hear the sound of his fingers moving along the strings of his instrument, though, as we listen repeat-edly, he is not himself present to us. As Cortez speaks in the place of her persona, filling the pronoun with her own voice as she reads, "I am essence of Rose Solitude" (*Mouth* 40), Davis slides in and out of citations. At one point he alludes briefly to the melody of Ellington's "Sophisticated Lady," surely one of the Ellington orchestra's most popular of collaborative works, thus doubling the signifying directions of the jazz text. For if Cortez's poem "Rose Solitude" is an overironized praise song for Elling-ton, then Davis's quotation from "Sophisticated Lady" must be taken not only as a further tribute to Ellington but also as an ironic praise for the praise song's author, Cortez.

A similar use of music to compound the ironies and directions of meaning is found in "If the Drum Is a Woman," included on *There It Is*. A smaller ensemble plays here than on most of the other tracks, the instruments being limited to drums. This poem, too, provides a sort of interrogation in the midst of praise for Ellington, by composing a form of answer song to his *a Drum Is a Woman*, released in 1957. Again there is a doubleness at play, for Cortez's jazz text is an antiphonal response to an album in which Ellington also mingles jazz with the spoken word. Cortez, of course, saw at once the irony in Ellington's identification of woman with an instrument that is played by beating upon it. While the drums of her son, Denardo Coleman, and those of Abraham Adzinyah and Farel Johnson converse rapidly with one another, Cortez asks the obvious question: "If The Drum Is A Woman / why are you pounding your drum into an insane babble?" (*Firespitter* 15). Still, as the presence of the male drummers implies, Cortez does not entirely reject the metaphor. Instead, she redirects it and asks the unnamed addressee of her poem to reconceive the trope along with her, rescuing the positive connotations Ellington had in mind from the objectifications of his expression:

> don't try to dominate your drum
> don't become weak and cold and desert your drum
> don't be forced into the position
> as an oppressor of drums
> and make a drum tragedy of drums
>
> (15)

There is nothing tragic about the drumming on this track, nor is Cortez trying to drum Ellington out of the canon or the community. What she attempts is a raid upon the aetheticization of the figure of woman and a return to the same metaphor, reclaimed, that served as the vehicle for that aestheticization. What she demands, and what she accomplishes on this recording, is a sweeping redefinition of the place of woman's voice in the communal creation and circulation of tropes.

Such antiphonal moments and instrumental use of instruments characterize all of Cortez's work in this genre. On her recording of "Festivals and Funerals" with Davis, Cortez's speaking voice completes a triad of descending, spoken scales to Davis's accompaniment. As she reads, "there are no tears / we have no friends / this is the word," her descending voice and the bass line intersect at the word "word." On the album *Unsubmissive Blues,* the trio of tuba, drums, and guitar that plays behind the spoken stanzas of "In the Morning" follows a traditional twelve-bar, slow-blues pattern. But the improvising lines of Bern Nix's guitar and Joe Daly's tuba depart at times from the traditional blues scale. The poem is not written in blues form but exists at a tangent to the blues, intersecting at a thematic and structural point, and it is recited within the twelve-bar structure, following the tonic–subdominant–dominant chords in their repeating patterns: I – IV – I – V – IV – I. The presence of Daly's tuba rejoins the urban blues to traditions of black marching bands and brass bands in jazz. Daly is one of a small cadre of inventive players of the instrument who gave the tuba renewed prominence during this period. (Taj Mahal's concerts with his blues-based tuba "choir" brought this revival to the pop music audience.) Bern Nix, frequent member of the Coleman bands, plays a blues guitar that jumps the tracks, departing from standard scales like a harmolodic T-Bone Walker. Cortez's poem, rather than adopt the pattern of statement and repeated statement followed by resolution, uses its refrain as an African-American blues objective correlative, a "mascon" phrase, to use Stephen Henderson's terminology, that summons a connotative wealth of blues history. The lines of the stanzas are once more compounded out of Cortez's compressed and hyperbolic imagery:

> Disguised in my mouth as a swampland
> nailed to my teeth like a rising sun
> you come out in the middle of fish-scales
> you bleed into gourds wrapped with red ants
>
> (*Mouth* 46)

In the same way that Daly's tuba lines root Nix's guitar solos in a recognizable blues context even as Nix flies out along the very edge of the chords (reminiscent of the way that Bobby Hutcherson's vibraphone chords provide a point of reentry for Shepp's soaring improvisations in "On This Night"), Cortez's refrain offers a still point of reference for her most extreme, supersurrealist inventions. Her reading of "In the morning in the morning in the morning" (46), in its reiterative chant, invokes the repetitions in one of the most frequently repeated blues lyrics: "In the evening, in the evening, baby, when the sun goes down."

With her temporal inversion of the song's trope (matched at times by Nix's inverted chords), Cortez signals her "repetition with a difference" of the blues. Her version of "the changing same" is an Afrocentric surrealism inspired by the imagery of folk imagination as well as by the surrealism of the Negritude poets Aimé Césaire and Léopold Sédar Senghor. For Cortez, the morning is "all over my door like a rooster," a simile that should be read in the plenitude of its continued inversions as well as for its immediate qualities. Cortez's simile calls to mind other legendary roosters of the blues tradition, particularly Howling Wolf's little red rooster that was "too lazy to crow for day." More important still, the morning "all over my door like a rooster" is antiphonal to the always ironic optimism of the blues, the optimism that tells us the "sun's gonna shine in my back door someday."

With each succeeding recording Cortez has deepened and complicated these techniques. By the time of *There It Is* she had expanded her group of musicians to seven, and the core of the band was composed of members of Coleman's Prime Time Band of the period, surrounded by additional drummers. Coleman himself had taken to the use of a "double" trio in forming his bands, using two drummers. On *There It Is*, bassist Jamaaladeen Tacuma, Bern Nix, and tenor saxophonist Charles Moffett are joined by three percussionists, including Denardo Coleman. (Ornette was to appear on Cortez's next album, *Maintain Control*, playing along with their son.) *There It Is* provides an opportunity to see how Cortez adapts her already written texts in their new harmolodic contexts. As she told Melhem, her poem "I See Chano Pozo" is different in each of its public presentations. The title piece of the collection, the poem "There It Is," is restructured slightly to accomodate the text to the fast twelve-bar blues played by Tacuma, Denardo Coleman, and Nix. Tacuma plays a sort of warped boogie on his electric bass, while Nix plays variants of standard blues chords (major ninths, sevenths, etc.) and harmolodic fills. Cortez expands her use of the refrain in this poem. In the version that appears in the book *Firespitter* (her band is also named "The Firespitters"), the title phrase appears halfway through the poem and then again as the last line. In her recorded version, Cortez repeats this line at the end of a stanza as a way of introducing the saxophone solo that is played by Charles Moffett:

They will spray you with
a virus of legionnaires disease
fill your nostrils with
the swine flu or their arrogance
stuff your body into a tampon of
toxic shock syndrome
try to pump all the resources of the world
into their own veins
and fly off into the wild blue yonder to
pollute another planet

(39)

When she adapted the poem for recording, Cortez inserted after these lines the refrain "There it is," and after she reads this line Moffett comes in with a shock syndrome of a saxophone solo. Since the next line of the poem begins with a conjunction, Cortez rejoins her text as if she is continuing Moffett's statement, saying, "And if we don't fight" (39). An intertext for this line is Claude McKay's sonnet "If We Must Die." Inverting the rhetorical direction of that canonical poem of the Harlem Renaissance much as she inverts the logical orders of the blues, Cortez warns of what will happen if we do not resist, rather than telling us that if we must die anyway we should die in resistance. If we do not fight, she predicts, all that awaits us is "The decomposed look of repression / forever and ever and ever / And there it is" (39).

At a much simpler level of adaptation, "U.S./Nigerian Relations" shows the rhetorical efficiency of the changing same; the poem consists of the same two lines, chanted twenty times in succession. The couplet of the printed poem reads, "They want the oil / But they don't want the people" (*Firespitter* 26). It would be difficult to read this rapidly exactly twenty times at every public reading (though it can be done with practice, and with the printed page as guide), and this is not what Cortez does on *There It Is*, where the title has even been altered. In *Firespitter* the poem is called "Nigerian/American Relations." On the record, Cortez chants her lines in excess of the indicated twenty repetitions, speeding up, slowing down, and altering her enunciation as the band plays an intense harmolodic improvisation around her. One of the astonishing things about a live performance of the Coleman band has always been the precision with which seven musicians, each playing what might at first sound like seven radically independent melody lines, can suddenly, with no visible signal being passed on the stage, stop on a dime and play a passage in unison. That same effect is achieved in "U.S./Nigerian Relations." With the proliferating repetitions of Cortez's script we begin to perceive deepening ironies in her couplet. In the past, Americans seemed to have an insatiable appetite for the people of West Africa. Slave traders could not get "enough" of them to satisfy the desires of whites in the Americas. Now a new order has arrived; now "They want the oil / But they don't want the people." At the conclusion of one series of chants Cortez leaves the microphone, and the band churns out a crashing but convoluted series of melodies and rhythms. Then Cortez reenters and reiterates her chanted script.

Cortez's work, both on the page and on the stage, simply refuses to countenance reductive distinctions between lyric poetry and vernacular song. Although she does insist upon an art that refuses to oblige the commercially driven markets for market-defined accessibility that determine the flows of commodity art in the United States, and will not be bound by audience desires for paraphrasable "messages," neither is she willing to concede that avant-garde poetry is inaccessible to popular audiences, and in fact her recordings may be more "listenable" than much currently available spoken-word product. Because Cortez's "supersurrealism" arises from within the same imagining cultures that have given us the blues and jazz in the first place, there seems little good reason to think her poetry any more opaque than the vernacular itself, a constant inventor of novel tropes. A jukebox that has in the past accommodated songs about "Smokestack Lightning," black-cat bones, and Mojo teeth should have room for Cortez and Davis's recording of "Lynch Fragment 2," whose last lines read, "i am zest from bad jaw quiver / of aftermath / / Come Celebrate Me" (*Scarifications* 12). The surrealist identifications of these lines should slow down any rush to incorporate them into curricular "units" on ethnic identity (and, in fact, I have yet to find this poem in any of our multiplying multicultural anthologies for college use), or those who might want to declare black verse free of the taint of such European avant garde movements as surrealism and dada. The syntactic and semantic displacements of these lines should give pause to any who wish to enlist Cortez's poetry in a celebration of unproblematic self-presence. Besides, such superficial readings are likely to overlook the intertextual rhetorics of Cortez's work, African-American intertextualities made doubly resonant in their musical contexts. Along with everything else that "Lynch Fragment 2" is doing, it is joining in a chorus with one of the most liberating pop anthems of the 1960s. Against a backdrop of the exploding social movements of the postwar decades, Cortez takes to the stage of history along with the Civil Rights movement, along with the Black Arts movement, along with Florence Ballard, Mary Wilson, and Diana Ross, to say to America, "Come See about Me."

Much rewarding work remains to be done with the significant body of jazz texts that I have only been able to survey rapidly here. We need published transcriptions, so that musicologists and literary scholars can conduct interdisciplinary analyses. More jazz texts need to be catalogued and examined, texts like Hammiet Bluiett's recording with Quincy Troupe of the poem "Snake Back Solos" on the *Nali Kola* sessions, and Roland Kirk's 1975 recording, which was quite popular for a time on FM radio, of Betty Neal's "Theme for the Eulipians." Comparative studies need to be done that will include works in which texts were written by the musicians themselves, such as David S. Ware's composition "Mind Time" on his *Great Bliss* volumes, and works that continue the practice of writing jazz melodies to free verse texts. Jazz texts need to be examined in comparison with the recordings that continue to appear of black poets reciting their works unaccompanied. Most importantly, perhaps, future, fuller studies of African-American jazz texts must be as open and free as the genre itself has been. Such studies must begin with the willingness to listen to texts that ask of the genre questions similar to those put to music by such black experimentalists as Sun Ra, Ornette Coleman, John Coltrane, Cecil Taylor, Jeanne Lee, Anthony Braxton, Alice Coltrane, Sonny Sharrock, and Amina Claudine Myers. As jazz audiences earlier found themselves attending to performances that raised the profoundest of questions about the very materials of music, about harmony, rhythm, melody, and measure, cultural studies must now listen to jazz texts that challenge common assumptions about what the human voice should do in music or in speech, about what constitutes a spoken text, about what sorts of sounds can be musical, and about the nature of listening to language. At a time when international symposia are held to honor and study the legacy of a white composer and poet such as John Cage, we cannot afford to continue the institutionalized hypocrisy that denies an equal level of attention to African-American artists like Sun Ra, Ronald Shannon Jackson, Joseph Jarman, and Cecil Taylor.

5

"OTHER PLANES OF THERE"

For a long time the world has dwelt on faith, beliefs, possibly
dreams, and the truth; and the kind of world you've got today is
based on those things.
  How do you like it?

Sun Ra, "Possibility"

this is about songs
about when they happen about
pieces and absences
of connection about for no reason

Ed Roberson, Lucid

When Elouise Loftin wrote, "you'll never understand what i'm
not saying" (*Barefoot Necklace*, 3), she was assuredly not offering
her poem in illustration of Jean-François Lyotard's then unwritten theory of the postmodern in art as the structural formation
indicating the presence of the unpresentable. Loftin's poem has
not been included in recent celebrations, condemnations, or
even explanations of postmodernity in the arts, seemingly fulfilling the prophecy of her poem. And despite continued scholarly
attention to orality in the structures of African-American verse,
to the vernacular as structuring principle in black American
poetics, and to the influence of black music upon black literary
arts, a large body of works in which jazz artists speak poetry has
gone almost completely unexamined, and to all appearances
unheard, by students of literature. Cultural studies have prolifer-
ated essays about the cultural contexts of Rap, about Rap poetry

as transgressive act, about Rap as vernacular theorizing, but even as more and more young people rediscover jazz (often by way of jazz samples on Rap recordings), critics, even critics of poetry, have evinced little inclination to listen to or read the works of black experimentalists interrogating the generic boundaries of jazz text, reading, playing, and reciting, as jazz musicians used to say, "outside." Whether or not anything can be said to be truly outside the text, these artists have taken the musical presentation of texts far outside anything attempted by the Beats, far outside the actually quite conservative (perhaps even reactionary) poetic forms of much Rap, often outside what some listeners would be willing to think of as either musical or poetic. Following the example of Amiri Baraka's writing and the New York Art Quartet's music, these artists have tested the limits of writing and musical languages and have found new things to do with sound and signification.

"But to say, 'it ain't supposed to be that way!' " These words come flying like a broken drumstick out of the sonic attack that makes up the second track of Ronald Shannon Jackson's 1984 recording, *Pulse*. Since that track represented itself among the album's titles as combining a recitation from Shakespeare's *Richard III* with a reading of Edgar Allan Poe's "Raven," already an audacious bit of literary miscegenation, this line may well represent, even literally, the response of someone listening to the track for the first time. Jayne Cortez asked that we not "make a drum tragedy of drums." Jackson drummed a tragedy, completely restructuring it and suturing it to yet another tragedy in the act. Readings to drums have been a cliché on the public reading circuit since the earliest days of coffeehouse verse and bongo drums. The sweat-shirted, goateed, sunglasses-wearing, coolly detached bongo player was such a familiar sight behind Beat poets that Hollywood films and television programs made a stock comic character of the figure. In the 1960s, that cliché transformed into another: the dashiki-clad, goateed, sunglasses-wearing, coolly detached conga drummer behind the militant black poet. Jackson represented a sight as unfamiliar among public representations as his music: the dread-locked drummer shouting and humming verses himself as he invented ever more complex rhythms to a poem as rhythmically complex as "The Raven."

Ronald Shannon Jackson may be best known among jazz audiences as the leader of a remarkably productive "harmolodic" ensemble that he called the Decoding Society. Jackson has been a prolific session player with other group leaders as well, and many of his "Decoders" have gone on to renown in their own right. The guitarist Vernon Reid, for example, has achieved post–Decoding Society fame among Rock audiences with his own band, Living Color, and was a founding member of the Black Rock Coalition. Jackson studied harmolodic approaches while playing with Ornette Coleman, and his Decoding Society was much influenced by the work of Coleman's Prime Time Band. The Decoding Society played a harder-edged and somewhat more tightly constructed harmolodic jazz, but their conception of improvising and of ensemble organization was much the same as Prime Time's.

Given that harmolodic music destroys the conventional view of the relationship between melody line and background musician, it should come as no surprise that Jackson should have proceeded to a destruction of common assumptions about the "lead" role of the reciting voice and the "accompanying" role of the drums. *Pulse* is a collection of drum solos and of literary works recited within percussion improvisations. No amount of listening to jazz texts by Kerouac, Shepp, Rexroth, Marion Brown, Baraka, or even Cortez can entirely prepare a listener for what will be experienced on *Pulse,* for Jackson's mode of recitation was as novel and transgressive as was Jimi Hendrix's approach to the electric guitar or, to return to jazz models, the guitar works of Sonny Sharrock. If Sun Ra dismantled the common knowledge about how to organize the sections of a post-Ellington big band, always retaining prominently the recognizable shards of that common knowledge, then Jackson took apart common sense about what it means to recite.

The first line of Cecil Taylor's poem "The Musician" is an apt description of Jackson's work on *Pulse:* "he pour'd floors talk" (12). The first track on *Pulse,* "Circus of Civilized Fools," is a virtuoso drum solo of the sort often featured by jazz bands in performance. Although the structure of Jackson's solo might seem unusual to listeners who are new to jazz, its forms will certainly be familiar to those who are familiar with post-Bop approaches to the instrument. There is little on this first number to warn of what comes next. One can hear a few odd vocal sounds coming from Jackson, but these might be taken for the sort of rumblings and hummings that can be heard coming from such jazz masters as Erroll Garner, Keith Jarrett, Jimmy Garrison, and Roland Kirk as they play their instruments. But when the second track gets going it becomes evident that Jackson intends to explore the possibilities of the human speaking voice as a percussive instrument in its own right. It has long been a high compliment to jazz singers to say that they play their voices like instruments, but we are not accustomed to hearing speech of the type recorded by Jackson. He is not simply adopting a dramatic voice; he is tearing away at the boundary between speech and music, and he is using written texts – reconstituted canonical written texts – to accomplish his deconstructions of speech. *Pulse* bears a request along with its album credits. Printed at the bottom of the notes we read, "Request: Play at significant volume for maximum enjoyment." The second track is eleven minutes and thirty seconds of lyric drum work and vocal distortions. As Jackson moves through his initial solo on the drums he begins to add a series of grunts, groans, and bits of language. It is only when we hear the words "Now is the Winter of my discontent" that we recognize Shakespeare in the midst of the glossolalia of Jackson's vocal effects. He reformulates the meters of his source texts as he invents polyrhythms around them on his drums. The opening lines of "The Raven" begin one of the best-known (maybe really the "best-loved") poems of the American people, their rhythms as instantly recognizable as those of Longfellow's *Hiawatha.* Jackson punches caesurae into the lines where there had been none. The interrupted and truncated poem, appended to Richard's soliloquy and poured across the surfaces of thundering drums, becomes a radically redesigned, though no less terrifying, form of recitation. Adding repetitions not indicated in Poe's script, exfoliating some parts of text by means of paraphrase and improvised response, Jackson's shattering revision of "The Raven" finds, as we hear him pronounce at one point seven minutes into the work, "the blues!" Melvin B. Tolson, in an aside during a poetry reading at the Library of Congress, wondered aloud whether Poe, a thorough racist raised in the Black Belt South, might have drawn inspiration for his rhythms from his experience of black ministers. Like Russell Atkins before him, Jackson reclaims Poe by reassembling his texts as black postmodernism. Having heard the text of "The Raven," Jackson's response was "to say 'it ain't supposed to be that way.' " In the neoclassicism of

Poe's verse Jackson found a source for the New World African-American baroque of his percussive readings.

The task he undertook with his recitation of poems by Sterling Brown is fundamentally different, though the results will no doubt be equally disturbing to those accustomed to more usual forms of dramatic delivery. Brown's materials were often taken directly from vernacular sources. Jackson returns with Brown to those source texts in folk-song and storytelling traditions, but he remasters them as well. In Brown's collection *No Hiding Place*, the book he had hoped would follow *Southern Road* but that did not appear in its entirety until his *Collected Poems* was published, he included a section entitled "Washington, D.C.," a series of sketches and folk lyrics dedicated to his hometown. (Late in his life Brown was declared the poet laureate of the District of Columbia.) What Jackson does with Brown's poem "Puttin' on Dog" is to restore it to its folk-song context. The rhythm Jackson uses to accompany his half sung and half spoken rendition of the poem recalls both the continuous Caribbean influence in African-American music and the traditions of marching bands in black music. In the third verse he shifts out of this pattern and speaks the lines with sound effects from his drums:

> He's about to use English on the lonesome eight ball
> Stops short when he hears what Buck has said,
> Winds up like Babe Ruth aimin' for a homer
> And bends his cuestick around Buck's head.
>
> (Brown 227)

By means of his arrangement, Jackson creates a pun that does not exist in the written text. He stops his choral rhythm and singing, going into a spoken recitation just as he is about to read the line "He's about to use English." As he narrates Scrappy's baseball-style windup, he plays a snare drum roll under the line, as a circus drummer might, and then punctuates Scrappy's cuestick blow to Buck's head with, appropriately, a rim shot. As he does with "The Raven," Jackson adds words to his source text. In keeping with the call-and-response form of the source, he responds to his own narrative with interjections. When he comes to the close of the last verse, which tells how Scrappy was still "a puttin' on dog" in his coffin, Jackson yells out, "Second line, y'all," and the last chorus of the poem is delivered to the rhythm of a New Orleans second-line marching drum.

Jackson sets up a similar, syncopated marching rhythm for his rendition of Brown's "Slim in Atlanta," and again he makes minor alterations throughout the text. The title is announced, as if to a curbside audience during Mardi Gras, "Slim in Atlanta, Y'all," implying that the announced lyric is one with which the audience has some prior familiarity. In some places Jackson alters Brown's line breaks. In the fourth verse, for instance, he moves the word "waitin' " from the end of line 3 to the beginning of line 4, changing enjambed lines to end-stopped lines. The line that ends the first quatrain, "From laughin' outdoors" (Brown 81), becomes "To do their laughin' outdoors." Likewise, he transforms the third line of the third verse, in which the Southern whites issue their bizarre command to newly arrived Slim Greer, inserting additional words. Jackson's longer line places greater emphasis upon the command. In his reading, what the "rebs" tell Slim is, "Dontcha do your laughin' in the street." None of these alterations is as radical as Jackson's revisions of Shakespeare and Poe. They seem instead to point to the small ways in which such a ballad gets altered at each stage of its transmission through a community. Jackson sets up his own form of call and response with his laughs, grunts, and humming between his own recited lines.

Jackson had guest artists on this recording for some tracks, but he made no attempt to get the guest poet, Michael Harper, to engage in vocal distortions similar to those Jackson applied to the texts he recited. In fact, Harper's reading on *Pulse* sounds much like his readings in public appearances or on his other recordings with jazz artists. A rendition of Robert Hayden's "Those Winter Sundays" lasts less than a minute, Jackson providing softly crackling percussion sounds to match the onomatopoeia of Hayden's text. Harper and Jackson also perform a duet with Harper's poem "Last Affair: Bessie's Blues Song." Harper reads each of his lines in his customary voice. Jackson provides a different rhythm for each verse, returning at the chorus to a rhythm he associates with the song alluded to in the title. At times Jackson drops out, leaving Harper's voice to resonate alone. Elsewhere Jackson offers literalizing effects, such as a chiming sound on his cymbal to match the word "chime" when it occurs in the poem.

The album cover features a repeating graph, unidentified. It could be a record of the artist's heartbeat. It could be a graph of his drumming. It could be a graph signifying nothing, appropriated from some unrelated context. It might even be read as a voiceprint, inscribing the trace of somebody's speech, or a polygraph, testing the veracity of what has been spoken. In each event, what we witness in Jackson's *Pulse* is the deformation and reformulation of traditional texts and of texts written in traditional forms. It would be left to musicians and composers who were themselves poets, artists like Joseph Jarman and Cecil Taylor, to set less normative poetic forms, texts formed within the aesthetic rebellions of the New American Poetry and the Black Arts, to an equally transgressive music.

The Art Ensemble of Chicago has long practiced what is these days called "performance art" (they began their work as a group in the era of "happenings" and "guerilla theater"), and their performances have often included spoken and recited materials. For most of their decades together, drummer Don Moye, bassist Malachi Favors, and reed player Joseph Jarman have appeared onstage dressed in Africanesque costumes (sometimes with an Afro-Asiatic touch), their faces covered with makeup that obscures their individual identities beneath an abstract diasporic figuration. For many years the trumpet player, Lester Bowie, has appeared with them dressed in a lab coat, as if to emphasize the experimental nature of their music, and wearing a hard hat, as if to underscore the danger implicit in such experiments. Roscoe Mitchell, the other reed player, usually appears onstage dressed in casual clothes, as if he had paused in the course of his ordinary day to play some of this extraordinary music (which, I suppose, *is* an ordinary day for Mitchell). But within the context of his costumed collaborators, Mitchell's attire, too, comes to seem an adopted costume. He appears in the guise of the ordinary man, and in the end that persona may be as unusual as those of the other ensemble members. The Art Ensemble's musicians are all multiinstrumentalists, and their passion for "little" percussion instruments and novel sound sources has continually expanded the array of equipment they take with them onto the stage. Typically, the five members of the ensemble position themselves at "stations" surrounded by their choice of instruments, but in the music that they proceed to produce it may sound as though more than five people are playing, and it is sometimes difficult to determine which artist is responsible for which ambient tone. It is not at all unusual for a voice to float out from the stage, uttering cryptic phrases. On those occasions when a poem is recited, the text is usually the work of Jarman, though poems by the group's other saxophone player, Mitchell, have also appeared on their album covers.

Joseph Jarman has worked with jazz texts since his earliest days as a recording artist and performer, and he was one of those members of Chicago's Association for the Advancement of Creative Musicians who pioneered text-based performance art in jazz. In reviewing a recording by the Last Poets in 1971, Kalamu Ya Salaam had complained that

> if you listen closely, [they] have obviously listened closely to Imamu [Baraka] but only close enough to imitate the form of what Imamu was doing. Listen to their speech patterns, then hear Imamu's voice. The Last Poets sound good, but meanwhile the content of what they're saying is confused . . . Is there soup in those cans or simple shit? (29)

Jarman had also listened closely to Baraka, particularly to works like his recitation with the New York Art Quartet, and Baraka's strong influence is not only felt but thematized in Jarman's texts, the earliest instance being "Non-Cognitive Aspects of the City," recorded on his *Song For* album in 1967. Even his calm and measured delivery, a stark contrast to the vocal distortions of Ronald Shannon Jackson, could have been modeled on Baraka's delivery of "Black Dada Nihilismus." But whereas the Last Poets took Baraka's attitudes and typography while leaving the details of his poetics and the incisiveness of his critique behind, Jarman's poem follows Baraka in its mixing of black urban surrealism with a form of projective verse.

It might seem that something entitled "Non-Cognitive Aspects of the City" should be composed of something less conducive to cognition than words, and J. B. Figi, author of the liner notes to *Song For,* found himself unwilling to engage in anything so cognitive as a discussion of the piece. " 'Non-Cognitive Aspects of the City' has its own words," Figi writes, "and needs no others." People rarely discuss poems simply because the poems themselves appear to need it, though, and Ekkehard Jost has discussed Jarman's text specifically as an example to oppose to the usual jazz-and-poetry efforts in which the two forms, as he put it, "run, as it were, on separate tracks." In contrast, Jost says,

Non-Cognitive Aspects of the City (among other pieces) demonstrates that a very intensive interaction between words and
music can indeed be attained . . . There is a feedback process in which Jarman's voice and phrasing, and the collective improvisations by his companions, influence each
other. Furthermore, there are passages in Jarman's *Aspects*
when the speaking voice not only has something to say
verbally, but clearly dominates as a rhythmic (and thus musical) element. (172)

Of course, there is a quite obvious reason this should be true.
Jarman is the composer of both music and text, and he has
designed his jazz text so that the poem dominates rhythmically.
This is not one of those sessions where, in the midst of a series of
solos, the director suddenly points to the poet in the studio and
cues him or her to read. Jarman has designed his poem and his
music together, and the poem determines the spaces for the
instrumental improvisations.

"Non-Cognitive Aspects of the City" is organized in a tripartite
structure in which the music and the poetic text shape one
another. The alto saxophone theme we hear at the beginning
and end of the composition matches the title phrase of the piece
in measure, though it forms a different rhythm. The triadic
structure of the poem also follows the trio pattern of Jarman's
accompanists, and thus the solos by the drummer, pianist, and
bassist are separated and cued by stanzas in the poem. (This
explains why the poem is composed for a smaller ensemble than
the septet that plays the other pieces heard on *Song For.*)

"Non-Cognitive Aspects of the City" begins with Jarman playing a deceptively light-hearted, quickly rising figure on his alto
saxophone, the figure that becomes the motivic pattern for later
portions of the composition. He is joined by the piano, bass,
and drums, played by Christopher Gaddy, Charles Clark, and
Thurman Barker respectively, as they sketch a tentative form for
their later improvisations. Barker then plays a drum solo that sets
the stage for Jarman's recitation of the poem's first section. As
the piano and bass provide a busy background, Barker moves to
small percussion instruments, and Jarman reads,

Non-cognitive aspects of the city,
Where Roi J.'s prophecies become the causes of children.
Once quiet black blocks of stone,

Encasements of regularity,
Sweet now intellectual dada
Of vain landscapes
The city
Long history   upheaval

(Here again I am forced to guess at line breaks and punctuation, since no printed version of the poem is supplied with the recording.) As a sort of praise song and invocation of the muses, Jarman records a tribute both to Baraka (LeRoi Jones) and to the next generation of black youth, who have taken up the causes of Black Arts and Black Liberation. He places that tribute within the ironic surroundings of what would normally be designated irrationalism. (His use of the term "non-cognitive" embraces both wider and narrower senses of cognition. He speaks at once of that which is unknowable and of that which is incapable of reduction to empirical statement.)

Clearly, one aspect of Jarman's postmodernity is his recognition of certain failures of modernity, failures that carried within them the implicit seeds of his posting. Chicago's architecture, for example, features many instances of the modernist attempt to plan formally functional structures for a brave new world, but that very rational planning, that encasement of regularity, produced "vain landscapes." By Jarman's time, the isolated alienation of the modernist intellectual looked increasingly like a vain affectation, and the upheavals of the cities in the 1960s went a long way toward demonstrating the vanity of those urban and social planners whose plans froze in place the economic castes and disparities that were the legacy of the premodern. At the same time, it was through cracks in the high modernist facade, Jarman's poem suggests, that a glimpse was to be gained of another way:

The frail feel of Winter's wanting,
Crying to leaves they wander,
Seeing the capital vision,
Dada,
New word out of the twenties of chaos
Returned in the suntan jars,
Fruits of education with others.
Non-cognitive, these motions,
Embracing sidewalk heroes.

Both formally and thematically, Jarman incorporates as a principle of his composition the dada of which he speaks. The image of dada "returned in the suntan jars" recalls Georges Ribemont-Dessaignes's definition, in "Les Plaisirs de Dada," that "Dada fills tubes of paint with margarine" (qtd. in Bohn xi). Jarman's surreal imagery has a racialized pattern of signifying absent from Dessaignes's, however, one more mark of its "post-" position. The suntan jar is the African-American container that returns a transformed dada (as in Baraka's poem "Black Dada Nihilismus") to its puzzled sender. The suntan jar also serves as one more ironic comment on the desires of white people to darken themselves (both culturally and epidermally) while remaining purely white. In his descriptions of the very nearly indescribable dada, Willard Bohn states that "Dada's one overriding concern was the achievement of total liberty: social, moral, and intellectual. In this vein, its adherents questioned the basic postulates of rationalism and humanism as few had done before" (xvii). I think it safe to say that black Americans had good reason to interrogate the rationality of humanism long before the *Brown v. Board of Education* decision could bring the "Fruits of education with others." One fruit of education was introduction to the word "dada," but black people had lived a dada life in America for generations before postmodernity made the questioning of dominant humanism a dominant academic enterprise. Black intellectuals in the 1960s confronted a white public discourse (and, as we called it in those days, a "power structure") that declared their very being irrational and that classified any and all of their efforts to achieve full liberation as irrational. The dada of the black experimentalist, of the suntan jar, would not be exactly the dada of Picabia, though, any more than the surrealism of Césaire was exactly that of Magritte. This was to be an art that said, "If humanism as practiced in America is reasonable, then we prefer not to be reasonable."

At the conclusion of the poem's initial sequence, Thurman Barker resumes his drum solo, and then Jarman's saxophone, the linking element in all of the improvisatory passages, joins in. The second portion of the poem mirrors the tripartite structure of the whole. In this portion Jarman recites a lengthy refrain three times, to a background of bass, drums, and piano. The refrain pronounces a promise that out of "The hell that is where we are" shall come a new beginning that is also a return. The signifying resistance of black arts, that which is seen as simultaneously irrational (indeed, primitive) and presumptuous by white thought, will rise within the power of the city:

Uppity,
The force of becoming,
What art was made to return . . .

Following the third repetition, the voice rests, and Clark plays a bass solo, bowing his strings. Jarman reenters on alto, they both fade as small percussion instruments fill the space they are vacating, and Gaddy plays the inside of his piano, plucking individual strings and strumming groups of open strings. The piano will return with a solo at the end of the text it introduces, as earlier Barker's drums led into and out of the poem's first segment, continually promising "what art was made to return."

In the concluding segment of his poem Jarman again echoes Baraka. In "Black Dada Nihilismus" Baraka had asked, "why / you carry knives?" (*Dead* 63). Jarman's poem, in lines that sound a good deal like Baraka's, supplies an answer, an answer self-evident to those who have seen pictures of Emmet Till's corpse:

Common tools, the knife and gun,
Castration in store,
The tarred spotlight against what hope we have.
Non-cognitive, these elements . . .

Again the poem strikes at humanist self-assurance and at appeals to reason and to the teleological progress of history. How is one to think of such things as lynching and castration and the public burning of black corpses, each of which had been documented in the pages of the *Chicago Defender?* What content can a term like "cognitive dissonance" even have in such a context? The poem closes on its most fatalistic note:

Internal, these states on plains far out,
Is what these lives become.
Thought's final last work. There
Spots forth treason.
Last word.
Non-cognitive doom.

The piano then plays its solo. When the other musicians return, they play lines built around that initial alto saxophone figure that Jarman played alone to open the piece. Despite the sadness of the poem's last segment, I believe that the repeated midsection and the band's closing statements point to a countermotion. The uprising figure of the alto saxophone that opens and closes "Non-cognitive Aspects of the City" I read as exemplifying "What art was made to return," that "Uppity / The force of becoming." The front cover of *Song For* (the title is another pun – the album consists of four songs) displays a figure–background shift replicating the figure–background shifts in "Non-cognitive Aspects of the City" between the dada of exhaustion and the dada of renewal. Modeling their work after those pictures in which one alternately sees a lamp or two faces, the artists, Billy and Sylvia Abernathy, have placed two silhouettes of Jarman facing each other, the brims of their identical hats touching at the edge, in such a way that the bright space between them becomes a lamp of sorts. The two sides of Jarman that we see gracing the cover of his album are, in fact, the same side.

Among the earliest recorded Jarman jazz texts with the Art Ensemble of Chicago is the composition "Ericka," which, at twenty-one minutes and thirty seconds, is a yet more complex and sinuous piece than "Non-Cognitive Aspects of the City," its structure less neatly arranged than that text's triadic movements. "Ericka" is part of the sessions recorded in Paris in 1969 entitled *A Jackson in Your House.* The sessions were dedicated to Charles Clark, the bass player on "Non-Cognitive Aspects," who had died in April of 1969. *A Jackson in Your House* was recorded during one of the early Art Ensemble's drummerless days, before Don Moye had joined permanently, and so the use of small percussion instruments was more than usually important to the band's work. "Ericka" addresses much of the same thematic material as "Non-Cognitive Aspects." There are specific allusions here to the Black Panthers, whose Chicago chapter had been particularly effective in organizing the black communities until its leaders were murdered by the police, aided by the Federal Bureau of Investigation. The "Ericka" of the title may be Ericka Huggins, the Panther activist whose husband was assassinated in Los Angeles in 1969. Jarman links his own music to the renewed spirits of the courageous young, writing,

Ericka,
Child of our uncharted microtones
Thrown through the dawn, the maze of, blown.
As she matures in black America,
The panther paying homage to the people

Torn with guns.
Television hero gone to madness
Seeking the answer.
Can we endure?

These last two lines are repeated at the close of the poem's second section, linking the stanzas together around the quietly moving melodies played on flute and marimba in the background. The third stanza marks a transition, both in the tone of the poem and in the music. The second stanza spoke of the mother; the third speaks of the father. In a thickening atmosphere of drums, bells, melodica, and an unexpected sitar, Jarman declares that

The bare facts of existence
Image the black saint,
Whom LeRoi calls
The heaviest spirit.

The poem returns to Ericka herself in the last stanza of the text proper, which describes a nation of nomadic seekers drifting away from one another. "Must she," Jarman asks, "Ericka, endure . . . visionless . . . alone?" At the close of his recitation, against the rising sounds of a saxophone, Jarman begins to sing the last word of his repeating line, "Rise up, alone." As he reaches the word "alone" with each repetition, he sings it in a quiet, high tone held for at least a measure. This is repeated four times, slowly fading into the rising music, eventually disappearing into a saxophone solo. Soon both saxophones are playing improvised lines around the faded and wandering tone, while the trumpet of Lester Bowie darts in and out of the mix.

During the extended group improvisations that follow, the Ensemble turns the piece from its somber beginning to characteristically ironic and humorous movements. Bowie can be heard growling through his trumpet. At one point a voice, perhaps representing that of a police officer, is heard telling someone to "Give me some help with these bodies." Later, another voice can be heard speaking the formulaic phrases that punctuate Caribbean folktales: "Crick Crack." The voice tells only parts of a tale, however, some lost narrative in which the hero advances "with his elbows far in front of him." When we reach the end of "Ericka," we are seemingly distant from the elegiac measures of Jarman's initial recitation. As the quartet brings their diverging lines of melodies to a ragged ending, a last voice can be heard. It might again be the voice of a crime-scene investigator finishing his work, or just the voice of a band leader calling it a day. "O.K. boys," the voice announces. "You can pack it up now, and take it home." Both "Ericka" and "Non-Cognitive Aspects of the City" are assemblages of phrases and imagery that are brought together along jagged lines, but "Ericka" is even more of a collage, with its highly disparate modes of speech and song, elegy and playfulness, and is in the end perhaps more typical of the Art Ensemble's *mixage*.

Four years later the Art Ensemble of Chicago, with AACM guest artist Muhal Richard Abrams on piano, recorded *Fanfare for the Warriors,* one of their first albums with a major label, Atlantic, and included among its compositions Jarman's recitation of his "myth poem" "Odawalla." The musical context here is quite different from that in either "Non-Cognitive Aspects of the City" or "Ericka." On those performances Jarman had composed both music and text. On *Fanfare for the Warriors* Jarman recites his poem within the performance of music credited to bassist Malachi Favors, entitled "Illistrum." A tone poem, more of the kind envisioned by Marion Brown than those of Romanticist composers, this piece begins with a loud crash and the sound of a human voice shouting the title word. A protracted series of honks and percussion sounds follows, the effect being much like standing at a crowded intersection as cars honk at each other. The drums and percussion next set up a syncopated rhythm, climaxing as a second voice shouts, "Odawalla." Then, as Abrams plays isolated notes on the piano and the other musicians play small percussion instruments, punctuated by occasional honks and growls on a number of different horns, Jarman reads his poem:

> came through the people of the sun
> into the grey haze of the ghost worlds
> vanished legions, crowding bread lines – the people
> of the Sun coated with green chalk
> all kinds of warm light between them
> destroyed for the silver queen of the ghost worlds
> wild beast such as dogs gone mad and lechers –
>   the wanderers

(33)

This is very much in the same spirit as "Non-Cognitive Aspects" and of the initial reading of "Ericka." We get the same sense of souls wandering in search of sustenance, beset by oppressive terrors, but here the action of the poem is set against an imagined ancient landscape of primal origins rather than in the specifically locatable scenes of the city. As a result, the later poem is able to assume a prophetic tone that we might otherwise resist. Because "Odawalla" has the feel of an originary myth translated from an ancient text, the tone seems to support the speaker's assumption of the prophetic stance, and the actions in the music around Jarman's voice seem to be fulfilling the prophecy. Odawalla, we are told, "came through the people of the sun" to warn them "and to teach them how they may increase their bounty / through the practice of the drum and silent gong" (33). All the while we hear whistling, gongs, small drums, and erupting horns, as though the teaching were in progress around us. The "silent gong" is a Zen-like impossibility that comes to make a good deal of sense in the final generative moments of the text:

ODAWALLA vibrated the movement of CAMBE GILL
                    O POIU
causing the silent gong to sound silent, the body whole
the grey haze
                    Sun people
                    drum
                    silent
                    gong . . .

Jarman's voice trails out into the music as Lester Bowie begins to solo insistently on his muted trumpet. In the last minutes of "Illistrum" we hear a shimmering curtain of vibraphones, gongs, and piano against the climbing trumpet of Bowie, giving the whole a still more mystical cast. The poem "Odawalla" is an odd exercise on its own. (It was reprinted in Chicago's evangelizing surrealist magazine *Arsenal* two years after the recording.) Like Armand Schwerner's *Tablets*, it reads like the partial transcription of an ancient and lost language, but in conjunction with Favors's musical composition it becomes a more intriguing piece. Full of synesthetic moments, such as "SEKA saw the sound of the silent gong," it is also filled with assonance and sharp consonantal sounds. The poem is less in the projective mode than Jarman's other texts, and a bit too much of an imitation "wisdom" narrative, but as a sound text it is most effective.

The one prominent artist in whom the experimental poetics of Baraka, the avant-garde musical methodologies of the Art Ensemble of Chicago, and the radical manipulations of the speaking voice undertaken by Jackson are all joined in one expressive art is Cecil Taylor. Taylor has been startling audiences (and sometimes his collaborators) since the 1950s, and he has been one of the most consistently radical of artists in his conception of form. He has also, since his earliest days as a performing artist, been intimately associated with the revolutions in postwar American writing, though he has infrequently offered his own writing for public circulation. He has, from time to time over the years, published his remarkable poems in magazines and among the liner notes to his recordings, but many fans of his piano work remain unaware of the extent of his literary activities, and no literary critics have included him in their surveys of American verse. Taylor often incorporates the speaking voice (if we can still call it that, when what it speaks is not "words") as part of the music he produces. His concert performances have sometimes included short bursts of words, along with abstract dance movements and percussion, as he moves to the piano to begin what can turn out to be a marathon recital and improvisation. An example of such techniques available on a recorded performance is the first composition on the collection *In Florescence,* where Taylor can be heard producing vocal sounds and reciting snatches of poetry in a fashion reminiscent of his one album of recorded poetry. In his comments on *In Florescence,* reprinted among Jim Macnie's liner notes, Taylor says, "I currently view the presentation of music from a very ritualistic point of view . . . The voice, the chanting, the poems and the movement are all things I've been working up to throughout my whole career."

Taylor assisted with the physical production of *Floating Bear* and was one of the many artists to pass through Baraka's New York gatherings. Taylor later associated with poets of the Umbra group, and now and then he has contributed his poems to the more adventurous of the little magazines. His poems "Scroll No. 1" and "Scroll No. 2," for example, were both published in a 1965 issue of *Sounds and Fury* magazine before they reappeared as the liner notes to his 1973 recording *Indent.* (That recording had first been released on Taylor's own Unit Core Records label in a limited edition prior to its rerelease by Arista Records.)

Taylor's interest in bodily performance also dates to those early years of his first New York jazz dates. It was Cecil Taylor who appeared with his band-mate Archie Shepp in a production of Jack Gelber's *Connection.* In later years Taylor created a musical adaptation of Adrienne Kennedy's *Rat's Mass,* which he then directed for La Mama Theater. He composed a work that premiered at the Alvin Ailey American Dance Theater.

Because the published record of Taylor's work in poetry is relatively sparse, in marked contrast to his prolific record as a composer and pianist, it would be difficult, without access to the artist's manuscripts, to comment accurately upon the evolution of his writing. The scattered early poems that have been printed, though, leave one with the impression that the characteristic elements of his poetics must have been in place fairly early, and they have remained the basis of his textual improvisations ever since. His poetry partakes of the surrealism and dada, crossed with the traditions of blues imagery, that we have seen so often among the black avant-garde artists of the latter half of the century, but Taylor has departed far more frequently from the visual image than do most of his contemporaries. Like Russell Atkins, also a composer, Taylor constructs objects as ideas by means of a form of deconstruction, and his poems are likely to mix the visual with the impalpable (noncognitive?), as in the closing lines of "Scroll No. 1," first published in 1965:

> Mirror born color squared
> difference excuse
> mountain organ hill bill
>   tongue tastes
> tar flesh trampled seeds.
>
> (*Indent,* n. pag.)

The paratactic organization of lines and phrases and the syntactic disruptions evident in this poem clearly belong in a lineage of radical poetics stretching from dada through such experiments as William Carlos Williams's *Kora in Hell* and Gertude Stein's *Tender Buttons* and into the postprojective poetics of Baraka. Those genealogies of modernist and postmodernist aesthetics intersect in Taylor's texts with such techniques of African-American poetics as "worrying the line" and ironic signifying (Do hillbillies pay the "hill bills"?), as they also intersect in the poetry of Baraka. Taylor's poems are equally clearly precursors to the "language-centered" writings of artists like Clark Coolidge, Ron Silliman, Bruce Andrews, Carla Harryman, Charles Bernstein, Lyn Hejinian, and Barrett Watten, though Coolidge is one of the only white poets to have discussed Taylor at any length in his published works.

Taylor's version of composition by field, and "open" poetry, also appears to be closely related to his approach to musical composition. His music was for many years built around what he calls "unit structures," sometimes very brief figures, other times more extended shapes. This is what led Baraka, when contrasting Taylor's mode of writing music with that of Ornette Coleman, to remark that "Taylor's seem much more works of composition, rather than notated solos" (*Black Music* 106). These unit structures, rather than a received form like the twelve-bar blues pattern, then determine the formation of the larger composition in their combination and their imbricating of improvisations. Likewise, the lines formed in the unit structures, rather than traditional major and minor scales and chords, indicate the tonal materials appropriate for the solos. As Shepp explained to Baraka in 1964,

> Cecil plays lines . . . something like a row or scale . . . that lends itself to the melodic shape of the tune, which is derived from the melody, so that the harmony many times becomes subservient to the body of the tune. And the chords he plays are basically percussive . . . Playing with Taylor, I began to be liberated from thinking about chords. (*Music* 152)

The individual words in Taylor's poems similarly provide the structuring and thematic materials for the poet's further improvisations. The words *and* their significations, rather than a traditional structure like iambic pentameter or the sonnet, furnish the formative impetus. In "The Musician," a poem that appeared in the same 1976 issue of *Arsenal: Surrealist Subversion* that included Jarman's poem and Franklin Rosemont's essay "Black Music and Surrealist Revolution," the names of the musicians Taylor chooses to invoke are unfolded to form improvising line structures. Hence, Jelly Roll Morton and Earl "Fatha" Hines, whose names when pronounced in succession can give us a five-foot line, lead to the following measures:

Morton jell'd gem pack'd Earl
Hines bobbin' natural placement
feelings connect older body orders
wailer found regional dictum

(13)

As these lines indicate, Taylor has a musician's ear for the sound of his texts. The percussive chord clusters of his piano music find their verbal analogue in the virtuoso sound clusters of his poetic line. The poet often uses infrequently heard words, words that might not ordinarily be thought "poetic," for their sound possibilities. He also uses invented words, words in foreign languages, and, again paralleling the work of Atkins, novel verb forms made from familiar nouns. Added to these techniques is Taylor's occasional use of the phonetic diction long associated in white writing with black characters, as an ironic way of turning that minstrel language back on itself in a resignifying deconstruction. In the final stanzas of the short poem that is printed with the Cecil Taylor Unit's 1977 album *Dark to Themselves*, Taylor puts all of these methods into play, summoning the *voudoun loa Legba*, American cousin to the West African Orisha:

Hewé-zo
 vertabraes seam'd atolling
 meteor pa-zzanin a hissing
 asson adorn bells past
  a 2nd month lain 7 side.
     churn/
Da
oldest ancestor/ fertilized seed
  /   making LegBa/
  /   phallic mystere/
     by the
     center post
     of Peristyle

Such poetry as this by no means represents a rejection of representation and referentiality. If anything, its rejection of an unproblematic assumption of the transparency of language leads to a flood of referential possibilities. The poet provides the grounding units, the lines and tropes, from which readers and listeners will construct those significations, but he only directs them; he does not determine them within a limited horizon of intentionality. The directions are given from a historically minded, radical political stance. Taylor's poems are generally marked by a repudiation of the false representations of freedom in a racialized culture. In "The Musician" we can read racial origins for the sham of constitutional representation:

> choice
> fielded in theft hull dimension dam'd
> bow of Middle Passage, plural choice
> depth grist incarnate slime theft ravaged.

The Constitution of the United States in its original passage extended the franchise only to property-holding white males, this at a time when America's constitutional government countenanced the holding of property in persons. Property was, more than usually, literal theft when the property in question was the persons of Africa stolen from their homes and shipped on the Middle Passage to slavery in the New World. That fatal choice that denied freedom of choice gave form to the founding Republic. "Scroll No. 2," a 1965 poem, begins:

> Nation's lost diplomacy
> lost nation's duplicity
> Demagogic democracy
> Damned dutiful
> Darned cloth
> blue serge   white white
> one someone   shirt floptic
> tank bat and "yeah bo"
> I'ma Senatah!
> You just sing dance unseen
>
>   (*Indent*, n. pag.)

For poets such as Baraka, Spellman, Cortez, and Cecil Taylor, moving to an avant-garde poetics was never motivated by the desire to evade the political imperatives of race and class. For them a radical politics and a radical poetics were virtually inseparable. From their writings during the last decades we would judge that they believed it unlikely that revolutionary politics could be adequately advanced within the forms traditionally associated with past social formations, though the traces of those earlier forms would always remain visible in the new, perhaps under some form of erasure. In this these African-American postmodernists again retrieved from their modernist precursors a more radical mode than that popularized by the New Critics. In the surrealists, they located a radically anticolonial politics given formal experimental expression. Although there were racists among surrealists, and political reactionaries, surrealists were far more likely than an Eliot or a Tate to align themselves publically with the cause of oppressed races. The Surrealist Group in Paris, for one example, contributed to Nancy Cunard's 1933 anthology *Negro* a statement opposing what they called "Murderous Humanitarianism." This contribution was translated by Samuel Beckett and signed by such prominent artists as André Breton, Roger Callois, René Char, René Crevel, Paul Eluard, and Yves Tanguy. The statement could easily have been written by Baraka himself. In citing the sins of the colonial apparatus, the Paris surrealists wrote that "The white man preaches, doses, vaccinates, assassinates and (from himself) receives absolution. With his psalms, his speeches, his guarantees of liberty, equality and fraternity, he seeks to drown the noise of his machine guns" (*Negro* 352).

With the exception of his invented words and scattering of foreign words, Taylor's registers of writing present no insurmountable obstacle to any sufficiently interested to undertake their reading. There is really little difficulty in making sense of so wonderfully ironic and melodic a line as this, from the poem "Choir": "I'se field, I'se rock, I'se time." And Taylor's alliterative and rhyming effects, like his musical units, give us sonic markers with which to orient ourselves in the denser passages of a poem on the order of "Choir":

> bone
> become dress'd skin talk'in syllabic
> monotone hidden from passage walk
> ovah
> delta thru crystal charged atmospheric
>
>> (*Embraced*, n. pag.)

Far from being escapist elitism (dictionaries are democratically available technologies), then, Taylor's postmodernist poetics are his mode of political practice. His writing is not an attempt to turn his back on traditional oral forms, and neither is it a denial of speech in favor of sign. His is the radical artifice of Atkins, but it is also the textual music sought by a number of other black jazz composers of his time.

Julius Hemphill, for one, described his own text-based works as compositions in which he "makes use of orchestral language that proceeds from the rhythmic impulses of the spoken word and does not obey the dictates of meter nor of melody except for the expressive inflections associated with speech in generally colloquial situations" (*Roi Boyé* n. pag.). As Ronald Radano suggests in his summary of Taylor's work in music, Taylor's writing exists within the supplemental logics of sign and song:

> Taylor's modernism took the form of a rhythmic propulsiveness and kinetic energy that supplanted traditional qualities of swing. Further, his technical essays, which betray a familiarity with the "scientific" theoretical literature of contemporary composition, owe equally to the rhythm and musical metaphor of contemporary black poetry, suggesting a complementary oral discourse. (110)

It would probably be more truthful to say that Taylor's rhythms supplemented Swing than to say that they supplanted it. Not content to repeat verbatim the rhythms of 1930s and 1940s Swing, Taylor devised new ways to turn a phrase in music. His new ways may have been disconcerting to any listeners who want African-American artists to stick to the traditional rhythmic vocabularies of Swing (Philip Larkin was an even moldier fig than that, to judge from his writings on jazz) and leave the theorizing to the (presumably white) nonswinging scientists of music, ("You just sing dance unseen"). But such attempts to oppose Swing to a presumptively emotionless and mathematical scientism at the piano are ultimately as futile as attempts to oppose experimental writing to the purported immediacy of speech. What could be more immediate, after all, than the act of reading, of taking the words of another into oneself through the organs of vision?

Taylor's written verse complements orality. What the poet is after, in both his music and his poetry, is outlined at the opening of "Garden":

> . . . energies of fusion
> the placing experiences metamorphosized
> human exchange toward complete submission

to the spirits conscious digestive response
the resulting process many level'd hitting
in various constructs:

> Group sound
> speech transported

(116)

Two pages later, the poem charts its own methodology in a line
that reads, "Sun's bounty transposing language" (118). Writing
has traditionally been seen as a vehicle for the spoken word, but
Taylor sees it more as the scene of "transport," in the sense of
ecstatic transcendence of speech. Just as a musician "transposes"
a melody into a different key, where the melody remains recognizable in its difference, writing affords the possibility of transpositions beyond those available in speech. Taylor's poetry sometimes marks this fact of transpositional supplementarity
graphically, as in the line, "parts travel   come sum='s" ("Musician" 12). The pun is audible, but it is not fully comprehensible
until we read the spelling of "sum." The equal sign that links
"sum" to its possessive apostrophe is not pronounced, though it
acts simultaneously as copula and sign of the sum. That same
sort of chirographic punning is at work in the line "hotcall
waiting synapse sinchange shaken chord" ("Musician" 12), in
which call waiting, the synapses communicating between our
neurons, sin, telephone cords, and musical chords are all riding
on the same line, all offering themselves as potential lines of
flight for improvisation, all forming a "group sound." As Bop and
post-Bop improvisors understood that a number of seemingly
conflictual lines of melody could pass through the notes of the
"same" chord, Taylor's poems demonstrate the polysemous and
overdetermined nature of all signs. If, in Coleman's harmolodic
theory, every note can sound like a tonic, as Don Cherry explained it, in the postmodern poetics of Taylor every inscribed
sign can sound like the tonal center for more than one line of
interpretative practice.

Clark Coolidge located the seeds of this poetics in Bop itself.
In a letter that he wrote to poet and guitarist David Meltzer in
1980, Coolidge spoke of the two "keystones" to Bop, "Time and
Changes" (measure and chord structures):

> The feel is that time has a precise center. Like tight-roping
> on a moving pulley clothesline, you're always trying to keep

up midway between the poles. It really gets that sharply physical. As a drummer you're holding time's cutting edge in your right hand (ride cymbal), a simultaneity of holding and shaping. You occupy the center of the sonic sphere, the world, and ride it and bear it, inviolable . . . And everything that happens there happens once and at once. Once and Ounce, Groove and Chord, Wave and Particle: the Complementarity of Bop. (Meltzer 251)

What we see at the end of Coolidge's commentary is that "transport" of speech and "transposition" of language that Taylor writes of in "Garden" and "The Musician." The "Complementarity of Bop" produced the post-Bop of Free Jazz as practiced by Coleman, the Art Ensemble of Chicago, and Taylor, and the music of Sun Ra's "Omniverse." In the same way we might argue that the "complementarity" of modernist poetics, locatable in dada, surrealism, constructivism, and vorticism, was unfolded as the "supplementarity" of postmodernism, locatable in the poetry of Coolidge and Taylor. This could go a long way toward explaining why, aside from the fact that they listened to the same music, Coolidge's and Taylor's poetics are so strikingly similar, a fact seldom noted in contemporary literary criticism. Not only are their poetics closely related; there are haunting similarities between their individual poems. In Coolidge's collection *Space* (1970), the first line of the first poem is "FELL FAR BUT THE BARN (came) up & smacked me" (3). In 1989, his poem "Comes through in the Call Hold (Improvisations on Cecil Taylor)" contains the line "Fell to this, house markings" (9). (The poem was printed in a special jazz supplement to the *Village Voice*.) Coolidge may have been on hold to Taylor's "hotcall waiting," but his lines also seem to intersect with Taylor's around a common tonal center. In "The Musician," published in 1976, Taylor wrote the very Coolidge-like line "stood stain fell tree sacrilege" (13). The first poem in Coolidge's *Space* was entitled "Fed Drapes." In Taylor's "Garden" an intertextual echo can be heard in the stream of language:

> fed shoulders as division nestles, anon nascent un-
> born yet wither spool unwinde under a natural kin'
> like cork churning unwound rope out of
> stream evenness uninterrupted leaves
>   too a good tone about

(118)

Among Coolidge's most significant poems inspired by his life-long immersion in jazz is the lengthy serial poem entitled "Registers (People in All)," in which his memories of people, and the textual qualities of their names, guide the transpositions between linguistic registers that occur in the poem. In "Choir," which was published along with Taylor's duets with pianist Mary Lou Williams, Taylor practices that same technique, as in his meditations on the figure of Bop piano great Bud Powell: "bud blown circular to the blessed skin / analagous [sic]/ ear from continuum light draw matter to / bone." In the concluding stanza to "Choir," Taylor sought to site his composition, as Coolidge does in "Registers (People in All)," in all registers at once:

> of space particular node
> betwix layers announce
> savor'd victuals in rapped
> basin resonate climb'in growth
> salvage time establish'd
> area agglutinized abyss
> being Astral & all registers
> between.

Far more important than the surface similarities that inevitably arise from the extensive practice of a common poetics is the fact of that commonality itself. There is sufficient idiomatic differentiation in their works that few readers would mistake Coolidge's poetry for Taylor's, but what is crucial to keep before us as we survey the history of recent American verse is the intertextual relationship between black and white avant-gardes. Historians of avant-garde movements in American poetry have tended to write as if black Americans had little direct involvement, and hence our histories have tended to elide the powerful influence of black poets on American verse in general and "experimental" verse in particular. By tracing the many ways that black music and postmodern poetics form the structuring assumptions of artists of such diverse backgrounds as Coolidge and Taylor, we can begin to formulate an understanding of how differing racial subjectivities move within language around a common axis. Taylor's sociohistorical positioning differed from Coolidge's, but it also became a part of Coolidge's own subjectivity as he read and listened to Taylor. This mirrors the interpollation of Euro-American modernism within the legacy of Taylor's African-

American modernist precursors. Taylor drew upon a resonant
history of black responses to white America, a written history:

> blind game stung history tag
> like rope mighty people rise
> rose 'tween ivory firm line

("Musician" 13)

These words arise out of a signifying genealogy that includes the
writings of Marcus Garvey *and* W. E. B. DuBois, as well as the
prophetic oral traditions of the African-American sermon. Taylor's poem is a rope trick that models prophecy in a time when
metanarratives of emancipation are often held suspect. It models
a prophetic stance that does not rest its hopes in a transcendent
telos, whether divine or historical, but in the past examples of
"transport" in music and writing that have continually been reborn in African-American culture.

Critics who privilege the spoken over the written, or who
privilege the oral as it enters literature, may not have in mind the
forms of orality that are to be heard in the recorded literature of
Taylor's *Chinampas,* a 1987 recording session (not released until
1991) that is the most extensive collection of his jazz poetry
widely available at this time. (The collection entitled *In Florescence* also included numerous musical compositions that feature
spoken voice and text, as well as one important poetic text.)
The shouts, screams, gagging noises, and hoarse whispers Taylor
recorded on *Chinampas* may not meet many scholars' expectations of black oral traditions, but when people "get happy" in
the Amen Corner transports of language may ensue. *Chinampas*
is an unusual jazz text in a number of ways. Most unusual is the
fact that Taylor does not play the piano on any of these selections. The music for these compositions is all played on drums,
bells, and small percussion instruments. No printed versions of
the poems are provided (at a time when nearly every Rap and
Pop album comes with its own small booklet of lyrics). The titles
of the poems are all numerical. Like the title of John Cage's most
famous composition for closed piano, the titles of Taylor's jazz
texts are indications of each piece's duration (the longest is the
one entitled "12′30"). In the liner notes, Taylor credits himself
separately for "poetry" and "voice," indicating that these practices exist in a supplementary relationship to one another. The
"poem" is not precisely coincident with the voice of the poet.

There is one selection, entitled "5′46" and beginning with the phrase "it be crystalized," that has no music at all. The remaining poems are all accompanied by percussion instruments, and many are recorded with double-tracked voice.

The occasional screams and choking sounds offer the listener a space in which to reconceive the nature of speech and our usual assumptions about the human voice in music. Because our languages make use of only a small portion of the sounds our vocal apparatus is capable of producing, we tend to hear any sound that is not a phoneme in a language we speak and that is not sung either as entirely nonsignifying or as signifying only at a metalinguistic or gestural level. Undoing that usual way of regarding the voice seems to be at least in part another of Taylor's modes of deconstructive composition. Willard Bohn has reiterated the suggestion that one subject of dada "is really the birth of language via the destruction and reconstruction of the word" (xvii). On his recording of poems such as "5′04" and "5′46," Taylor destroys what we would normally take to be the "natural" phonetic orders of English and reconstitutes them otherwise. Sometimes a recognizable word will be stretched to the breaking point, falling into constituent vocables. Other times seemingly nonmeaningful word forms will come together as if giving birth to a new language, forms that sound scriptable: "Ayida, ayida wedō," for instance, my poor transcription of one passage recited in "5′04." Such moments show, too, that Taylor's most radically transgressive works are a following through of the more radical suggestions in the work of William Carlos Williams. In *The Great American Novel*, Williams's narrator sounds very much like the Taylor of *Chinampas:*

> Break the words. Words are indivisible crystals. One cannot break them – Awu tsst grang splith gra pragh og bm – Yes, one can break them. One can make words. Progress? If I make a word I make myself into a word. Such is progress. I shall make myself into a word. One big word. (*Imaginations* 160)

The term *chinampas* is, according to the liner notes, an Aztec word meaning "floating gardens." The recordings are subtitled "Hot Points." Both terms are metaphorical expressions of Taylor's conception of the compositions. The jazz text as hot point parallels the functioning of the unit structures in Taylor's ensem-

ble compositions, texts that provide a shaping line for subsequent improvisation and a point of juncture for the attachment
of additional units. The jazz text as floating garden calls to mind
both the imaginary gardens cited by Marianne Moore, with their
real toads, and Jorge Louis Borges's garden of forking paths.
These jazz texts are landscapes for wandering that float free of
quotidian ground without ever losing sight of it. Despite the lack
of printed texts, *Chinampas* has the effect of enmeshing us further in the grammatology of signs rather than fostering the
illusion of a self-present voice. At the most basic level, any recording of the speaking voice participates in the same logics of
difference, deferral, and absence that form the conditions for
the possibility of writing. The digital coding carried on a compact
disk is a form of electronic calligraphy that allows us to defer
listening and to listen to one who is not present. The speaking
voice has been encoded in a stream of information, to be reconstituted through the reading lens of the disk playback device. To
further compound these displacements, Taylor makes use of the
technology of the studio to double-track his own recitations. His
voice is taken down, marked so that later his voice can join itself.
We hear two Cecil Taylors calling and responding to each other
on tracks like "5'07" and "12'30." One of the doubled voices
remarks upon this very process of deferral and repetition. "For
the letter after body acknowledges space," one of the two Taylors
intones to a background of finger snaps, handclaps, drum, and
his own mirroring voice. The voice, which sings at the beginning
of "12'30," also echoes the music around it. "Damballah half
oracle bells," it pronounces to a responsive soundtrack that includes bells (and what sounds to me like finger cymbals).

Such thickening of affect also returns our attention to the
materiality of the signifiers, in good twentieth-century modernist
and postmodernist fashion. The last text, "3'36," pronounces an
edict applicable to the entire project: "magnetized, they have
been concretized." This text triple-tracks Taylor's voice, and it
makes extensive use of stereophonic separation effects to produce the illusion of a reciting voice in motion within our listening room. This is yet more effective when the listener uses
headphones, as Taylor's voice then seems to emanate from various floating "hot points" within one's own head. On two pieces,
"9'20" and "6'56," Taylor uses sheets of paper as a percussion
instrument. On "9'20" they provide the only music accompa-

nying the recitation. As Taylor asks hurriedly, "Guess what? Guess what?", the sound of pages being turned, shuffled, and shaken rhythmically takes the place of the rattles and cymbals heard on the other pieces. We are left in the dark ("darkness of movable screen," Taylor reads on "3'36") as to whether these noises are made by the pages of his actual reading text or are simply made by sheets of paper chosen for their superior sound-making properties.

Taylor's characteristic dada humor surfaces at several points. By the "water's edge" of "5'07," Taylor tells us excitedly, "Quadraped's got a plan!" In "5'46" he reads a definition of the word "synechdoche" rather than read a synechdoche. Thus we hear "a substitution of the part for the whole" as a substitution for a trope. The poems additionally pay ironic tribute to the past of poetry, most notably at the very beginning of *Chinampas*. The first piece, "5'04," is read to a background of somber soundings on the tympani, as if in homage to Ezra Pound's own odd recordings, where he performed somewhat pompous dramatizations of his verse while beating on the tympani. This piece opens with the words "Angle of incidence," a line that, more than coincidentally enough, has as its intertext Walter Arensberg's dada poem "Theorem":

> For purposes of illusion
> the actual ascent of two waves
> transparent to a basis
> which has a disappearance of its own
> is timed
> at the angle of incidence
> to the swing of a suspended
> lens
> (qtd. in Bohn 13)

The poems of *Chinampas* also have that mixture of dada-esque and Zen counterlogic that produces images like Jarman's silent sounding gong or Taylor's image in "3'43" of "mirrors manicured without touch."

Taylor's jazz texts share with the neobaroque of Atkins a scripting of abstract imagery. Taylor speaks in "5'46" of "non-repetitive spatial openings" and on "5'04" of "the florescence of a perpendicular." Like the "color squared" of his early poem "Scroll No. 1," these are linguistic objects that parallel the imagery of the visual but cannot, strictly speaking, be visualized. If we try to imagine spatial openings, repetitive or not, we will probably end by thinking of something with a hole in it. If we attempt to envision a florescent perpendicular, we will probably have to have some object in mind placed perpendicularly to some other object and then imagine it glowing. Taylor's words, like Atkins's, sometimes create noncognitive aspects of the material world or, to use Williams's terminology, the imaginative qualities of actual things. They are metaphysical poems for real readers and audiences, but to keep us from getting too serious about this most serious art, Taylor deliberately stutters on several successive attempts to utter the word "metaphysics" as he recites "5'46."

Admittedly, some of Taylor's vocal effects are more interesting to listen to than others. In the same way that his extended passage of moaning along with his own piano on *The Great Concert of Cecil Taylor* is finally more annoying than revealing, some of the gagging sounds emitted here may tempt listeners to regard them as a form of auto-critique. In the end, though, Taylor has undertaken a courageous exploration of the detritus of vocal signifying, and he has not only expanded the vocabulary of jazz; he has expanded the vocabulary of vocabulary. For Cecil Taylor, writing is never just the recording of either speech or thought, nor is it just a matter of getting it all down for posterity. Taylor's jazz texts are reports of an experiment in progress, of his excavations of human languages and music. They are, as he writes in "5'04," "deposits of hieroglyphic regions," a statement that places him in the company of Melville and Baraka, Poe and Atkins, Ed Roberson and the ancient Ethiopian authors.

For years jazz critics have listened to the music of Cecil Taylor and asked each other, "But is it jazz?" Taylor has attempted to transport the music beyond the level of such a concern (though the formal histories of jazz are always visible in his compositions). Many will listen to a work like *Chinampas* and ask, "Is it poetry?" or even, "But is it speech?" The "Hot Points" of *Chinampas* in their continual transgressions of genre and transpositions of form may end by rendering such questions moot. In any event, "the darkness of the movable screen" is here recorded, and that moving screen must inevitably change the shape of our listening rooms. Some critics may still ask, "But is it black?" The more significant question for us to address, as we read and listen to Russell Atkins, Percy Johnston, Jayne Cortez, Harold Carrington,

and Cecil Taylor may be, What does it mean to our understanding of ourselves and of American language that black people
make these orders of art? Baraka, in his article "Present Perfect
(Cecil Taylor)," published in the radical poetry magazine *Kulchur*
as far back as 1962, said,

> Taylor and the others are making music that is exactly where
> we are. It is as exact in its emotional registrations and as
> severely contemporary in its aesthetic as any other Western
> art . . . But what can you say of a society that sends Benny
> Goodman and Robert Frost to Russia as cultural avants. I
> am convincing myself that it is the least of our worries.
> (*Black Music* 109)

Baraka raises the question of cultural representation but does
not want to get ahead of himself. The real cultural "avants" of
America are not the sort of emissaries that our cultural ministries
want to send out as an advance guard for the New World Order,
and in representing our culture to ourselves we have too quickly
settled for the representations of the modal average. As the
histories of America's post–World War II literary arts have taken
shape, they have been mostly silent on the subject of black experiment, and that silence, in the midst of unceasing debate over
the question of subjectivity in the latter half of the century, does
indeed speak volumes. But, to give Ed Roberson's poetry the last,
as well as the first, word:

> the music's fact is
>   a glossolalia
>   sound's meaning.
>
>   (*Lucid* 60)

WORKS CITED

Addison, Lloyd. *The Aura and the Umbra.* London: Paul Bremen, 1970.
  Letter to Jonathan Williams. Poetry and Rare Book Collection: Jargon Papers, B97F46. Library of the State University of New York, Buffalo.
  Letters to Rosey Pool. Rosey Pool Papers. "Correspondence, 1959–1967." File folder no. 4. Moorland–Spingarn Research Center, Manuscript Division. Howard University, Washington, DC.
Alexander, Will. *Vertical Rainbow Climber.* Aptos, CA: Jazz Press, 1987.
Anderson III, T. J. "Review of *Moment's Notice.*" *Lift* 14 (1994): 79–80.
Art Ensemble of Chicago. *Fanfare for the Warriors.* Atlantic Records, SD 1651. 1973.
A Jackson in Your House. Affinity Records, AFF 9. 1970.
Ashbery, John. "The New Realism." *The Tennis Court Oath.* Middletown, CT: Wesleyan UP, 1962. 59–63.
Atkins, Russell. "Abstract of the Hypothetical Arbitrary Constant of Inhibition's Continuumization Becoming 'Consciousness' (Nervous System Etc.)." *Free Lance* 11.1 (1967): 24–36.
"Éloge." *Free Lance* 14.2 (1970): 26–7.
"Henry Dumas: An Appreciation." *Black American Literature Forum* 22.2 (1988): 159–60.
Here in The. Cleveland: Cleveland State University Poetry Center, 1976.
Heretofore. London: Paul Bremen, 1968.
"How Would I Come upon a Corpse?" *Free Lance* 3.1 (1955): 26.
"The Hypothetical Arbitrary Constant of Inhibition's Continuumization." *Free Lance* 8.2 (1964): 33–62.
"Langston Hughes and the Avant-Garde." *Podium* 1.3 (1965): 14–15.
"Letter to *Input.*" *Input* 1.4 (1964): 6–7.
Maleficium. Cleveland: Free Lance Press, 1971.

"May Twenty-Second, Nineteen Sixty Seven." *Free Lance* 11.2 (1967): 20–3.

"Notes on Negro Poets." *Free Lance* 2.1 (1954): 16–18.

"Of." *Free Lance* 7.1 (1963): 21–3.

"Of." *Free Lance* 11.1 (1967): 49–54.

"Of." *Free Lance* 20.1–2 (1980): 1–5.

"Of: The Invalidity of Dominant-Group 'Education' Forms for 'Progress' for Non-Dominant Ethnic Groups as Americans." *Free Lance* 7.2 (1963): 19–32.

Phenomena. Cleveland: Free Lance Poetry and Prose Workshop/Wilberforce UP, 1961.

"A Phenomenalist Perspective for Poetics Based on C (Negative) and B (Positive) Probabilities for Maxima and Minima." *Free Lance* 18.1–2 (1977): 16–24.

A Podium Presentation. Brooklyn Heights, OH: Poetry Seminar Press, 1960.

"Pseudo-problematical Critical Values for 'More' in Poetry as Opposed to Technique." *Free Lance.* 16.1–2 (1973): 45–59.

"A Psychovisual Perspective for 'Musical' Composition." *Free Lance* 3.2 (1955): 2–17.

"Psychovisual Perspective for 'Musical' Composition." *Free Lance* 5.1 (1958): 7–47.

"Review of *Musophilus by Samuel Daniel.*" *Free Lance* 10.1 (1966): 12–13.

"Some Thoughts Defining 'Mainstream' . . ." *Free Lance* 8.1 (1964): 26–7.

"Special Russell Atkins Issue." With Commentary by Casper L. Jordan and J. Stefanski. *Free Lance* 14.2 (1970).

Spyrytual. Cleveland: 7 Flowers Press, 1966.

2 by Russell Atkins. Cleveland: Free Lance Poets and Prose Workshop, 1963.

Whichever. Cleveland: Free Lance Press, 1978.

Babb, Valerie M. "William Melvin Kelly." *Dictionary of Literary Biography 33: Afro-American Fiction Writers after 1955.* Ed. Thadious Davis and Trudier Harris. Detroit: Gale Research, 1984. 135–43.

Baker, Houston A. *Afro-American Poetics: Revisions of Harlem and the Black Aesthetic.* Madison: U of Wisconsin P, 1988.

Modernism and the Harlem Renaissance. Chicago: U of Chicago P, 1987.

Baraka, Amiri. *The Autobiography of LeRoi Jones/Amiri Baraka.* New York: Freundlich Books, 1984.

Black Magic: Poetry, 1961–1967. New York: Bobbs-Merrill, 1969.

Black Music. New York: Quill, 1967.

The Dead Lecturer. New York: Grove, 1964.

Home: Social Essays. New York: 1966.

"Introduction: Pfister Needs to Be Heard!" *Beer Cans, Bullets, Things & Pieces* by Arthur Pfister. Detroit: Broadside Press, 1972. 4–6.

"Lowdown." Poetry and Rare Book Collection: Intrepid Collection, B54F18. Library of the State University of New York, Buffalo.

"A Meditation on Bob Kaufman." *Sulfur* 29 (1991): 61–6.

New Music–New Poetry. With David Murray and Steve McCall. India Navigation, 1048. 1981.

New York Art Quartet. With the New York Art Quartet. Base Records, ESP-1004. 1965.

"Note." *The Floating Bear: A Newsletter.* Ed. Diane di Prima and LeRoi Jones. LaJolla, CA: Laurence McGilvery, 1973. 56.

"Notes on Lou Donaldson & Andrew Hill." *Cricket* (1969): 46.

"Revue." *The Floating Bear: A Newsletter: Numbers 1–37, 1961–1969.* Ed. Diane di Prima and LeRoi Jones. LaJolla, CA: Laurence McGilvery, 1973. 15–16.

"Suppose Sorrow Was a Time Machine." *Yugen* 2 (1958): 9–11.

Baraka, Amiri (LeRoi Jones), and Hettie Cohen, eds. *Yugen* 7 (1961).

Barrett, Lindon. "(Further) Figures of Violence: *The Street* in the American Landscape." *Cultural Critique* 25 (1993): 205–37.

Berkson, Bill, and Frank O'Hara. "F.Y.I. 6/26/61 (The Picnic Hour)." *Locus Solus* 3–4 (1962): 104–5.

Bérubé, Michael. *Marginal Forces/Cultural Centers: Tolson, Pynchon, and the Politics of the Canon.* Ithaca, NY: Cornell UP, 1992.

Bluiett, Hammiet. *Nali Kola.* Soul Note Records, 121: 188–2. 1987.

Bohn, Willard, ed. *The Dada Market: An Anthology.* Carbondale, IL: Southern Illinois UP, 1993.

Braxton, Joanne. *Sometimes I Think of Maryland.* New York: Sunbury Press, 1977.

Bremser, Ray. *Angel.* New York: Tompkins Square Press, 1967.

Blowing Mouth/The Jazz Poems, 1958–1970. Cherry Valley, NY: Cherry Valley Editions, 1978.

"drive suite." *beat coast east: AN ANTHOLOGY OF REBELLION.* Ed. Stanley Fisher. New York: Excelsior Press, 1960. 71–3.

Drive Suite: an essay on composition, materials, references, etc. . . . San Francisco: Nova Broadcast, 1968.

Brooks, Gwendolyn. *Blacks.* Chicago: David, 1989.

Brown, Marion. *Afternoon of a Georgia Faun.* ECM Records, ECM 1004 2310 444. 1970.

Geechee Recollections. ABC Records, AS-9252. 1973.

Sweet Earth Flying. ABC Records, AS-9275. 1974.

Brown, Sterling. *The Collected Poems of Sterling A. Brown*. New York: Harper and Row, 1980.

Bryan, John. "Poetry's Floating Crap Game." *Poetry Flash* 103 (1981): 3, 8.

Carrington, Harold. *Drive suite*. London: Paul Bremen, 1972.

"Lament." Amiri Baraka Papers, 1958–1966. Special Collections, file C. UCLA.

Letters to Amiri Baraka. Baraka Papers, UCLA.

Letters to Jonathan Williams. Poetry and Rare Book Collection: Jargon Papers, B27F30; B146F37; B146F38. Library of the State University of New York, Buffalo.

"Woo's People." Poetry and Rare Book Collection: Jargon Papers, B27F30. Library of the State University of New York, Buffalo.

Césaire, Aimé. *Return to My Native Land*. Trans. John Berger and Anna Bostock. Baltimore: Penguin Books, 1969.

Chambers, Stephen. "HER." *Journal of Black Poetry* 1.11 (1969): 21.

Cherkovski, Neeli. "Bob Kaufman: The President of Poetry." *Poetry Flash* 78 (1979): 7–8.

Chow, Rey. *Writing Diaspora: Tactics of Intervention in Contemporary Cultural Studies*. Bloomington: Indiana UP, 1993.

Coleman, Ornette. *Science Fiction*. With poem by David Henderson. Columbia Records, KC 31061. 1971.

Skies of America. Columbia Records, KC 31562. 1972.

Congdon, Kirby. "A Reply." *Input* 1.4 (1964): 9.

Coolidge, Clark. "From Comes through in the Call Hold (Improvisations on Cecil Taylor)." *Village Voice*, "Jazz Special." June 26, 1989. 9–10.

"Registers (People in All)." *Temblor* 10 (1989): 59–67.

Sound as Thought: Poems, 1982–1984. Los Angeles: Sun and Moon Press, 1990.

Space. New York: Harper and Row, 1970.

Cortez, Jayne. *Celebrations and Solitudes*. Strata-East Records, SES-7421. 1974.

Coagulations: New and Selected Poems. New York: Thunder's Mouth Press, 1984.

Firespitter. New York: Bola Press, 1982.

Maintain Control. Bola Press Records, BP-8601. 1986.

Mouth on Paper. New York: Bola Press, 1977.

Scarifications. New York: Bola Press, 1978.

There It Is. Bola Press Records, BP-8201. 1982.

Unsubmissive Blues. Bola Press Records, BP-8001. 1980.

Crouch, Stanley. "*Black Fire*: A Review." *Journal of Black Poetry* 1.11 (1969): 65–9.

"Books." *Journal of Black Poetry* 1.10 (1968): 90–2.

"Toward a Purer Black Poetry Esthetic." *Journal of Black Poetry* 1.10 (1968): 28–9.

Cumberbatch, Lawrence S. "I Swear To You That Ship Never Sunk in Middle-Passage!" *We Speak as Liberators: Young Black Poets.* Ed. Orde Coombs. New York: Dodd, Mead, 1970.

Davis, Miles. *doo-bop.* Warner Brothers, 9 26938-2. 1992.

Live – Evil. Columbia Records, G 30954. 1970.

Delany, Martin R. *The Origin of Races and Color.* Philadelphia: Harper and Brothers, 1879; Facs. Baltimore: Black Classic Press, 1991.

Dent, Tom. "Lorenzo Thomas." *Dictionary of Literary Biography 41: Afro-American Poets since 1955.* Ed. Trudier Harris and Thadious Davis. Detroit: Gale Research, 1985. 315–26.

"Umbra Days." *Black American Literature Forum* 14.3 (1980): 105–8.

Derrida, Jacques. *Aporias.* Trans. Thomas Dutoit. Stanford: Stanford UP, 1993.

Dorn, Ed. Letters to Amiri Baraka. Amiri Baraka Papers, 1958–1966, Special Collections, Ed Dorn file. UCLA.

Dumas, Henry. *Play Ebony, Play Ivory.* Ed. Eugene Redmond. New York: Random House, 1974.

Ellingham, Lewis, and Kevin Killian. "*Cock Drill:* Jack Spicer, Steve Jonas, The 'Boston Renaissance' and After." *The Poetry of Stephen Jonas.* 40–3.

Emeruwa, Leatrice W. "Black Art and Artists in Cleveland." *Black World* 22.3 (1973): 23–33.

Fabio, Sarah Webster. "Tripping with Black Writing." *The Black Aesthetic.* Ed. Addison Gayle, Jr. Garden City, NY: Doubleday, 1972. 173–81.

Farnsworth, Robert M. *Melvin B. Tolson, 1898–1966: Plain Talk and Poetic Prophecy.* Columbia, MO: U of Missouri P, 1984.

Fields, Julia. Letter to Rosey Pool. Rosey Pool Papers. "Correspondence 1959–1967." Box no. 52. Moorland–Spingarn Research Center, Manuscript Division. Howard University, Washington, DC.

Slow Coins: New Poems (& Some Old Ones). Washington, DC: Three Continents Press, 1981.

Fletcher, Bob. "A Lovedirge to the Whitehouse/(or, It Soots You Right)." *Umbra Anthology, 1967–1968.* Ed. David Henderson. New York: Umbra, 1968. 11–12.

Foster, Frances Smith. *Written by Herself: Literary Production by African American Women, 1746–1892.* Bloomington: Indiana UP, 1993.

Fraser, Al. "To the 'JFK' Quintet." *Black Fire.* Ed. LeRoi Jones and Larry Neal. New York: Apollo, 1968. 272.

Frost, Robert. *The Poetry of Robert Frost.* New York: Holt, Rinehart and Winston, 1969.

Garcia Lorca, Federico. *The Selected Poems of Federico Garcia Lorca.* Ed. Francisco Garcia Lorca and Donald Allen. New York: New Directions, 1955.

Gehr, Richard. "On the Road Again." *Village Voice.* June 7, 1994. 17–18.

Gilroy, Paul. *The Black Atlantic: Modernity and Double Consciousness.* Cambridge, MA: Harvard UP, 1993.

Ginsberg, Allen. "Kerouac." *The Jack Kerouac Collection.* Rhino Records, 1990. 8.

Giscombe, C. S. "Fugitive." *A Poetics of Criticism.* Ed. Juliana Spahr, Mark Wallace, Kristin Prevallet, and Pam Rehm. Buffalo: Leave Books, 1994. 49–54.

"From Giscome Road." *Writing from the New Coast: Presentation.* Ed. Peter Gizzi and Connell McGrath. Stockbridge, MA: O blek Editions, 1993. 94–6.

Goldberg, David Theo. *Racist Culture: Philosophy and the Politics of Meaning.* Cambridge, MA: Blackwell Publisher, 1993.

Golding, Alan. *From Outlaw to Classic: Canons in American Poetry.* Madison: U of Wisconsin P, 1995.

Goodman, Nelson. *Ways of Worldmaking.* Indianapolis: Hackett, 1978.

Govan, Oswald. "The Angry Skies Are Calling." *Burning Spear: An Anthology of Afro-Saxon Poetry.* Washington, DC: Jupiter Hammon, 1963. 22–3.

Gruttola, Raffael de. "A Reminiscence." *The Poetry of Stephen Jonas.* Somerville, MA: *Lift*, 1992. 29–30.

Gunn, Giles, *Thinking across the American Grain: Ideology, Intellect, and the New Pragmatism.* Chicago: U of Chicago P, 1992.

Hall, Stuart. "What Is This 'Black' in Black Popular Culture?" *Black Popular Culture: A Project by Michelle Wallace.* Ed. Gina Dent. Seattle: Bay Press, 1992. 21–33.

Hamalian, Linda. *A Life of Kenneth Rexroth.* New York: Norton, 1991.

Hamilton, Bobb. "Biographical Notes." *For Malcolm.* 2nd ed. Ed. Dudley Randall and Margaret G. Burroughs. Detroit: Broadside Press, 1969. 100.

Harland, Richard. *Beyond Superstructuralism: The Syntagmatic Side of Language.* London: Routledge, 1993.

Harper, Michael S., and Anthony Walton, eds. *Every Shut Eye Ain't Asleep: An Anthology of Poetry by African Americans since 1945.* Boston: Little, Brown, 1994.

Harrison, De Leon. "The Room." *The Poetry of Black America: Anthology of the Twentieth Century.* Ed. Arnold Adoff. New York: Harper and Row, 1973. 394–5.

"Yellow." *The Poetry of Black America.* 395.

Hemphill, Julius. *Roi Boyé & the Gotham Minstrels.* Sackville Recordings, 3014/15. 1977.

Henderson, David. "Editor's Column." *Umbra Blackworks* 1 (1970): n. pag.

Henderson, Stephen. *Understanding the New Black Poetry: Black Speech and Black Music as Poetic References.* New York: Morrow, 1972.

High, Ronald Henry. "Russell Atkins." *Dictionary of Literary Biography 41: Afro-American Poets since 1955.* Ed. Trudier Harris and Thadious Davis. Detroit: Gale Research, 1985. 24–32.

Hughes, Langston. "The Twenties: Harlem and Its Negritude." *African Forum* 1 (1966): 18–19.

Weary Blues. With Charles Mingus and Leonard Feather. Verve Records, 841 600-2. 1990. (Recorded in 1958.)

Hughes, Langston, ed. *New Negro Poets U.S.A.* Bloomington: Indiana UP, 1964.

Hughes, Langston, and Arna Bontemps. *Arna Bontemps – Langston Hughes Letters, 1925–1967.* Ed. Charles H. Nichols. New York: Paragon House, 1990.

Hughes, Langston, and Arna Bontemps, eds. *The Poetry of the Negro.* Garden City, NY: Doubleday, 1970.

Hunt, Erica. "Notes for an Oppositional Poetics." *The Politics of Poetic Form: Poetry and Public Policy.* Ed. Charles Bernstein. New York: Roof Books, 1990. 197–212.

Ismaili-Abu-Bakr, Rashidah. "Slightly Autobiographical: The 1960s on the Lower East Side." *African American Review* 27.4 (1993): 585–9.

Jackson, Gerald. "Untitled." *Umbra Anthology, 1967–1968.* Ed. David Henderson. New York: Society of Umbra, 1968.

Jackson, Ronald Shannon. *Pulse.* Celluloid Records, CELCD5011. 1984.

James, C. L. R. *The Black Jacobins: Toussaint L'Ouverture and the San Domingo Revolution.* 1938. 2nd ed. New York: Random House, 1963.

Jameson, Fredric. *Postmodernism, or, The Cultural Logic of Late Capitalism.* Durham, NC: Duke UP, 1991.

Jarman, Joseph. "Odawalla." *Arsenal: Surrealist Subversion* 3 (1976): 33.

Song For. Delmark Records, DS-9410. 1967.

Joans, Ted. *Black Pow-Wow: Jazz Poems.* New York: Hill and Wang, 1969.

Johnson, Abby Arthur, and Ronald Mayberry Johnson. *Propaganda & Aesthetics: The Literary Politics of African-American Magazines in the Twentieth Century.* Amherst: U of Massachusetts P, 1991.

Johnson, Georgia Douglass. "Resolution." *Phylon* 21.3 (1960): 265.

Johnson, Helene. "Bottled." *Shadowed Dreams: Women's Poetry of the Harlem Renaissance.* Ed. Maureen Honey. New Brunswick, NJ: Rutgers UP, 1989.

Johnston, Percy Edward. "BLAUPUNKT." *Dasein/Muntu* 12 (1988): 151.

"Confessions of Whitey." *Dasein* 7–8 (1968): 39.

"Dewey Square, 1956." *Burning Spear: An Anthology of Afro-Saxon Poetry.* Washington, DC: Jupiter Hammon, 1963. 42–3.

"Minton's Midtown, Baby!" *Dasein* 7–8 (1968): 44–7.

"Pax Romana." *Dasein* 1.1 (1961): 43.

Phenomenology of Space and Time: An Examination of Eugene Clay Holmes' Studies in the Philosophy of Time and Space. New York: Dasein Literary Society, 1976.

"Round about Midnight, Opus 6." *Dasein* 4–5 (1966): 232.

"Round about Midnight, Opus 17." *Understanding the New Black Poetry.* Stephen Henderson. New York: Morrow, 1973. 192–3.

Sean Pendragon Requiem. New York: Dasein–Jupiter Hammon, 1964.

Six Cylinder Olympus. Chicago: Jupiter Hammon, 1964.

"Variations on a Theme by Johnston." *Burning Spear: An Anthology of Afro-Saxon Poetry.* Washington, DC: Jupiter Hammon, 1963. 46.

Johnston, Percy E., and LeRoy Stone. *Continental Streamlets.* Washington, DC: Stone and Johnston, 1960.

Jonas, Stephen. "distend." Baraka Papers, UCLA.

Exercises for Ear: Being a Primer for the Beginner in the American Idiom. London: Ferry Press, 1968.

Four Letters. :that: 23 (1994).

" 'I' BEFORE E-quality OR I THE FEW, YOU THE MINNIE-SINGERS." Baraka papers, UCLA.

"III." Poetry and Rare Book Collection: Robert Kelly Papers, B272, F14. State University of New York at Buffalo.

Letters to LeRoi Jones. Baraka Papers, UCLA.

Letters to Robert Kelly. Poetry and Rare Book Collection: Robert Kelly Papers, B66F1; B66F3; B66F4; B66F5. Library of the State University of New York, Buffalo.

"Orgasm 0." Baraka papers, UCLA.

"Orgasm X." Baraka papers, UCLA.

"Orgasm XXVIIII: First Series." Baraka papers, UCLA.

"Orgasm 52." Baraka papers, UCLA.

"Orgasm XXXVI–Second Series." Baraka Papers, UCLA.

"About the Poem and about Measure for George Stanley." Baraka Papers, 1958–1966. Special Collections, Stephen Jonas file. UCLA.

The Poetry of Stephen Jonas. Ed. Joseph Torra. *Lift* 10–11 (1992).

"A Poet's Word to a Blue Painter." Baraka Papers, UCLA.

Selected Poems. Ed. Raffael de Gruttola. Boston: Stone Soup Poetry, 1973.

Selected Poems. Ed. Joseph Torra. Hoboken, NJ: Talisman, 1994.

"Subway Haiku." Diane di Prima and LeRoi Jones, eds., *The Floating Bear.*

Transmutations. London: Ferry Press, 1966.

"What Made Maud Hum." Baraka Papers, UCLA, Jonas file.

Jordan, Casper LeRoy. Afterword to *Phenomena,* by Russell Atkins. 76–8.

Jordan, June. *Some Changes.* New York: Dutton, 1971.

Jost, Ekkehard. *Free Jazz.* New York: Da Capo, 1981.

Joyce, Joyce A. "The Black Canon: Reconstructing Black American Literary Criticism." *New Literary History* 18.2 (1987): 335–44.

——— " 'Who the Cap Fit': Unconsciousness and Unconscionableness in the Criticism of Houston A. Baker, Jr., and Henry Louis Gates, Jr." *New Literary History* 18.2 (1987): 373–84.

Judy, Ronald A. T. *(Dis)forming the American Canon: African-Arabic Slave Narratives and the Vernacular.* Minneapolis: U of Minnesota P, 1993.

Kaufman, Bob. *Does the Secret Mind Whisper?* San Francisco: City Lights, 1960.

Kelly, Robert. "Llanto for Steve Jonas." *Hearse* 13 (1970): n. pag.

Kelly, William Melvin. *Dunfords Travels Everywheres.* New York: Doubleday, 1970.

"Interview with Ishmael Reed and Quincy Troupe." *Konch* 1.2 (1990): 1–7.

"Jest Like Sam." *Negro Digest* 17.12 (1969): 61–4.

"Letter to Melvin B. Tolson." Melvin B. Tolson Papers, container no. 1: "General Correspondence," folder K. Library of Congress, Washington, DC.

Kirk, Roland. *The Return of the 5000 Lb. Man.* Warner Brothers Records, 0698. 1976.

Kubernick, Harvey, ed. *JazzSpeak: A Word Collection.* New Alliance Records, NAR CD 054. 1991.

Kutzinski, Vera. *Against the American Grain: Myth and History in William Carlos Williams, Jay Wright, and Nicolás Guillén.* Baltimore: Johns Hopkins UP, 1987.

Laforgue, Jules. *The Last Poems of Jules Laforgue.* Trans. Madeleine Betts. Elms Court, UK: Stockwell, 1973.

Legall, Walter de. "Psalm for Sonny Rollins." *Dasein* 6 (1966): 76–7.

Litweiler, John. *Ornette Coleman: A Harmolodic Life.* New York: Morrow, 1992.

Loftin, Elouise. *Barefoot Necklace.* Brooklyn: Jamima House, 1975.

——— "Haitian Heritage." *Celebration.* With Andrew Cyrille and Maono. IPS Records, IPS ST002. 1975.

Lorde, Audre. *Coal.* New York: Norton, 1976.

Zami: A New Spelling of My Name. Watertown, MA: Persephone Press, 1982.

Lowensohn, Ron. Letters to Amiri Baraka. Amiri Baraka Papers, Lowensohn file. UCLA.

Lucas, W. Francis. "Norman H. Pritchard, Poet." *Liberator* 7.6 (1967): 12–13.

Lund, Mary Graham. "Atomic Bombs." *Phylon* 21.2 (1960): 143.

Mackey, Nathaniel. *Discrepant Engagement: Dissonance, Cross-Culturality, and Experimental Writing.* Cambridge: Cambridge UP, 1993.

School of Udhra. San Francisco: City Lights, 1993.

Madhabuti, Haki. "Only a Few Left." *Free Lance* 11.2 (1967): 48.

Major, Clarence. *The Dark and the Feeling: Black American Writers and Their Work.* New York: Third Press, 1974.

No. New York: Emerson Hall, 1973.

"A Petition for Langston Hughes." *Free Lance* 11.2 (1967): 49.

McLucas, Leroy. "Graph." *Umbra* 1.1 (1963): 39.

"Negotiation." *Umbra* 1.1 (1963): 38.

Melhem, D. H. *Heroism in the New Black Poetry: Introductions and Interviews.* Lexington: UP of Kentucky, 1990.

Meltzer, David. *Reading Jazz.* San Francisco: Mercury House, 1993.

Metz, Christian. *The Imaginary Signifier: Psychoanalysis and the Cinema.* Trans. Celia Britton, Annwyl Williams, Ben Brewster, and Alfred Guzzetti. Bloomington: Indiana UP, 1982.

Miller, May. "The Wrong Side of Morning." *Phylon* 21.4 (1960): 316.

Mingus, Charles. *Let My Children Hear Music.* Columbia Records, C31039. N.d.

Town Hall Concert. Solid State Records, SS 18024. 1962.

Monson, Ingrid. "Doubleness and Jazz Improvisation: Irony, Parody, and Ethnomusicology." *Critical Inquiry* 20.2 (1994): 283–313.

Mullen, Harryette. "Visionary Literacy: Art, Literature and Indigenous African Writing Systems." Lecture delivered at Intersection for the Arts, San Francisco, May 24, 1993.

Napier, Winston. "The Howard Poets." *Washington and Washington Writing.* Ed. David McAleavey. Washington, DC: Center for Washington Area Studies, 1987. 57–67.

Natambu, Kofi. "Words & Music in America." *Moment's Notice: Jazz in Poetry & Prose.* Minneapolis: Coffee House Press, 1993. 342.

Nicosia, Gerald. "Kerouac as Musician." *The Jack Kerouac Collection.* Rhino Records, 1990. 9–11.

O'Hara, Frank. Introduction to *The Beautiful Days* by A. B. Spellman. New York: Poets Press, 1965.

Ong, Walter J. *Orality and Literacy: The Technologizing of the Word.* London: Methuen, 1982.

Oppenheimer, Joel. "Letter to LeRoi Jones." *Yugen* 7 (1961): 59–61.

Oren, Michel. "The Umbra Poets' Workshop, 1962–1965: Some Socio-Literary Puzzles." *Studies in Black American Literature:* Vol. 2, *Belief vs. Theory in Black American Literary Criticism.* Ed. Joe Weixlman and Chester J. Fontenot. Greenwood, FL: Penkevill, 1986. 177–223.

Outlaw, Lucius. "African, African American, Africana Philosophy." *Philosophical Forum* 24.1–3 (1992–3): 62–93.

Patterson, Raymond. Letter to Rosey Pool. Sept. 5, 1960. Rosey Pool Papers. Moorland–Spingarn Research Collection. Manuscript Division, Howard University. Washington, DC.

Perloff, Marjorie. *Poetic License: Essays on Modernist and Postmodernist Lyric.* Evanston, IL: Northwestern UP, 1990.

Perry, David. "The Jack Kerouac Collection." *The Jack Kerouac Collection.* Rhino Records, 1990. 2–7.

Pitcher, Oliver. *Dust of Silence.* New York: Troubador Press, 1958.

"Introduction: At Random." *Atlanta University Sampler.* Ed. Oliver Pitcher. Atlanta: Atlanta University Center, n.d.

"Tango." *Yugen* 2 (1958): 17.

Postell, Tom. "Gertrude Stein Rides the Town Down El – to New York City." *Yugen* 1 (1958): 9.

"harmony." *Yugen* 2 (1958): 8.

"I Want a Solid Piece of Sunlight and a Yardstick to Measure It With." *Yugen* 1 (1958): 10.

Pound, Ezra. *Selected Letters, 1907–1941.* Ed. D. D. Paige. New York: New Directions, 1950.

di Prima, Diane. Introduction to *The Floating Bear: A Newsletter.* Ed. Diane Di Prima and LeRoi Jones. LaJolla, CA: Laurence McGilvery, 1973. vii–xviii.

di Prima, Diane, and LeRoi Jones, eds. *The Floating Bear: A Newsletter.* LaJolla, CA: Laurence McGilvery, 1973.

Pritchard, Norman H. *EECCHHOOEESS.* New York: New York UP, 1971.

"From Where the Blues?" *Umbra* 2 (1963): 51.

"Magma." *Liberator* 7.6 (1967): 12.

The Matrix: Poems, 1960–1970. Garden City, NY: Doubleday, 1970.

"Metagnomy." *The New Black Poetry.* Ed. Clarence Major. New York: International, 1969. 100–1.

".–.–.–." *Dices or Black Bones: Black Voices of the Seventies.* Ed. Adam David Miller. New York: Houghton Mifflin, 1970.

Ra, Sun. "To the Peoples of Earth." *Black Fire: An Anthology of Afro-American Writing.* Ed. LeRoi Jones and Larry Neal. New York: Morrow, 1968. 217.

"The Possibility of Altered Destiny." Talk given at Soundscape, New

York City, Nov. 10, 1979. *Live from Soundscape*. DIW Records, DIW-388B. 1994.

Radano, Ronald M. *New Musical Figurations: Anthony Braxton's Cultural Critique*. Chicago: U of Chicago P, 1992.

Rattray, David. "Lightning over the Treasury." *The Poetry of Stephen Jonas*. 36–9.

Redding, J. Saunders. *To Make a Poet Black*. 1939; rpt., Ithaca, NY: Cornell UP, 1988.

Redmond, Eugene. *Drumvoices: The Mission of Afro-American Poetry: A Critical History*. New York: Doubleday [Anchor], 1976.

Roberson, Ed. *Etai-Eken*. Pittsburgh: U of Pittsburgh P, 1975.

Lucid Interval as Integral Music. Pittsburgh: Harmattan Press, 1984.

When Thy King Is a Boy. Pittsburgh: U of Pittsburgh P, 1970.

Rowell, Charles H. "Between the Comedy of Matters and the Ritual Workings of Man: An Interview with Lorenzo Thomas." *Callaloo* 4.1–3 (1981): 19–35.

Shepp, Archie. *Attica Blues*. ABC Records, AS-9222. 1972.

Fire Music. ABC Records, A-86. 1965.

Live in San Francisco. Jasmine Records, JAS 75. 1966.

On This Night. ABC Records, A-97. 1965.

A Sea of Faces. Black Saint Records, BSR 0002. 1975.

There's a Trumpet in My Soul. Arista Records, AL1016. 1975.

Shepp, Archie. With John Coltrane. *New Thing at Newport*. ABC Records, A-94. 1965.

Silliman, Ron. "Wild Form." *lower   limit   speech* 9 (1994): n.pag.

Simon, Adelaide. "Salvos for Atkins." *Input* 1.4 (1964): 8–9.

Spellman, A. B. "Baltimore Oriole." Diane di Prima and LeRoi Jones, eds., *The Floating Bear*. 283.

The Beautiful Days. New York: Poets Press, 1965.

Four Lives in the Bebop Business. New York: Pantheon, 1966; rpt. New York, Limelight, 1985.

"I Looked & Saw History Caught." *The New Black Poetry*. Ed. Clarence Major. New York: International, 1969. 126.

"there is in the atlanta." *Journal of Black Poetry*. 1.10 (1968): 19.

"THE TRUTH YOU CARRY IS VERY DARK." *Yugen* 2 (1958): 22–3.

"when black people are." *Journal of Black Poetry* 1.10 (1968): 19.

Spivak, Gayatri Chakravorty. *Outside in the Teaching Machine*. London: Routledge, 1993.

Stone, LeRoy. "Flamenco Sketches." *Understanding the New Black Poetry*. Ed. Stephen Henderson. New York: Morrow, 1973. 194–5.

Subryan, Carmen. "A. B. Spellman." *Dictionary of Literary Biography 41: Afro-American Poets since 1955*. Ed. Trudier Harris and Thadious Davis. Detroit: Gale Research, 1985. 311–15.

Such, David. *Avant Garde Jazz Musicians Performing "Out There."* Iowa City: U of Iowa P, 1993.

The Surrealist Group in Paris. "Murderous Humanitarianism." Trans. Samuel Beckett. *Negro: An Anthology.* Ed. Nancy Cunard. 1933; abridged ed., New York: Ungar, 1970. 352–53.

Taylor, Cecil. *Chinampas.* Leo Records, CDLR 153. 1991. (Recorded in 1987.)

Dark to Themselves. Inner City Records, 3001. 1977. (Recorded in 1976.)

Embraced. With Mary Lou Williams. Pablo Records, 2620-108. 1978. (Recorded in 1977.)

"Garden." *Moment's Notice: Jazz in Poetry & Prose.* Ed. Art Lange and Nathaniel Mackey. Minneapolis: Coffee House Press, 1993. 116–37.

Indent. Arista Records, AL 1038. 1977. (Recorded in 1973.)

In Florescence. A & M Records, SP 5286. 1990.

"The Musician." *Arsenal: Surrealist Subversion* 3 (1976): 12–15.

Thomas, Lorenzo. "Alea's Children: The Avant Garde on the Lower East Side, 1960–1970." *African American Review* 27.4 (1993): 573–8.

The Bathers. New York: I. Reed Books, 1981.

Chances Are Few. Berkeley: Blue Wind Press, 1979.

"The Shadow World: New York's Umbra Workshop and Origins of the Black Arts Movement." *Callaloo* 1.4 (1978): 53–72.

Torra, Joseph. Introduction to *Stephen Jonas: Selected Poems.* Ed. Joseph Torra. Hoboken, NJ: Talisman House, 1994. 1–12.

Wallenstein, Barry. "Poetry and Jazz: A Twentieth Century Wedding." *Black American Literature Forum* 25.3 (1991): 595–620.

Ward, Jerry. "N. J. Loftis's *Black Anima:* A Problem in Aesthetics." *Journal of Black Studies* 7.2 (1976): 195–210.

Ware, David S. *Great Bliss.* Vol. 1. Silkheart Records, SHCD 127. 1990.

Warren, Kenneth W. *Black and White Strangers: Race and American Literary Realism.* Chicago: U of Chicago P, 1993.

Weinberger, Eliot. *American Poetry since 1950: Innovators and Outsiders.* New York: Marsilio, 1993.

Letter to the editor. *American Poetry Review.* 23.4 (1994): 43–4.

West, Cornell. *Beyond Eurocentrism and Multiculturalism I: Prophetic Thought in Postmodern Times.* Monroe, ME: Common Courage Press, 1993.

Beyond Eurocentrism and Multiculturalism II: Prophetic Reflections: Notes on Race and Power in America. Monroe, ME: Common Courage Press, 1993.

White, Joseph. "Black Is a Soul." *The Poetry of Black America.* Ed. Arnold Adoff. New York: Harper and Row, 1973. 262–3.

Williams, William Carlos. *Imaginations.* Ed. Webster Schott. New York: New Directions, 1970.

Ya Salaam, Kalamu. "On Record." *Black World* 20.9 (1971): 28–33.

Yau, John. "Neither Us nor Them." *American Poetry Review* 23.2 (1994): 45–54.

Young, Kevin. "Signs of Repression: N. H. Pritchard's *The Matrix.*" *Harvard Library Bulletin* 3.2 (1992): 36–43.

INDEX